IN PRAISE OF
Marriage

"Ah, love, let us be true
To one another! for the world, which seems
To lie before us like a land of dreams,
So various, so beautiful, so new,
Hath really neither joy, nor love, nor light,
Nor certitude, nor peace, nor help for pain;
And we are here as on a darkling plain
Swept with confused alarms of struggle and flight,
Where ignorant armies clash by night."
— Matthew Arnold

IN PRAISE OF
Marriage

by
Edith Atkin

New York
THE VANGUARD PRESS

Copyright © 1982 by Edith Atkin
Published by Vanguard Press, Inc., 424 Madison Avenue, New York, N.Y. 10017.
Published simultaneously in Canada.

Library of Congress Cataloging in Publication Data
Atkin, Edith Lesser, date   In praise of marriage.
Includes bibliographical references and index.
1. Marriage—United States. 2. Family—United States.

I. Title.
HQ536.A88 1982   306.8   81-16324
ISBN 0-8149-0854-3   AACR2

Designer: Tom Bevans
Manufactured in the United States of America.
1 2 3 4 5 6 7 8 9 0

ACKNOWLEDGMENTS

I owe so much to so many in writing this book that it would be impossible to acknowledge them all. I would like, however, to express my indebtedness first and foremost to the many friends, relatives, colleagues, acquaintances, and patients — above all, patients — who shared with me their experiences, their thoughts, and their fantasies about love and marriage and family life.

One friend to whom I feel particularly indebted I would like to mention by name — Arlette (Mrs. Paul) Brauer. She encouraged me to continue writing whenever I felt myself sinking under the morass of material, so much of it ephemeral and contradictory, and wanted desperately to quit.

I would like to record my gratitude to my publishers, the Vanguard Press: the perceptive, gentle yet strict Miriam Shrifte; the charming, astute Evelyn Shrifte; and my editor, Bernice Woll, surely the most ideal of editors, whose intelligence, grace, and clarity of thought enormously enriched my work. Whenever I felt stymied they welcomed me to bounce my ideas off them, over lunch of V-8 juice, tuna fish sandwiches on thin rye toast, and ginger cookies, in their Dickensian quarters, until I could see my way clear to get moving again.

Finally, I reserve my deepest thanks to my husband, who would patiently listen to me whenever I felt the compulsion to kick around an idea, be it while we were fishing for snappers off our dock or huddled around the fireplace on cold winter nights. He never failed to enrich my knowledge, sharpen my perceptions, and expand my thinking, whatever the subject I was mulling over. Without his constant support I could not have produced this book.

— The Author

A Note about the Author by Her Husband

When my wife asked me — "allowed me" is more exact — to read her manuscript, it was with a certain amount of trepidation that I did so. As I endured her typing far into the night for many many nights, I had wondered at her daring — indeed, at the daring of anyone short of Westermark or Sigmund Freud to tackle so complicated, so colossal a subject as marriage, one that encompasses all the ambiguities and paradoxes of life itself.

What *chutzpah*, I thought to myself. In the three decades I have been married to her I can vouch that brashness is not a quality she possesses. Where did it come from, this audacity? Was it the women's movement that had given her that kind of brazen courage? Was it perhaps a personality change, a side effect of the postmenopause?

There were also vague fears. Would she write about our private life, an occupational hazard for psychoanalysts with literary wives? Reveal our sex life, our habits, our fights, our reconciliations? This too seemed strange, since she is a very private person. We had been married more than twenty years before I learned she had won a poetry prize while still in college. When I asked, "Why didn't you ever tell me this?" she replied, "You never asked me."

As a psychoanalyst I am subject to considerable curiosity by my patients about my personal life. Would the book be upsetting to them? Interfere with the transference? Complicate the treatment?

I need not have worried. I found the book objective,

informed, and scientifically sound, on the whole a wise and compassionate treatment of a very difficult subject. Better yet, I found it eminently readable, even in spots amusing and delightful. I trust the reader will find it the same.

— Samuel Atkin, M.D.

CONTENTS

Contents

PART FOUR
Love and Sex in and out of Marriage

PART FIVE
Affirmation

INTRODUCTION

How I Came to Write This Book

I was sitting on the deck of our summer cottage facing the bay watching Cindy and Buck digging for clams about a quarter mile offshore. Littlenecks were selling for $50 a bushel that season, and by pooling their labor they could make as high as $300 a day. They were saving their money to go to Europe in October, where they intended to "knock around" for a year before returning to school. Cindy had completed her second year; Buck, his third at a small upstate college. The two had met the year before at a party after a football game in which Buck had made the winning touchdown and, to hear Cindy tell it, it was "love at first sight." They had dated for several months before Cindy moved out of her dormitory and into Buck's tiny basement apartment off campus. They share expenses and housekeeping chores. Buck is entirely self-supporting, so extras, like an occasional movie or rock concert, come out of Cindy's monthly allowance from home.

Cindy is the granddaughter of our summer neighbors, Ernestine and Frank Johnson. I have known the Johnsons for more than twenty-five years. They are what we mean when we say someone is "the salt of the earth" — decent, dependable people of integrity, people one can rely on to do the right thing. Both Johnsons are third-generation Americans of Scandinavian descent. They have been married almost fifty years and are as devoted a couple as one could hope to find. Frank is a retired IBM executive. He participates actively in com-

munity affairs, serving on the school board and various charitable institutions. Ernestine had worked for two years as a
receptionist in a doctor's office before she married Frank. Although it happened many decades ago, she still speaks with
pride and nostalgia of those halcyon days of her girlhood
when she earned her own money and ate her lunch in restaurants.

The Johnsons have three living children (two died in
infancy). John, 46, a chemical engineer, is married and the
father of three grown children. He lives in the Midwest. The
Johnsons seldom see him, though they keep in touch by
phone. Marian, Cindy's mother, is 43. She was divorced when
Cindy was 7. Marian works as a pediatric nurse in a large
hospital. She is the sole support of Cindy, who is 19, and
Luke, 14. The father contributes nothing for their support,
having remarried within a year of the divorce. He has all he
can do to take care of his second brood of children. Luke is
beginning to show "problems" at school and in the community and is a source of worry and grief to his grandparents.
Gloria, 37, is also divorced. She is the mother of a 14-year-old
girl and a 12-year-old boy. She works as an editorial assistant
in a publishing house. Gloria expects to marry a man with
whom she has been living the past two years as soon as his
wife, a practicing Catholic, from whom he has been separated
five years, will give him a divorce.

The Johnsons are a closely knit family, sharing in one
another's troubles and joys. The brothers and sisters of the
older Johnsons keep in touch with one another through letters, greeting cards, and gifts to mark birthdays and other
special occasions. Every Thanksgiving the entire clan on both
sides of the family, some traveling from distant places, gather
in the Johnson home to celebrate the holiday.

Here is a stable, traditional, "old-fashioned" American
family with solid, Protestant middle-class virtues, the kind of
family we like to think of "as American as apple pie," a family
like those upon which our nation is said to have been built
and whose children, we have been led to expect, would follow

in their parents' footsteps and continue the traditions in which they and their parents before them had been raised.

As I watched these two young people — did I mention that Buck was black? — who were openly living together with no intention of getting married, at least in the foreseeable future, I wondered what had happened to our society in general and marriage in particular in the course of the two generations that separated grandmother from granddaughter to make Cindy's and Buck's unsanctified living arrangements almost a commonplace in today's world.

And what about the even more startling difference in *one* generation between the staid, conventional, traditional marriage of the senior Johnsons, soon to celebrate their golden wedding anniversary, and the marriages of their offspring? Two of their three children are divorced (one of them living in open adultery). I know nothing of John's marital situation. What I do know is that his oldest daughter, Jacqueline, 24, recently abandoned her husband and 4-year-old retarded child to go off with a married man twice her age.

A thousand questions ran riot in my mind. What is happening to marriage these days? Is monogamous marriage really going down the drain, as the media keep drumming? What does it mean that one out of three marriages ends in divorce? (In Marin County, California, it is said to be one out of two.) Is this shockingly high divorce rate a portent of marriage in the future? Or is it a transient social phenomenon reflecting a period of rapid social change?

Perhaps the most striking change in the contemporary social scene directly affecting marriage is the marked increase in working wives. What impact on marriage does the working wife have? Is there a change in or a diminishing of the differences in traditional roles of husband and wife? A trend toward more egalitarianism in the spousal relationship now that the wife is also a wage earner? Has the women's liberation movement affected marriage, and if so, how?

Other questions began to plague me. What about the

so-called sexual revolution that we are told has swept the country? There is little question that there is greater sexual freedom, at least among the young, than in the days of the older Johnsons. Has this helped or hurt marriage? And what about the role of sex in marriage (about which, for all the millions of words on the subject, there is much confusion and contradictory opinion)? Does the quality of the sexual relationship necessarily make or break a marriage? What happens to the sexual relationship in marriage over time? Do love and sex mean different things to the husband than to the wife?

Is there a "new morality" abroad in the land — a "culture of narcissism," to use Christopher Lasch's phrase? Are there indeed new sexual life-styles? How prevalent is "open marriage"? Are there a lot of "swinging" couples? What about infidelity? Is it more prevalent in Cindy's or her mother's generation than it was in the elder Johnsons'? If so, what effect does it have on present-day marriage? Are married women "playing around" more? Have husbands become more tolerant of infidelitous wives than they were in former generations?

And what about the family? What is happening to it these days? We are told that the small nuclear family puts an enormous emotional strain on its members. The intensity of the emotional ties between parents and children, thrown upon one another in the nuclear family for emotional sustenance, is said to breed neuroses and worse. Is the nuclear family the culprit responsible for the psychological ills of our time?

We are also told that the greater mobility of families has seriously weakened kinship ties, and for the urban family such ties are practically nonexistent. Yet here is the Johnson clan, who keep in touch with one another and travel far distances to celebrate Thanksgiving together. Is the Johnson clan unique? Or are kinship ties still around, even in big cities?

What about the effect on the children of the working mother? We know that the mother-child relationship in the first few years of life is crucial in the emotional development of a child. Yet 42 percent of working mothers have children under six years of age. Does the mother's absence have an adverse effect upon the young child? Can this be countered in other ways — say, with day-care centers or day foster homes? Are the children of working mothers more neglected than those of mothers who stay home? Is there any connection between the increase in working mothers and the increase in delinquency? Or has her employment been good for the children? Made them more self-reliant?

Finally, I dared to ask myself the sixty-four-dollar question: *Is marriage necessary?* Many authorities think not.

However, when one considers that marriage and the family have endured for thousands of years, contrary questions come to mind: May there not be something in the human being that reaches out for bonding with another human being? Some "social instinct," if you will, that needs family?

And what of the future? What will marriage and the family be like in the year 2000?

These were only some of the questions that harried me as I watched Cindy and Buck and contemplated their future. It was my search for answers that led to the writing of this book.

No sooner had I begun that search than I was confronted with the vastness of the project. First off, in our pluralistic society there are marked differences in many aspects of behavior, attitudes, habits, values, customs, beliefs, and rituals among different social and economic classes, let alone among different ethnic, cultural, and religious groups. Even in so seemingly basic a biological fact of life as sexual behavior there are marked class differences.[1]

While the influence of the ubiquitous television has tended to homogenize some aspects of contemporary culture, such social phenomena as marriage, family life, and child-rearing practices are deeply entrenched in the class structure and are not easily uprooted.[2]

If I was not to be drowned in an ocean of unmanageable material, I saw that I would have to carve out for myself a discrete swath to examine. I therefore decided to confine my search largely to marriage and family life in that part of our society I know best — middle-income and middle-class white urban America. Whatever observations and conclusions I reach will pertain for the most part to that segment of American life.

Facts and Figures

To gather first hand material for this book I interviewed friends, colleagues, relatives, and acquaintances, many of whom referred me to others whom I did not know (and with whom I felt more at ease in asking intimate questions about their sex lives than with those men and women I knew personally). I also drew upon my wide experience of more than twenty-five years as a therapist with private and clinic patients.

I interviewed men and women from every socio-economic class. However, the bulk of my material in this book is derived from my observations and interviews with white people from the upper-middle, middle-middle, and lower-middle classes, to use sociological terminology. Most of them had had at least some high school education, many had attended college, and a few held doctorate or other professional degrees.

Interviewees ranged in age from 18 to 81 years. Length of marriages ranged from 4 months to 56 years, the bulk falling within the 8 to 22 year span.

Their occupations ranged from waiter and garage attendant to business executive, theatrical producer, and college president. They included doctors, lawyers, accountants, architects, actors, beauticians, salesclerks, call girls, housewives, teachers, writers, engineers, computer analysts, social workers, psychologists, psychoanalysts, editors, artists, typists, and secretaries.

In all, I interviewed 143 persons, of whom I included 127 in this book. Of these there were forty-two couples in their first marriage, twelve in their second. One woman was on her fifth husband (happily married, I might add), four men on their third wives. Five couples were living together without benefit of clergy. Four women and two men were currently divorced. One woman was a widow, two were unmarried mothers. All save five couples had children. (The children of two couples were adopted.) A number of couples were raising stepchildren as well as their own. *

These figures do not include the countless informal talks and mini-interviews I had with casual strangers. On long bus, train, or airplane rides, on the beach, on a park bench, I would lose no opportunity to engage my erstwhile neighbor in conversation on some aspect of marriage or family if an occasion presented itself and if he or she seemed promising material. (I live near a children's playground and in my spare time I like to watch the children at play. Their bored or tired mothers are only too glad to engage in "adult" conversation while keeping an eye on their children.) I gleaned what I could from these random contacts.

One of my most productive interviews was with a man who sat next to me on a five-hour plane trip from New York

---

* Of the sixteen interviewees whose data I did not utilize in this book, eight were middle-class blacks. Since I believe that the black experience is something a white person at this period in our society cannot fully appreciate, no matter how knowledgeable or understanding, I make no claims for the pertinence of my findings to black persons. I also interviewed four homosexual men who had long and deep emotional relationships with male partners and four Lesbians (two of whom had been married), including one Lesbian couple who were raising the two children of their former marriages. I have not included their material in this book, as I do not feel "married" homosexual experience is sufficiently pertinent to its purpose.

As a mental health consultant in day care centers, I had an opportunity to observe and talk with many people at the lower end of the socio-economic scale — unmarried mothers, welfare mothers, fathers whose wives had deserted them and the children, unemployed men and women — people for whom the task of providing rice and beans for their children was a never-ending struggle. Since most of them were single parents, I did not include them in this study although my knowledge of their lives served as an invaluable backdrop to it.

to Los Angeles. (I was traveling first class, the trip having been paid for by a California industrial outfit that had asked me to lead a seminar on "The Divorced Father.") This man, a top executive in the production end of the television industry, was returning to Los Angeles after a two-day business conference in New York with a major network. He was about 48, I would guess, handsome, urbane, "happily married for the second time around," he said. He had a grown son from his first marriage and two small children in his present one. He had a mistress in New York and several on the West Coast.

When I told him I was writing a book on marriage it did not take long before he started to tell me his ideas and experiences. (Here was a nice, middle-aged lady from New York, a good listener, whom he would never see again once we touched down in the L.A. airport, he probably thought, so he could afford to talk freely.) For me this accidental meeting was a bonanza, since it was most unlikely that in the normal course of my life I would have had an opportunity to interview a person from his social milieu. (He was a member of the so-called "international jet set," his name not infrequently mentioned in gossip columns.)

I had other informal sources for gathering people's thoughts, opinions, experiences, and prejudices on the subject of marriage. Hosts who knew I was working on this book would bring up the topic at dinner parties and it never failed to elicit a wealth of discussion, often heated and controversial.

Last but not least, I used the experiences of my own two marriages — the passionate, madly-in-love marriage of my youth, full of laughter and weeping, which, after fifteen years, "got used up,"[3] and the present marriage of my maturity, durable, serene, and deeply gratifying.

This book is not a "scientific" treatise on marriage and the family. My interviewees were not selected in any "scientific" way. I interviewed whomever and wherever I could. I made no surveys, distributed no questionnaires. Most of my interviews were conducted informally, often over lunch or a cup of coffee, rarely in my office. A lot of the people I talked with didn't realize that they were being interviewed. We were just conversing. I counted on my ability to "draw people out" and my skill and experience in conducting interviews — an essential tool in the armamentarium of anyone working in the helping professions — to elicit "in-depth" material. And I also utilized my knowledge of the social, psychological, and biological sciences as well as my wide experience of more than twenty-five years as a therapist with private and clinic patients.

I have tried to be as objective as possible. I have presented facts and figures as reported by such relatively unimpeachable sources as the U.S. Census Bureau; the Department of Labor Statistics; the National Opinion Research Council; the Harris and Roper organizations; public opinion surveys by newspapers and other media (e.g., the *New York Times*–CBS polls); and research studies conducted by universities and professional organizations.

But a book on a subject so emotionally loaded is bound to be biased by the writer's own life experience and by his or her temperament. Let me warn the reader: I am optimistic about marriage, past, present, and future. My researches in the course of writing this book have confirmed my belief that marriage for all its stresses and strains, its frustrations, disappointments, restrictions, and pains, is (or can be) a life-enriching, liberating, and fulfilling institution. As for the family, it is the best arrangement man has devised for raising children. To paraphrase Winston Churchill about democracy, the family may be the worst possible system, but there is nothing better.

A further warning to the reader: If you are looking for a book on How to Be Happy Though Married, or Ten Ways to Please Your Spouse, or How to Save Your Marriage, this is not it. Nor will you find here formulas for improving your sex life or making you a more skillful lover. If, however, you are looking for fresh insights into those institutions in which you and practically all mankind are involved — marriage and the family — and if you would like to glean a fuller understanding of yourself as spouse, parent, or lover (or all three), I think you have found the right book.

PART ONE

Marriage in a Changing World

CHAPTER

1

The Marriage Bond

"Hail, wedded love, mysterious law, true source
Of human offspring."

— *John Milton*

Marriage Is Dead — Long Live Marriage

Experts have been predicting the death of marriage for generations. Back in 1927 John Watson, father of behavioral psychology, announced that, on the basis of statistical projections, by 1977 marriage would no longer exist. In the last twenty-five years books and articles excoriating marriage have proliferated like rabbits. *Marriage is Hell, Is Marriage Necessary?, The Mirages of Marriage, The Baby Trap, Marriage is a Miserable Institution* — titles like these are commonplace. As proof of the bankruptcy of marriage their authors cite the high divorce rate and the hordes of men and women living in "single blessedness" or with members of their own or the opposite sex without benefit of clergy. Many of the predictors of doom sing hosannas to alternative mating rituals, like open marriage, serial marriage, or group marriage. Among some fashionable circles, bearing children out of wedlock has become chic — the "in" thing.

"Who needs marriage?" scoff the "singles," the live-

° 3 °

togethers, the communards. "Unnecessary." "Reactionary." "An outmoded convention."[1]

Who needs marriage? Just about everybody. According to the Bureau of the Census,[2] 95 *percent of all Americans marry at some time in their lives.* By the age of 30, nine out of ten women have been married at least once. Even those persons of the divorced population who, one would assume, found marriage wanting, must also have found something desirable about that hoary institution, since four out of five divorced persons remarry. And most of them within five years. Whether one agrees with Samuel Johnson's quip that remarriage marks "the triumph of hope over experience," clearly the majority of divorced men and women prefer the state of marriage, whatever its flaws, to its alternatives.

Marriage today, while not exactly bursting with health, is alive and kicking, despite the lamentations over "that curious institution already in a state of advanced decay,"[3] if not already on the verge of "complete extinction."[4] Over the decades marriages in America have been steadily increasing. The most recent nationwide statistics, those sober reminders of facts rather than fancies, show that in 1979 there were more marriages per 100,000 population than at any time in our history.[5]

Marriage, it seems, is here to stay.

Marriage Is Good for the Health

Whatever the shallows and miseries of individual marriages, nationwide studies indicate that across the board married people are healthier, happier, and better off than the unmarried. Death rates on average are lower for married men and women than for single, widowed, or divorced at all ages.[6] Suicide rates are lower — the rate of suicide for single men is almost twice as high as for married men. Married people make the least demand on the health care system.[7] Married men are in better physical and emotional shape than single, widowed, or divorced men. (Married women have a higher rate of some physical and mental disorders than single women or married men.[8]) Married men and women are more likely to say they are "very happy" than are single, widowed, or divorced men and women.[9]

The difference in the prevalence of serious mental illness necessitating hospitalization among the different categories of marital status is striking. According to the National Institute of Mental Health, in 1975 the rate of admissions to psychiatric hospitals was seven and a half times higher for unmarried persons than for married and almost ten times higher for the separated and divorced.[10]

What Is Marriage?

"A life allied with mine . . . that is the miracle of marriage. Another life that wills my good as much as its own, because it is united with mine . . ."[11]

De Rougemont's sentiment expresses to my mind the essence of marriage: a union — sexual and spiritual — of a man and woman who commit themselves to love, honor, and comfort each other. An all-embracing intimacy between two people who have broken through their shells of "selfness" — that protective covering which isolates us from others — to mingle their hearts and minds and bodies together into a "we." A covenant between a man and woman who pledge to share their lives and their love with each other.

Intimacy, commitment, companionship, bonding. These make the mortar of marriage. Without them a marriage, no matter how smooth surfaced, is a hollow thing. With them the meanest dwelling is solid.

What do we mean by these rather fanciful words?

Intimacy: [12] "And he came in unto her and he knew her." I like to think that this Biblical phrase means more than knowing the intimate recesses of her body. I like to think it means his knowing her thoughts, her moods, her tastes, her preferences, her aversions, her diffidences, her delights. And her knowing his. I like to think it means the intimacy of a man and woman who share not only the joys of the flesh — for these can be found outside the marriage bed — but the homey intimacies of domestic life.

The poet and the novelist always say everything better. Here is John Cheever describing that homey intimacy in marriage:

"He followed her into the bathroom and sat on the shut toilet seat while she washed her back with a brush. 'I forgot to tell you,' he said, 'Liza sent us a wheel of Brie.' 'That's nice,' she said, 'but you know what? Brie gives me terribly loose bowels.' He hitched up his genitals and crossed his legs. 'That's funny,' he said. 'It constipates me.' That was their marriage then — not the highest paving on the stair, the clatter of Italian fountains, the wind in the alien olive trees, but this: a jay naked male and female discussing their bowels." [13]

Intimacy does not mean the invasion of the other's inner privacy. Everyone carries within the hidden crevices of the psyche secret fantasies and desires, alien, sometimes even repugnant, to one's ideal self, which one may not wish to reveal to anyone. "To love," writes Carson McCullers, [14] "is always to accept the otherness, the mystery of the other, and to refuse to violate that mystery." Rilke expresses a similar thought when he writes: ". . . a good marriage is that in which each appoints the other guardian of his solitude . . . once the realization is accepted that even between the closest human beings infinite distances continue to exist, a wonderful living side by side can grow up, if they succeed in loving the distance between them." [15]

Some people are afraid of intimacy, though they may crave it. Deep down all of us long for closeness, for that blissful state when as infants we lay snug at mother's breast. But some of us, for whatever unconscious reason, may shy away from it, as though to yield to the wish might bring hurt or disaster. So we suffer our loneliness. Our days may be filled with people, things, activities; we may sleep with any number of partners, even imaganing ourselves to be in love with one or another of them, but we dare not risk the leap over the chasm that separates people to reach real intimacy.

Of course, if both mates prefer emotional distance, as sometimes happens, the marriage can work. We all know couples who live amicably together back to back, as it were. But generally lack of intimacy hurts a marriage.[16]

Rita, 33, a housewife, is contemplating divorce after twelve years of marriage in order to marry a much older man with whom she has fallen in love. She blames her self-centered husband for her disaffection. "We've lived together twelve years, had three children together, not counting two miscarriages; but he hasn't the faintest idea of what I'm really like. He'd die if he thought I even looked at another man. He thinks our marriage is great. He lives with this image of me as his sweet little wifey because I cater to his every wish, like his dear old mom did. He doesn't know the real me at all! With Jack [her lover, an expansive, fun-loving guy] I can be myself, warts and all."

In therapy Rita learned to see how she fostered this unreal image of herself as "the perfect wife and mother" because deep down she feared that if she revealed her "real, nasty self" to her husband he would dislike her, perhaps ever leave her. She traced this fear to her childhood relationship to her mother, a powerful woman whom she was always trying to please. She had prided herself on being the "good girl" in the family in contrast to her flighty younger sister, "the black sheep," whom she both scorned and envied. Insight into her contribution to the unrealistic picture-book marriage she was trying to live up to, and support from the therapist to risk "being herself" with her husband, may help put this marriage on a more intimate and realistic basis, "warts and all."

Commitment: Commitment is what we affirm, at that awesome moment in the wedding ceremony when, in response to the minister's question, "Do you, John [or Mary] . . . forsaking all others . . . promise to love and cherish, in sickness and in health, for richer or poorer, till death do you part?" we declare, "I do."

Commitment goes beyond intimacy. It implies the resolve to share your life with another — to share not only your worldly goods but your strengths and your weaknesses, your victories and your defeats, your hopes and your disappointments, your dreams and your realities. The exigencies of life or, all too often, human weakness, may mock our intentions or vitiate their fulfillment. Even people whose marriages end in divorce, I believe, start out with the intent to commit themselves to it.

To commit your love and your life to another person requires what Erikson calls "basic trust." The capacity for basic trust is established during the first years of life. It depends to a large extent upon the quality of "mothering" (whether by a mother, father, or mother surrogate) a child received when it was dependent for its very survival upon those around him. If he has been wrapped in loving parental care during this crucial period, he will acquire "basic trust" — trust that the world is a relatively safe place, that no one is necessarily out to deprive him of his substance or do him in. If a child is to mature into an adult capable of loving others without undue fear or suspicion, basic trust is an essential ingredient in its emotional development.

Like fear of intimacy, some men and women are fearful of committing themselves to marriage, or, if mated, to their marriage vows. In treatment of such persons one often discovers a history of a seriously disturbed parent-child relationship during their earliest years. Therapeutic intervention may be necessary to undo or mitigate the damage.

Companionship: "This is my beloved, and this is my friend. . . ." Those tender words in the Song of Solomon epitomize to me what is best in marriage. The two do not necessarily go together. We all know lovers who are not friends. "I'm madly in love with Sally," Hugh confided to me, "but I can't honestly say I like her." Chemistry, propinquity, fantasy, lust — these may catapult two people into a passionate affair. But the rigors of married life demand sterner stuff.

Companionship assuages Man's existential loneliness. The Bible tells us, "And the Lord God said, 'It is not good that the man should be alone; I will make him an helpmeet for him.' " I believe there is a deep human need that longs for connection with another. Being and having a "helpmeet" comes close to answering that need.

Companionship transcends the shared experience, the pleasure of "doing things together." Beyond them is the comfort companionship bestows upon the married couple who can sit silently in each other's presence, gazing at a fire, reading a book, or listening to Bach, knowing that neither words nor actions are needed to express the bond between them.

Edward Abbey sums up in lyrical fashion what companionship in marriage is. "Only one thing is lacking to complete my happiness. I want to wake up at dawn with a woman in my arms. I want to share the morning with her, while woodpeckers drum on hollow snags and the sun rises into the fiery clouds. I want to share an orange, a pot of black cowboy coffee, the calm and common sense of breakfast talk, the smiles, the touch of fingertips, the yearning of the flesh, the comradeship of man and woman, of one uncertain human for another." [17]

Last week I had lunch with my friend Marie. She lost her husband, a physician, ten months ago after twenty-eight years of marriage. Heart attack. Her daughter, married, with two small children, lives hundreds of miles away. Her unmarried son teaches at a distant university. Both children, kind, considerate, write or telephone her regularly on birthdays and holidays. Both have offered to have her come and live with them. But Marie prefers to live alone in the city apartment she had shared with her husband. Marie had never worked outside the home during her marriage. She had been quite content with her roles as wife, mother, homemaker, and community volunteer. Now she works as a saleslady in a women's specialty shop, partly because she can use the money and partly because she felt she should be "among people."

"I miss Jeff at every turn," she said. "I miss him in bed, of course. It's so . . . well, empty. I'm not talking just about the sex part. I mean lying next to him, having him there next to me when I wake up. There's nothing to get up for. I miss fixing his breakfast. Sewing a button on his shirt. I miss all the things that used to bug me: leaving his clothes around; the hair in the sink; the cigarette butts in the coffee cup. Now I do it myself just to remind me of him. I miss his noise. The house is so damn quiet. Of course I miss all the wonderful things about him — his hearty laugh that would ring through the house, his bear hug when he'd get home from the hospital. His surprise presents, like only a few days before he died he brought home a bunch of carnations because, he said, it was Groundhog Day.

"But you know what I miss most? Not having him around to share my happenings with. I never realized until he was gone how much richer my ordinary experiences were by knowing I'd be telling Jeff about them later. Little nothings, really. The yakitori I had for lunch with Sarah. The brash butcher who asks his women customers when he's about to wait on them, 'Getting yours?' The long-distance call from my sister telling me Chris was accepted at Haverford. Going to a movie and not having him to discuss it with. And my silly little worries, like that funny wart on my back."

Bonding: Bonding is a mysterious process not easily defined. Bonding in marriage is an unconscious emotional attachment between a man and woman that grows through living together. In many ways it is not unlike our earliest emotional attachments to our original family, which, no matter how emancipated we may think we are from its ties, we are never entirely free of.

Bonding insinuates itself in the marriage through sharing the millions of things that make up married life, from furnishing the first apartment and the birth of the children through fights, reconciliations, illnesses, disappointments, promotions and celebrations, to grandparenthood. Despite disillusionment of one's expectations, disappointment with the spouse, even falling out of love, bonding is what keeps marriages together.

I wonder if it is not the sundering of that mysterious marriage bond that makes divorce so painful; if it is not the incomplete sundering of that bond that makes ex-spouses hang on to each other, though it be through recriminations and legal battles, sometimes even after each has married another. I wonder too whether it is the unhealed wound of sundering that bond that accounts, at least in part, for the onset of illness that so frequently follows the death or divorce of a spouse.[18]

The Heart of the Matter

The foregoing was my personal catalogue of the essence of marriage. I wanted to know what my informants, who ranged from newlyweds to great-grandparents, thought about the matter. "In a word," I asked them, "what would you say is the essence of marriage?" Here are a few responses. They show how various are the meanings of marriage to different people and at different stages of marriage.

"The essence of marriage," said my good friend Arlette B, who has been happily married for thirty-five years and is the wisest person I know, "is *caring*. Marriage is an alliance between two people who have concern and compassion for each other, who support each other in their weaknesses."

"It's going through troubles together, like buddies who go through war together," said Cora G, married eighteen years. "Troubles bond people." The Gs recently had to hospitalize their schizophrenic adolescent son. Theirs had been a troubled marriage, almost from the start, on the verge of disruption many times. Their son's illness shocked them, Cora said, into realizing how much they had suffered through together and how much they needed each other for strength and support to endure their common grief.

"It's having someone there when you need him," said Sally D. "Someone you can count on." This is Sally's second marriage. Last year she underwent a mastectomy, a frightening experience that her present husband, unlike her first, who would disappear in times of stress, helped her live through with courage and grace.

"It's having a baby," said Margy C, 28, mother of her first infant after five years of marriage. A dance therapist, she readily gave up her professional career for the career of motherhood and homemaking. She intends to return to work someday, she said, but not until she's had all the children she wants, which at this moment she numbers eight!

"It's a balance between being independent and dependent on each other," said Eileen A. "It's being close to your partner yet letting the other have his own space." Eileen is a middle-aged, highly successful fashion designer whose work entails frequent entertainment of potential customers and occasional trips away from home, with little time for "family life." She has been married over twenty years, has no children. Her husband, a lawyer, while ostensibly proud of his wife's achievements, has been chronically irked by her intense involvement in her business affairs. He finally settled matters for himself by acquiring a steady, adoring mistress.

"My children," said Anthony, an auto mechanic, age 35, an Italian-American Catholic married to a girl of similar background whom he'd known since grammar school. They have three children, ages 8, 6, and 4. They live in their own home in the suburbs. "My children give meaning to my life. I like the responsibility of taking care of them. I enjoy watching them grow — their minds as well as their bodies. It's like a miracle. I like to teach them things. On Sundays after church my wife and I take them to the zoo or the Museum of Natural History. Once I took them to the Aquarium in Battery Park. They loved it. When I come home, the kids tell me what happened to them at school, and they sing for me the songs they learn at school. My children are the best thing that ever happened to me."

"Coming home to someone you love, take your tie and shoes off, be yourself, munch crunchies while you watch the Late Show together." This from a television producer, age 46, an ex-bon vivant and notorious man about town who married for the first time at 44. His wife is a quiet divorcée in her early 40s, mother of two grown children. "The 'eligible bachelor' bit gets mighty wearying after a while," he added.

"Commitment," declared Joseph A, a theological student, married two years and father of an infant. "Commitment to take on the obligations and responsibilities of family life. Commitment to the person you want to be the mother of your children and whom you want to spend your life with."

"Having a lover who is also your friend. Someone you can share your fantasies with, your thoughts, your hopes, your fears, your defeats, and not be ashamed." This from a young psychoanalyst who spends his days listening to other people's dreams and hopes and fears and fantasies.

"Companionship," said Danny T, age 76, a retired public servant. "And our four children, our nine grandchildren and six great-grandchildren," he added. "They came from all over the United States to celebrate our golden wedding anniversary last year," he said proudly. His wife nodded in agreement. "When we go to Florida in the winter and I see all those lonely old people sitting on a bench, alone, doing nothing, my heart breaks for them," she said. "I thank God Danny and I still have each other. To have a companion in your old age, it is a blessing from God."

A Dissenting Voice

I let my friend Herbert read a draft of this chapter. Herbert, 62, has had three wives and countless mistresses. He is currently divorced. "Rubbish!" he sputtered. "Sentimental piffle. I'm surprised you'd write such stuff. Look around and what do you see? Husbands cheating on their wives. Wives cheating on their husbands. Outrageous unions. Men and woman who despise each other imprisoned in a so-called marriage out of fear or greed or apathy. Or religion. Or the pitiful, cowardly excuse of 'children.' Most likely they stay together because, if you remember Freud's famous remark, 'their revenge is not yet complete.'[19]

"Husbands and wives who haven't what you psychologists call 'communicated' with each other for years, who day after dreary day go through the motions of mundane talk and routine sex, their boredom with each other heavy as lead. Marriages so empty they don't even bother to quarrel anymore."

I am well aware of the untold numbers of wretched marriages. Of the millions of battered wives, tormented husbands, abused children. The men who stop in at the neighborhood bar after work to put off going home, knowing that a nagging or slatternly or complaining wife awaits them. The women who dread the arrival of a sodden or sadistic or accusing husband. The women who loathe their husband's touch yet submit regularly to the sexual act. Marriages from which love or even caring has fled, held together by habit or apathy or neurotic interdependence. Marriages that, in the words of Colette, inflict "small deaths" on husbands and wives.

There have always been ill-conceived marriages, marriages that should never have been consecrated in the first place. Marriages of immature or self-centered or hedonistic persons who expected gratification of their own needs without thought or care of what the partner needed in return. Marriages consummated in love and hope and promise that sputtered out for lack of tending. Marriages based on unrealistic expectations, consummated in the euphoria of infatuation disguised as love, doomed to disappointment. Marriages held together by neurotic ties from which love or concern have fled.

Nor do I deny that there are wretched times in every marriage, the happiest as well as the sorriest. Times when the most loving spouses hate each other, if only for a moment.

The Marriage Bond

Times when one ardently wishes one were free, unencumbered by another's needs. Times when arguments and angry shouts and accusations pollute the air, when one storms out of the room in frustrated fury if only to restrain the impulse to hurl a lamp at the mate. Times when the loved one seems crude and insensitive and one wonders whatever possessed you to marry such a monster.

The Nitty-Gritty of Marriage

To paraphrase Marcus Aurelius's definition of life, marriage is "a battle and a sojourning in a baleful land." It is an imperfect union of two imperfect people, full of conflict and strife, joys and sorrows, comedy and tragedy, battered by strains and pains and "grievances foregone," constantly beset by crises large and small.

Always there are minor crises: Her overdrawn check. His bringing home an unexpected guest for dinner the night they're having leftover meat loaf. His "making a fool of himself" disco-ing with a 17-year-old minx at his son's high school graduation party. Her crushing the fender of the new car. His interfering mother-in-law. Her forgetting to pick up his suit from the cleaner.

And sometimes major ones: Losing one's job. Unpaid bills. Sitting up all night tending a baby with pneumonia. A miscarriage. Going to the police station to collect 13-year-old Jimmie after he was picked up with a gang of school kids smoking pot. Being called at 2 A.M. by a hospital to be told that your 18-year-old son was in a serious auto accident. Arranging for 16-year-old Janie's abortion. Falling in love with your best friend's spouse. A heart attack. Major surgery. Placing your aged parent in a nursing home. Mandatory retirement.

Marriage is never easy. Though nearly everyone tries it at one time or another, some men and women just aren't suited for it. It takes a certain degree of maturity to "hack it"

— to share the responsibiities of married life and to withstand its hardships. Some people aren't up to such heroics.

What makes the hardships of marriage worthwhile? The answer, I believe, lies somewhere in that mysterious, elusive state called love, or caring. That indefinable bond that holds a man and woman together for a lifetime. For most of us it is what makes life, even a life full of holes, worth living.

CHAPTER
2
Why Marriage?

"Any marriage, happy or unhappy, is infinitely more
interesting and significant than any romance, however
passionate."
                                          — *W. H. Auden*

It was a lovely wedding. The bride wore her mother's wedding gown — slipper satin trimmed with pearls and Alençon lace in Empire style. Instead of the traditional veil she wore a crown of daisies in her hair. As she walked on her father's arm to the strains of Telemann, performed by friends on flute, violin, and cello, to meet the groom awaiting her under a bower of vine leaves and white roses (the wedding took place on the lawn of her parents' country house) her radiance evoked a hum of admiration from the assembled guests. The marriage ceremony (replete with poetry from Elizabeth Barrett Browning and Yeats) had been written by the couple itself. Several women brushed a tear from their eye, recalling their dreams and hopes on a similar occasion in their own lives, as the minister declared, "I now pronounce you man and wife."

Soon after the congratulations and kisses by friends and relatives the happy couple ran, amid a pelting of rice, to an awaiting horse and carriage to go off on their honeymoon. Where were they going? To Paris? To Martinique? To a cottage in the Maine woods? Not at all. They were returning to their apartment on East Seventy-third Street in Manhattan, where they had been living together for two years. On Monday the groom had to return to the hospital, where he was working as a second-year resident in pediatrics, the bride to her job as an assistant curator in a museum.

What prompted this couple to get married, she at 23, he at 27, when they could have continued to live together without the hassles of matrimony? Perhaps the bride was pregnant? By no means. Indeed, they would not consider having children until he had completed his residency and established himself in his profession. And she was seriously thinking about getting a doctorate in ethnography first.

Is Marriage Necessary?

Until not so long ago the question, "Why are you getting married?" posed to an affianced man or woman, would have been met with puzzlement. *Everyone* was expected to get married. And almost everyone did. An unmarried woman verging on 30 was in danger of becoming, God forbid, "an old maid." Unless she had a good excuse, like sacrificing herself for a sick or aged parent, a woman who never married was looked upon with pity or suspicion. (An old Art Young cartoon showed a bedraggled woman, babe in arms, a brood of raggedy kids hanging onto her skirts, dragging her drunken husband from a saloon, who, upon seeing a nurse in neat uniform pass by, hisses scornfully, "Old maid!") A man who defied God's law to be fruitful and multiply by remaining unwed was considered odd, selfish, irresponsible, or if the truth were only known about him, "queer" (meaning homosexual). As recently as the late 70s a girl who went to college was expected, at least by her parents and most likely by herself and friends as well, to catch, whether or not she obtained an education, a prospective husband.

In those olden days when virginity, at least female virginity, was ostensibly surrendered only after the wedding or promise thereof, the regularization of sex relations, sanctified by God and society only within the holy state of matrimony, was a compelling reason for marriage. Today virginity in either sex beyond the age of consent is considered an encumbrance to be gotten rid of as quickly as possible. "Holding out" for marriage is looked upon by many young folks as a quaint anachronism.

Traditionally, procreation, along with companionship, was the basic purpose of marriage.[1] Today many young people question the wisdom of bringing children into an already overpopulated world, moreover a world under the constant threat of blowing itself up in a nuclear holocaust. Others, wrapped up in themselves and their own delights, don't want children to complicate their hedonistic lives. As for companionship, legal commitment to each other before a minister or judge is a non sequitur. Living together before marriage has become almost de rigueur. According to the Census Bureau, there are over a million unmarried couples living together, double the number in 1970.[2]

Cohabiting with little risk of unwelcome offspring, thanks to the availability of contraception and legal abortion, men and women can eschew the obligations of marriage altogether while enjoying the companionship and sexual privileges heretofore reserved for the properly wedded. Yet sooner or later almost everyone takes the marriage vows.

True, there is an increasing proportion of single adults of 30 or under in our population, most notably in urban centers. But across the nation the average age at first marriage is 21 for women and 23 for men. More than one quarter of the 18-year-old females in the United States are already married. Even college women, who in today's climate might be expected to consider other options, look forward to marriage. Surveys show that while most of them plan to work and enjoy the single life for several years after college, with or without a male live-in companion, practically all of them see themselves as eventual wives and mothers.[3]

It is understandable that women, who, whether by nature or nurture, look to wifehood and motherhood as their manifest destiny, should seek marriage. It is less understandable that men do so,[4] since marriage entails not only restriction of their "ingrained instinct for promiscuity"[5] but for many of them enslavement to a lifetime of labor, often dreary and energy-sapping labor, to support their families.

What is there about that barnacled institution, despite centuries of anti-marriage propaganda,[6] that continues to lure nearly every man and woman even in this heyday of "new morality"? I was particularly interested to learn why those who were married less than ten years took the vows of marriage. Practically all of them had had sex relations with the spouse before marriage and many had lived together for months or years. Many had the option of continuing to live together without assuming the responsibilities of marriage. Yet they chose to legalize the relationship.

Why, I asked? The replies were widely diverse. They ranged from "I got pregnant"; "she got pregnant"; "you're expected to get married"; "my mother nagged me to get married"; "all my friends were getting married"; "I wanted to get away from home"; to "I was tired of working"; "I wanted to settle down"; "I wanted a home"; "I wanted a child"; "I wanted a family."

Some gave plain down-to-earth answers: "Her father said he'd put me in business." "She had the capital. I had the know-how [for real estate]. We decided we'd make a good team." "Our landlord wouldn't give us a lease; he claimed there was some regulation against non-related people living in one household."

Some claimed family pressures. "My parents were terribly upset about our living together. They gave us separate rooms when we visited them, though they knew we were sleeping together. It relieved them enormously when I told them we were getting married. My dad gave us a thousand dollars for a wedding present."

One 45-year-old former divorcée who had lived with a male companion for six years said: "My son was getting married to a girl who came from this uptight WASP family from Connecticut. They were planning a fancy wedding in church with all their goyishe relatives there. My son asked me how he should introduce Joe, like, this guy is my mother's boy friend?

So Joe and I said 'What the hell. We might as well get married too.' So a week before my son got married, Joe and I went down to City Hall and got hitched."

A majority said they wanted to make a permanent commitment. "It solidified our relationship, enriched it," one man said. Another man, divorced three years and who had lived with his second wife six months before marriage, said, "I wanted to confirm publicly our commitment to each other. Although we got married on our lunch hour in a grungy office before a bored civil service clerk, when we signed that paper I felt like shouting for joy." In an interview with Gregory Hines, the great tap dancer, upon announcing his impending marriage to his companion of seven years, said, "It's a way of getting even closer than before."[7]

The following interviews of couples married less than a decade illustrate the diversity of motivation for committing themselves to a permanent and exclusive relationship:

Security: Valerie, 19, is a typist in a large insurance company. She has been married seven months to Frank, 25, a construction worker. They live in Brooklyn, in a tightly knit Italian neighborhood with a largely proletarian population, where both grew up. They rent an upstairs flat in her parents' home. "I knew Frank for years," Valerie said. "He used to hang around our house with my brother Al but we didn't start going together until about two years ago." When I asked Valerie why she got married so young, she said, "That's what my girl friends asked me. I told them, 'Why not?' I went out with a lot of boys in high school. All they ever wanted was one thing. When Frank asked me for a date the first time I wasn't sure I wanted to go out with him. I knew he'd been around with a lot of girls — his reputation wasn't so good — and I was a little scared. He had tickets for The Grateful Dead at Madison Square Garden. But I took a chance and went. Afterward he took me to a nice Chinese place to eat where we could dance too. He was real nice, a gentleman. He just kissed me good night, that's all. Then he went away for two weeks to visit his married sister in California. I kept thinking about him while he was gone. When he came back we started going steady. He took me to a lot of places I never was before. I got to like him a lot. I suppose you could say we were in love.

"My folks kept kidding me about when Frank and I were getting married. When the neighbors upstairs moved out my mother said if we got married we could have the apartment. That isn't why we got married, but it kind of made us decide not to wait. We had a big wedding. The whole neighborhood was invited. [Here Valerie describes in detail her wedding dress, the bridesmaids' gowns, the double-ring ceremony, the reception, the orchestra, the food and drink, etc.] We went to Jamaica on our honeymoon. We stayed for a week at the Holiday Inn at Montego Bay. It was beautiful."

"Yes," she said in response to my question, "I'm glad I got married. Frank is a steady worker. We're nearly all furnished. [She describes her furniture.] We're saving up to buy our own house someday." I ask about children. "Oh sure, but not until another year or two. We want to buy a new car first."

Ready to Settle Down: I asked Frank why he got married. "To tell the truth," he said, "I wasn't keen on getting married. If Valerie and her family hadn't pushed it I guess I'd still be making the singles scene, getting stoned with the guys, scoring with different girls. The year before we got married, Valerie and I went steady — and I was beginning to get tired of all that boozing and chasing around anyway. I liked being with Val. It was good to have someone you could talk to, not just fool around with. I could tell her about my work, the fellas on the job, my ambitions, my troubles at home, whatever was on my mind. Valerie's a good listener. And she used to make me feel good when I was downhearted." "What finally made you pop the question?" I pressed. "Well," he said, "we had a scare. She missed her period one month and she was crying and upset. So I said, 'Let's get married.' A week later she gets the curse. So she said I didn't have to marry her if I didn't want to. But then I thought to myself, why not? I was twenty-five, I had my fill of wine, women, and song. I liked her better than any other girl I went out with. She was sweet and loving. She didn't argue, she wasn't a flirt or anything like that. She had a practical head on her shoulders. I liked her folks. I figured she'd make a good wife. I guess I was ready to settle down. That's about it."

Children: In contrast to Valerie is Phyllis. Phyllis is a stunningly beautiful woman, sophisticated, urbane, a feminist, who was married at 29. Phyllis epitomized to me, in life-style, attitude toward love, sex, marriage, and relationship between the sexes, the prototype of many professional and career women I have known.

Now 35, Phyllis has been married for six years to Roger, 37, a partner in her father's law firm. They have two girls, 5 and 3. They met at a party when Phyllis was a graduate student in anthropology at Columbia University and Roger was an instructor in the law school.

Phyllis, an only child, comes from a wealthy, upper-middle-class Jewish family. Her father is a well-known corporation lawyer, her mother a volunteer fund raiser for several charitable organizations. Roger, the eldest of four children, comes from a lower-middle-class Jewish family. His father runs a hardware store in the Bronx. His mother is a housewife. His brother is a dentist. His two sisters are married and are housewives.

When Phyllis was 17 she became pregnant by a high-school classmate, Juan, a Puerto Rican lad from a disorganized, lower-class "welfare" family. He never knew his father. Her pregnancy was not discovered by her parents until the sixth month, when it was too late to have an abortion without undue risk. (This was in the days before legalized abortions.) The young couple was hurriedly married in order to legitimize the coming child. Two weeks later Phyllis had a miscarriage. An annulment was arranged. Phyllis never saw Juan again.

The following fall Phyllis entered college. At college Phyllis became "revirginated." She dated many young men, engaged in heavy petting, but refused to have sexual intercourse with anyone until her senior year, when she fell in love with a fellow student. It was a serious relationship that ended after six months, when the young man left for Oxford as a Rhodes scholar.

Before she met Roger, Phyllis had three more serious love affairs, all with brilliant, talented, but neurotic men — "very destructive relationships," Phyllis commented. "Roger was different from any of the guys I hung out with before. He was quiet, low-keyed, nothing scintillating or challenging about him. I felt comfortable with him. I didn't feel I had to be the most dazzling woman on earth when I was with him. He didn't rush me about sleeping with him, like just about every other guy I went out with. Besides, when I met him I was involved with George and I was never one for sleeping with two guys at the same time.

"On our fifth date, we were in his apartment, he was fixing dinner for us before we were to take off to hear Bucky Fuller, who was lecturing that night on campus, and it started to rain cats and dogs. So we didn't go to the lecture. Later it seemed ridiculous to go out in all that downpour to get back to my room; so I stayed. He was so sweet and thoughtful. We talked half the night. And he listened so patiently to my ravings against my parents and my professors and my roommate, without criticizing me or siding with me — he just listened. He told me of some of his experiences with his parents and professors but quiet-like, not the rantings I was used to hearing from my friends.

"I can't say I fell in love with him. The earth didn't move when we made love, but I sure as hell liked him a lot. I remember thinking, 'He's the first marriageable man I've known.' The next week I told off my roommate, packed my stuff, and moved in with him. We lived together for about a year before we got married. Oh, it wasn't all sweetness and light. We had our share of arguments. I don't know why he put up with me. He's calm; I'm quick-tempered. He's neat; I'm a slob. He keeps appointments; I'm always late. He's fussy about food; I don't care what I eat. He thinks everything out carefully before he undertakes something; I'm rash and impulsive. He's conservative politically, I'm a so-called liberal."

"What finally decided you to get married?" I asked. "I always took for granted that someday I would be married and have children," Phyllis replied. "So did all my friends," she added, "even the radical feminists. When I was a little girl I used to imagine myself a mother, with four darling little children, two boys and two girls. I even had names for them [not the names of her real children]. I gave each one a different personality, made up stories about them, where we'd go, what we'd do —"

"Was there a husband in this fantasy?" I asked.

"No, I didn't picture a husband or father, only myself and the children and the house we'd live in.

"So about deciding to get married — I had just gotten my Ph.D. I had a job offer to teach anthropology at a small college in the boondocks of Ohio. They wanted me to sign a two-year contract. Well, here I was, twenty-nine. I always wanted a family. I figured that if I was going to have a couple of kids before I got too old, I'd better get married before too long. Rog had broached the subject of marriage all year but I hadn't considered it until the night of my twenty-ninth birthday. It seemed like the right time. We called up our folks and told them. They were very happy."

Infatuation: I asked Roger the same question. He laughed. "I fell in love with Phyl the first time I laid eyes on her. I didn't know who she was. She was walking down the corridor of Ferris Hall. I thought she was the most beautiful creature I ever saw. Then I met her a few weeks later at a party. I took her home. She was as enchanting as I had dreamed she would be. I would have married her then and there."

Religion: The most unequivocal reply to my question I received from Jacob C, age 33, married nine years, father of four children and a fifth on the way. Jacob is the principal of a parochial day school to which I am a mental health consultant. He is an ultra-orthodox Jew, member of a Hassidic sect.

"What did you say?" he asked in astonishment. "Why did I get married?" He looked at me as though I had suddenly lost my senses. "What do you mean, 'Why did you get married?' Everybody gets married! It is the religious obligation of a Jew to get married." I explained the reason for my question.

Jacob shook his head sadly. "Sit down," he said. [We were leaning against a blackboard in a classroom.] "I will tell you." I sat down at a school desk while Jacob remained standing. He spoke in a rhetorical manner.

"Marriage in Judaism," Jacob intoned, "is a divine institution, part of the scheme of Creation for all mankind. It is the ideal human state. To marry and raise a family is a mitzvah [commandment] a Jew is expected to fulfill. Its holy purpose is to build a home and family. Marriage is also for companionship. A man's wife is his other self. It says in the Mishnah that a man is dependent on a woman for joy, happiness, and blessings.

"The Hebrew word for the marriage ceremony is *kiddushin*, or consecration." Jacob quoted in Hebrew the declaration under the *"huppah"* [the canopy] that formalizes the bond of matrimony. " 'Be thou consecrated unto me.' " He continued, "Only through marriage do men and women fulfill themselves to the highest. In the Cabbala," he added, "an unmarried man is called a *palga gufa* [half a body]. In Mishnah it says 'A Jew without a wife lives without joy, blessing, or good.' "

I broke in at this point to ask, "Does love figure in Judaic law? Did you love Rivka when you married her?" He looked at me scornfully. "Of course I loved Rivka," he said. "But to a Jew marriage is more than a physical union or a legal union. It is a sacred relation between husband and wife, sanctified by God. In bringing forth children, the man and woman are continuing creation; they are partners with God." There were a few moments of silence. Then Jacob smiled and asked slyly, "Did I answer your question?"

Love: What about love, the reader may well ask? Don't most people get married because they're in love? Indeed they do. Every survey on marriage (of which there are no end) shows that "love" is the reason most frequently given by both men and women for getting married, as it was in my own search. Now, being in love can propel a man and woman into bed together, but in these days when love can be, and frequently is, consummated without legal trappings, that conventional answer is too pat.

All the responses to my question seemed reasonable enough. But they gave no clues to account for the persistence of marriage through the centuries. I would see what the social scientists had to say.

Societal Pressures: Sociologists tell us that it is the concerted pressures of society that ensnare men and women into assuming the responsibilities of marriage and the family. Society depends upon the institutions of marriage and the family to perpetuate the race, pass on the cultural heritage from one generation to the next, and keep the social order stable.

Ours is indeed a marriage-oriented society. Kathryn Perutz calls society "the vast matchmaker." She writes, "Mothers hanker for grandchildren or your happiness . . . married friends arrange dinners and outings."[8] I myself no sooner spot an eligible male, single, divorced, or widowed, than I begin to ponder who among my unmarried female friends would make him a good wife.

Despite the wisecracks of stand-up comics, the deprecatory novels of disillusioned writers (happy marriages are rare in literature), marriage is glorified in song and story. If you need convincing, watch television for a day, the commercials as well as the entertainment.

The married couple is our social medium of exchange. Ask any widow or divorcée. She will tell you that she finds herself socially abandoned once she is no longer part of a pair. A friend of mine, age 50, who had been a popular hostess and, with her husband, a much sought-after dinner guest, told me that after her husband died, except for a few close friends and family members, she was socially isolated. "I can understand the Indian custom of purdah," she said bitterly.

Women are not alone as targets of social prejudice against the unmarried. The single man, I am told, is at a disadvantage in business, particularly at the corporate executive level. Less reliable, it is said. Banks regard him as a poorer credit risk than his married peer. It seems that single men and women "of a certain age" are still looked upon half disapprovingly, half envied, as a nonconformist "immoral minority."

Desire for Progeny: Some social psychologists tell us it is the desire for progeny through whom one can extend one's mortal existence that motivates many people to marry and raise a family. Some tell us that when men and women reach that adult stage of psychosocial development in the life cycle Erikson calls "generativity," they seek fulfillment in the social responsibility of bringing forth and raising a new generation.

Biological Roots: Without for a moment minimizing the immeasurable weight of societal pressures upon men and women to marry after reaching adulthood, or the developmental push in the course of the life cycle toward generativity, or the many diverse reasons given by my informants and those in national surveys, I believe there are also deep biological roots (aside from the sex drive) that account for the persistence of marriage and the family. (And why I believe that marriage and the family, however changed in form over time, will endure forever.)

The eminent sociobiologist, Edward O. Wilson,[9] believes that there are some "instinctive tendencies," perhaps programmed in the genes, that seek bonding. He thinks that many features of man's social behavior assumed to be culturally determined, *including marriage* (italics mine), may have a genetic foundation. Indeed, he claims that in the evolutionary framework the primary role of sexual behavior is not procreation but "to enhance male-female bonding," since the survival of the human species depends upon the long period of parental care of the young until they can fend for themselves.

I don't know much about genes. I do know that there seems to be a human propensity toward bonding. I believe the roots of bonding go back to the moment of birth when the newborn infant emerges or is wrenched from the warm, sheltering darkness of its mother's womb and thrust into the harsh light of day, its umbilical cord that had bound it to her throughout its fetal existence severed forever. That moment of aloneness I imagine must be the most terrifying moment of a human being's life, more terrifying than torture or the approach of death, so terrifying that it is repressed beyond all memory. We can hear it in the helpless infant's first angry, protesting, anguished cry. It is assuaged only when the infant is placed in its mother's arms and she holds it close to her warm, comforting breast. It is at this moment that bonding begins.

I believe it is in the imperative need for attachment to a succoring mother at birth — an attachment reinforced by the biological necessity of nurturing the dependent child over a long period of time if it is to survive — that the origin of the pair bond lies. We see it much later in a transmuted form in the marriage bond.[10]

First Attachments: Let us digress for a moment and examine the early mother-child relationship — what Selma Fraiberg calls "first attachments."[11] During the first five months of the infant's life, there is a state of oneness with the mother.[12] He regards her as an extension of himself. (And she him of herself. Many mothers speak of a "mystical bond" between themselves and their newborn infant.) By the sixth month he recognizes her as separate from himself (though he considers her and the others in his environment as there to do his bidding.) In the security of her presence he begins to try himself out as a separate person. He dares to leave the safety of her lap and crawl around the fascinating space before him. Under the spur of his developing muscles and brain he begins to walk! Now he can explore the wonders and delights of his ever-expanding environment, but at first only with the assurance that his mother is nearby and he can see her or run back to her for what Mahler calls "emotional refueling."[13]

Around 18 months, now fully aware of their separateness from the mother — their "I-ness" — most normal children, overwhelmed by a sense of aloneness, go through a crisis in which they both cling and push away the mother, shadow her and dart away, hold on and let go.

In the maturation process the child gradually "internalizes" the loved and needed mother; that is, he carries her image within himself so that she is with him even when she is no longer physically present. By three, for example, he is able to go off to nursery school without being distraught by her absence. "Borrowing strength from the loving parent," writes Dr. Willard Gaylin, "he will learn the courage to bear separation, for ironically it is only in such separation — with all its anxieties — that one can explore the world and begin the process of self-confidence and pride that leads to an independent state."[14] In the course of the individual's physical and psychosocial development to adulthood, he eventually leaves the security of his home altogether and in time marries, procreates, and begins a new generational cycle.

Later Attachments: "The past is never dead; in fact it is not even past," William Faulkner once said. I believe that buried deep inside every man and woman, the grumpiest misanthrope, the most suspicious hermit, the most self-sufficient man or woman, there lives an insecure child afraid of aloneness, who yearns for that blissful attachment to the mother it once had (or wishes it had had).

Being in love (or its illusion) re-creates that bliss. And so, in a metamorphosed way, does marriage born of love. It holds the promise of unreserved closeness with mother we once knew* and yielded up in order to fulfill the contrary need for separateness, for individual autonomy. I believe it is

* The failure of many marriages stems, however unconsciously, from this unrealistic expectation.

in the remains of our first attachments, however outgrown, transformed, distorted, or denied they may be in later life, and however multi-layered with the social, psychological, economic, and cultural aspects mentioned earlier, that we must dig for the answers to the question "Why Marriage."

CHAPTER 3

Marriage Yesterday and Today

*"The old order changeth, yielding place to
the new. . . ."*
— Alfred, Lord Tennyson

"The ever-whirling wheele of Change, *the
which all mortall things doth sway."*
— Edmund Spenser

In Chapter 1 we viewed marriage as a *private affair*, a sacrament between a man and woman who commit themselves to "love, honor, and cherish" each other.

Marriage serves another and, from society's point of view, more essential purpose. Throughout the history of mankind marriage has been first and foremost a *social institution* for the continuance of the human race. It arose out of the imperative to keep a man and woman together long enough not merely to procreate but to rear their offspring in a protected environment until they were able to fend for themselves.

As an institution marriage provides for the founding and maintenance of family life, upon which our social structure rests and through which the culture is transmitted from one generation to the next. Over the centuries the institution has become encrusted with a variety of religious, legal, moral, social, and economic sanctions, but its *purpose* — the establishment of family life, in which the children are nurtured and the culture is passed on — has persisted.

The *form* of marriage — whether monogamous, polygamous, polyandrous, or variations thereof — has varied from culture to culture and from age to age. So too has the basis upon which marriages have been contracted as well as the nature of the relationship between husband and wife. For example, marriage as we know it in Western culture today is premised on romantic love and free choice of mate. But this is a relatively recent phenomenon.

Until the late nineteenth century most formal marriages in Western societies were a businesslike affair arranged by the parents of the bride and groom.* The choice of a marriage partner was considered too important to be left to the young people. So their parents, presumably with wiser and more practical heads, chose their mates, weighing such indispensable matters as money, social status, bloodlines, and family connections.

Among some ethnic groups the bride and groom did not meet until the wedding day. My own grandmother first saw my grandfather at the betrothal ceremony, and then only to steal shy glances at this stranger with whom she was destined to live out her life. "What did Grandpa look like when you first saw him?" I once asked her. "I was disappointed," she said. "He was short and had red hair." Then, after a pause, she added, "And his nose looked like a potato." A month later she was wedded and bedded with a man with whom she had barely exchanged a sentence, who would father her thirteen children (six of whom would be buried in infancy).

"Did you love Grandpa?" I once asked my grandmother in a confidential moment. "Love, shmove," she replied. "You live with a man, you respect him, you take care of him, you go through hard times with him, so you love him." After some coaxing she revealed that before her betrothal to my grandfather she had been in love with Shimin, the glazier's son, who was tall and dark and beautiful, "like King David." But

---

* Of course, arranged marriages exist today not only in some Oriental societies, but among certain social strata in Western culture, notably in aristocratic and financial dynasties.

marriage of a rabbi's daughter to the son of a manual worker was unthinkable in that tightly knit caste-ridden Lithuanian village in the days before it was razed in the Holocaust. "Did you ever wish you had married Shimin?" I shamelessly pressed. Grandma gave me a reproving look. "What kind of a foolish question is that?"

In my grandmother's day marriages were expected to endure "till death do us part." If the couple didn't get along, their families generally intervened on the implicit assumption that marital troubles could be solved if one tried hard enough. If the troubles persisted, well, they had to be borne. Divorces did occur, but they were rare and considered shameful. When I was a small child I remember whisperings about my Tante Sarah's having been divorced "back in the Old Country." She had what was called a *get* (divorce). I did not know what the word meant, but from the tone of my mother's voice I gathered it was something bad, like a loathsome disease. Even in America at the turn of the century divorce was considered something of a disgrace. Upper-class divorced women were not "received" in high society, if one is to judge from the literature of the period.[1]

Contrast this attitude toward the sanctity of marriage vows with the following incident circa 1980. At a lavish wedding reception I attended recently, the father of the bride, an eminent jurist, said to his daughter, ostensibly as a bit of wry humor, "Remember, darling, I'm only paying for the first wedding. The next, you're on your own."

While most young people today undertake marriage as a serious commitment and anticipate a life together "till death do us part," some enter it with the sober, if unromantic, expectation that "if it doesn't work out we can always get a divorce."

Social and Economic Changes

Marriage and family life in America have undergone enormous changes since 1900. Since World War II they have been occurring at breakneck speed. Changes in social and economic forces of any time are reflected in its institutions. A brief glance at the cataclysmic upheavals in our social and economic structure over the last 75 years should make the changes in today's marriage and the family today more comprehensible.

In the early part of the century, the industrialization of society, with its intense economic growth, spurred by the rapid technological advances, had a profound impact on marriage and the family. It shifted the nation's way of life from a largely rural, agricultural subsistence economy to an urban, commercial one. People who for generations had been scratching the land for a bare living left the farms in droves and moved to the cities, where the jobs and money were. Their migration often took them far away from their kinfolk, who had served not only as a bulwark against the hazards of sickness, hard times, and old age, but as a dependable source of social and emotional support.

The loss of close kinship ties had many ramifications. It put a greater burden on the immediate family members — the nuclear family — to provide this support for one another, intensifying the emotional ties, both positive and negative, among them. Moreover, living in an impersonal environment, traditional social restraints on behavior were loosened. Old imperatives that bound families together lost their force. As children were increasingly exposed to outside influences, parental authority, which had characterized the traditional family, was weakened. In addition, other institutions, such as the school, the police, health, recreational, and welfare organizations, stripped the parents of their responsibilities for many aspects of family life that had been their province in earlier days.[2]

Our present-day society, with its mind-boggling scientific and technological advances, has spawned still other changes in family life. As social and geographic mobility has been accelerated and educational opportunities expanded, the generation gap has widened. Children no longer look to their parents as guides in making their way in the world. In many instances they seem to come from different worlds. The son of an immigrant tailor becomes an advisor to presidents; the daughter of a cleaning woman wins acclaim in nuclear physics. Social and economic advances scarcely dreamed about fifty years ago have brought unimagined material benefits to families. They have brought unimagined disruptions as well.

The Working Wife

Perhaps the most far-reaching change in the current American way of life that has affected marriage has been the unprecedented number of married women in the labor market. Of the 42 million women in the labor market (almost half the total labor force), more than half are married. This revolution in the role of women is perhaps the most outstanding social phenomenon of the twentieth century — more important, according to economist Eli Ginsburg, than the rise of Communism or the development of nuclear energy.

The working wife is no new phenomenon. Poverty has always forced some women to work outside the home. And professional or career women have, by and large, preferred to follow their chosen work, given the opportunity, than to forsake it for domesticity. Also, at various times in our nation's history, notably during wartime, women were encouraged to work in factories, offices, and fields. But when the men returned from military duty, the women, particularly mothers of young children, were expected to resume their accustomed role as homemakers. Most of them did so. Others, however, having found the fruits of paid labor sweet, remained in the marketplace. Moreover, the tremendous increase in clerical, sales, and service industries — "women's jobs" (a euphemism for low-paid) in stores, restaurants, hotels, offices, schools, hospitals, social agencies, and other community services, proliferated. To supplement the family income housewives flooded into them by the millions.[3]

By the middle '70s, with inflation a stark reality, many married women who previously had had the choice of remaining at home were being forced to take paying jobs in order to make ends meet. "More and more women are working out of necessity," said A. M. Herman, director of the Women's Bureau of the Labor Department. "Women don't have the option of working inside or outside the home anymore. Economic needs require that they go out and find a job." Many of these women are the sole support of their families, either because their husbands are unable to work or are unemployed. Of working women with working husbands, almost half the husbands earned $10,000 a year or less. "Often," Miss Herman explained, "a second income means the difference between poverty and an adequate standard of living."[4]

It is not only the wives of low-wage earners who are taking jobs to supplement the husband's income. Middle-income women are going to work to keep the family budget solvent or maintain their standard of living in the face of inflation. Said Amy G, who is working as a clerk in her brother's pharmacy, "Judy needs braces on her teeth. Do you know what that costs?"

In addition, many privileged women, whose husbands earn enough to support their families, are choosing to work in order to achieve traditional middle-class goals — down-payment on a home, college education for the children, a summer place, a vacation trip. "I'm working to put my kids through college," said my secretary, whose husband is a computer analyst. "With two kids in college at the same time, it's a tight squeeze to make it on my husband's salary." The high cost of that American dream, a home in the suburbs, what with soaring interest rates, has made it beyond the reach of many one-income families that only a generation ago could have afforded it. Often it is the wife's paycheck that makes the difference in the family's quality of life. In more than 40 percent of intact families, husbands and wives hold jobs. The two-paycheck family is fast becoming the rule in our nation.

The Changing Shape of Marriage

The working wife has changed the very shape of marriage. It has altered to some degree the traditional task-oriented roles of husband and wife. The everyday job of running a household — the cooking, the cleaning, the shopping, the laundry, not to mention the care of the children — tasks that have traditionally been considered "woman's work," has become almost impossibly burdensome for the working wife to shoulder alone. To be faced with dirty dishes, dirty clothes, and dirty kids after working all day is tough. It is bound to make a woman feel resentful and exploited unless she gets some help from her husband, and the children if they are big enough.

Tradition dies hard. Some husbands take umbrage at such an expectation. They point out that they do "the man's job" around the house. Mow the lawn, put up and take down the storm windows, paint the ceiling, tile the bathroom, fix the washing machine, unclog the sink. Some are willing to take out the garbage and carry home the groceries but balk at doing the dishes.

I have observed, however, that more and more husbands, particularly the younger ones, are sharing household responsibilities with their working wives. Many of those whom I interviewed admitted, some proudly, some amusedly, some sheepishly, that they rather enjoyed it. One boasted that he was a better shopper than his wife. Another gave me his recipe for the popovers he bakes every Sunday morning for the family's breakfast. When one considers that most of these men have been brought up to be waited on by their womenfolk, they are to be congratulated upon their conscientious efforts to change their accustomed habits.[5]

The following interview with Marjorie L, 28, a secretary, married for six years to Jeff, 30, an accountant, and mother of four-year-old Judy, contrasts this aspect of modern marriage with the patriarchal marriage of her parents when she was growing up.

"On my way home from work I pick up Judy at the day-care center and I buy whatever fresh stuff, like bread, milk, and vegetables, we might need for dinner. While I'm cooking dinner Jeff sets the table. After dinner he cleans up while I put Judy to bed. On Saturday morning we do our big shopping for the week at the supermarket. Then Jeff takes the clothes to the laundromat while I clean the house. He likes to vacuum, so I leave that job for him.

"Before Judy came we used to eat out a lot, but now it's gotten so expensive we don't do it except on special occasions, like Judy's birthday or our anniversary. Two weeks ago we really splurged to celebrate a ten-dollar raise I got. We asked my sister to stay with Judy and Jeff took me to this fancy French restaurant." Marjorie laughed as she added, "Jeff said he liked my beef stew better than this *boeuf à la* something or other that cost twelve seventy-five. To tell you the truth, so did I. But I must say I loved being seated at the table with the white damask cloth and the fine china and candlelight. And best of all, being waited on. I had to laugh to myself when the waiter, he wore a red jacket, asked, 'What would madam like?' I wanted to say 'Madam would like to do this every night.' But maybe it's more fun if you can only do it once in a while."

I asked about entertainment. Marjorie said, "We used to go to the movies a lot but reliable baby sitters are hard to get and besides, movies cost too much, especially if you add in the expense of the sitter. We save sitters for when we're invited to someone's house for dinner or a party. Sometimes one of us will go to a movie while the other stays home with Judy but it's not much fun to go alone. Sundays the three of us go out together — to the park or a museum or to visit friends or our folks."

Marjorie described how different things were in her family when she was growing up. "When Papa came home from the store supper was waiting for him on the table. We kids had already eaten so Papa could have peace and quiet. After supper Mama and us girls did the dishes while Papa sat himself down in the living room with his pipe and tobacco and read the paper. Three nights a week he would go to his social club upstairs of a cigar store to play cards with his fellow Greeks. Saturday nights he would go out, I think it was to a Turkish bath. The only time he went out with Mama was to a wedding or a funeral. They'd take us kids along if it was a big family affair or some Greek festival. Papa never went to church with us except on Christmas and Easter. Mama had her neighbors and relatives nearby to socialize with. I don't think she gave a second thought to Papa's having his own private social life, because that's how it was in Greece with her parents and grandparents when she grew up. To her that was how it was supposed to be."

Shifting Traditional Sex Roles

The wholesale entry of women in the labor market has wrought even more fundamental changes in the traditional relationship between husband and wife. Until not so long ago the role of each sex was clearly defined. *He* was the breadwinner, *She* the homemaker. As the breadwinner upon whom wife and children depended, sometimes for their very survival, *he* was the boss, *she* his handmaiden. Almost every aspect of a married woman's life was defined by her husband's. Even her name. He was John Smith, she, his adjunct, Mrs. John Smith. As someone remarked, "Marriage made them one flesh — his."

For hundreds, probably thousands, of years, man's "rightful" domination over woman was taken for granted, not only because of his greater physical size and strength but because of his God-given "natural superiority" — "how it's s'posed to be." Feminists have pointed out that society is a man-made structure that keeps women in a subservient role.

Now, dependence, particularly economic dependence, fosters a master-servant relationship between provider and recipient that no amount of love, assurance, or concrete gifts can altogether disguise. It inevitably breeds certain attitudes and behaviors in each toward the other, attitudes of dominance and submission, of power and powerlessness.

Women have, of course, been unwitting accomplices in this arrangement. For most women marriage and family have always been — and still are — their goal.[6] A little girl learns at her mother's knee that her task in life is to captivate, capture, and — toughest job of all — hold on to a man who will take care of her for the rest of her life. "Much of a woman's identity," writes Erik Erikson "is . . . defined in her kind of attractiveness and in the selective nature of her search for the man (or men) by whom she wishes to be sought."[7]

She learns, almost with her first "da-da," the importance of being pleasing to men (and the power she derives thereby) — pleasing to look at, to touch, to amuse. I watch three-year-old Susie turn her executive-type father into a lump of putty with her beguiling smile. She will be well-experienced by the time she catches a husband.

Over a hundred years ago George Eliot described the heroine of *Middlemarch* thus: "She was always trying to be what her husband wanted, and was never able to repose on his delight in what she was." Eliot's observation of Dorothea Brooke remains more or less true for most women today, at least for those who grew up before the Women's Liberation movement took hold. (A radical feminist described women's liberation as "the right not to please.")

If a woman is dependent upon a man for support, she soon learns to conciliate, to placate, to nod her head in agreement, regardless of what she thinks, in order not to "make waves." She even learns certain styles of discourse to get what she wants: to "beat around the bush," to ask indirect questions, to wheedle, and if necessary, to resort to tears. These entrenched "feminine" behavior patterns seem to persist even among the younger generation whose women are taking their place alongside men in the work force.[8]

Slowly, almost imperceptibly, women's way of relating to men as the *Herrenvolk* is being modified. Their entry into the workplace and their *cash* contribution to the family exchequer have loosened the underpinnings of traditional sex roles.

Once a woman has tasted the fruit of knowledge that she can support herself and, if need be, the children, her way of thinking about herself and about her relationship to her husband has been irrevocably altered. Abetted by the women's movement, which has raised women's (and men's) consciousness about their place in society (whether or not they are aware of its impact on their lives and whether or not they are in sympathy with the movement), the married woman who can earn her own living has begun to define herself in roles additional to those of wife and mother. This is true for women who love their husbands deeply and who put their roles of wife and mother far above that of wage earner. For the woman in an intolerable marriage, her greater economic independence makes it at least possible for her to consider ending it, something she could scarcely have done were she and the children entirely dependent upon the husband for economic survival.

This turn of events is redefining the old dominant-subordinate pattern of marital relations and is shaking the hierarchical power structure of the marriage institution itself. Of course, married women have always had certain circumscribed powers granted them by their husbands. There is the old joke about the man who declares that in his family he makes all the important decisions, like what to do about the oil crisis, nuclear energy, the mid-East situation, and Salt II, while his wife makes the minor ones: where they should live, the children's education, and handling the family finances.

And there has always been the immeasurable power inherent in her role as creator and nurturer of the children and as the chief sustainer of family life. These are no mean powers. The modern woman's discontent, I have found in my research for this book, has not been so much with her role as wife, mother, and homemaker as in the underlying assumption still extant in our "liberated" society, that she is intrinsically inferior to men, as witness the differential in pay for the same work or exclusion from certain occupations or positions of authority. (To argue that those over whom one wants to maintain power are inferior, be it biologically, intellectually, socially, or morally, has been a ploy as old as history itself.)

Working Wives and Marital Stability

On the whole, the experience of working outside the home has been good for wives. Studies show that working wives are in better physical health, have fewer psychosomatic illnesses, and are happier than full-time housewives.⁹ On the other hand, working wives are not so good for marriage. Marriages, at any rate those of young working wives, are more fragile, to judge from the divorce statistics.¹⁰

The change in the traditional role of wife — and the shift in the traditional balance of power — can be a threat to a husband's "masculinity." If the family needs the wife's income — and it generally does these days — he is in a tough spot. "She's gotten so uppity just because she earns more than me," a distraught husband complained, "She's getting hard to live with." He can't tell her to quit her job because "we need the dough." So he complains about her housekeeping, which indeed may be scanted, or about her neglect of the children.

Fulfilling his creature comforts may no longer be the center of her universe. Her hours of work may interfere with her former running of the house around his needs. Meals that had been planned to suit his schedule may have to be rearranged. Roasts, stews, and other foods he likes that take long, careful cooking may give way to franks and hamburgers. Even the couple's sex life may be adversely affected. After working on a job all day and doing the housework besides, she may be too tired to make love when he wants to, and now that she earns money, she may feel she has the right to say No.

The tradition-bound husband may have other, less outspoken, complaints. Henry G, a computer analyst, worries that his attractive wife, a secretary to a television executive, may "have an affair with one of those flashy TV guys she has to deal with."

George F tells me, "I hate it when I come home and she's not there and I have to heat up the supper for myself because she has to work late. I usually end up getting a bowl of chili at the corner hash joint."

Jud R, a lawyer married to a psychologist, resents her often not being available to entertain his clients because of her evening work.

Relations between the Gs, married five years, are

strained because he would like to start a family while she wants to postpone childbearing until she has established herself in a legal career.

On the other hand, many marriages have benefited, not merely financially, from the wife's working. This is particularly true for the well-educated and well-heeled couple, especially where both have gratifying careers. (And can afford good household help!) "Our lives are happier, fuller," reports the wife of a leading architect, who started to work as a secretary when her children entered school and is now, twelve years later, a vice president of the firm. "Ed's very proud of me, and very supportive," she said, adding "It wasn't easy at first, when I had to spend long hours away from home, going to meetings at night and taking trips out of town. I was filled with guilt about neglecting Ed and the kids for the job. But I managed to work out my priorities — they come first — and of course now that the kids are on their own and doing well, I don't have to feel guilty about them anymore. I must say that if it wasn't for Ed's patience and willingness to look after the kids when I had to be away I could never have done it."

Dual Career Couple [11]

As more women are entering the professions and filling executive and managerial positions, a new life-style seems to be emerging. By and large, the woman still takes major responsibility for child rearing and seeing to it that the house runs smoothly, but the man pitches in to help and, when necessary, takes over the job. Thus when Sally M, an intern, is on night duty, her husband, a physician, arranges to stay home with the children those nights, even though they have a live-in housekeeper.

I have noted, however, that among older professional couples the traditional husband-wife relationship prevails. I know many couples both of whom are physicians. The wife, though equal in rank and accomplishment, tends to "take a back seat" where her husband's professional status is involved.

One woman physician told me she would feel very uncomfortable earning more than her husband. When an opportunity for advancement arises for either one that requires moving to another community, it is generally the husband's career that takes priority in the decision to change living arrangements.

Years, no, centuries of ingrained attitudes explicit or implicit toward woman as somehow inferior to man, put on earth to serve him, are not easily uprooted, even when she is working side by side with him in the hospital, the laboratory, the law chambers or the executive suite. This is true, I have noticed, even among the most enlightened of men, men who take pride in the professional accomplishments of their wives. Here is a scene in the library of a happily married professional couple who have a (more or less) egalitarian relationship: (I shall leave it to the reader to guess whose it is.)

The wife is sitting at the typewriter working on a book about marriage. The husband is reading the *New York Times*. He: "Listen to this." He then reads to her an article by Anthony Lewis on the Op Ed page about some complicated impasse between the United States and the Soviet Union over missile bases. At this moment she couldn't care less about missiles, but she listens patiently (as patiently as her impatience to get back to her work allows) until he finishes reading and then presents his own ideas on the subject. When she finally gets back to her work, her train of thought about what she'd been writing has vanished. Eventually she thrashes out a few labored sentences. They don't sound quite right to her. She: "How does this sound to you? Does it make sense?" He, in a plaintive tone: "Darling, can't you see I'm reading?"

All in all, marriages of dual career couples come nearest to an egalitarian relationship and are among the most stable and gratifying of all those I had studied. Leon Eisenberg, professor of psychiatry at Harvard Medical School, who is married to Carola Eisenberg, dean of students at Harvard Medical School, in a symposium titled "Women Physicians in

Contemporary Society," sums it up thus: "Our wives are our best friends. No, it is not because friendship between men is difficult. We have men to whom we are close, whose friendship we treasure, with whom we can share our private thoughts.

"It is that our wives are all that and more. They do not replace friends or make them unnecessary. But our wives, our successful professional women are our lovers, our friends, and our comrades in lives of high adventure." [12]

Some authorities see the growing equality between men and women as a threat to the future of marriage and as incompatible with family life. They believe it breeds a power struggle for dominance between husband and wife, "destroying the bonds of affection that make marriage and family life worthwhile." [13]

True, the assaults on old patriarchal strongholds have not been without casualties. Some marriages, which in an earlier day would have remained intact, have been broken because a tradition-bound husband could not accept the demands of his wife for certain privileges and a rebellious wife would not give in. [14] As with all revolutions, there has been some overkill. And extremists have whipped up strife that might have been avoided had there been more understanding and patience on both sides.

In the long run, however, greater egalitarianism can only enrich the relationship between husband and wife and strengthen the marriage. For equality does not mean merely that the husband will do the dishes three times a week, diaper the baby at bedtime, go to the supermarket on Friday, and vacuum the rugs on Saturday. It means recognizing the wife as an equal person with needs and rights to be respected. I have found that most men, at least most young men, are trying. As they gradually liberate themselves from the cultural "macho" stereotypes that, while giving them certain powers have also burdened them, they find themselves able to love their partners in a more open and more mutually gratifying way.

Changing Pattern of the Marriage Cycle

Until not so many years ago parenting absorbed most of a couple's married life. This is no longer true. Today, with the trend toward fewer children, the couple completes its child-rearing job much earlier than did their forebears, giving them more time to do other things with their lives.

Moreover, with people living longer,[15] the couple will spend many years free of children in the home. This can be seen dramatically in comparing the marital life of my mother and her granddaughter. My mother, married at 19, a mother at 20, bore seven children over a period of twenty years. She was 45 when her youngest child trotted off to kindergarten, 60 when he left home for college. She had five child-free years before she died, two of them widowed. Her granddaughter, married at 21, has had two children within three years, all she plans to have. She will be 28 when her youngest enters nursery school, in her early 40s when he goes off to college. According to the life-expectancy charts she will have some thirty child-free years, many of them spent with her husband after his retirement. Small wonder that today's women expect to augment their mothering role with a career, to be pursued if not during, at least after they've completed their child-rearing task. This is especially true of today's college-educated women.

The Sexual Revolution and Its Effect on Marriage

The push for equality, goaded by the women's movement, has gone beyond the workplace, the kitchen, and the nursery. It has pervaded the bedroom, threatening entrenched assumptions about the sexual nature of men and women and their sexual rights and duties in the marital bed. For centuries as part of the marriage contract it has been the husband's prerogative to expect sexual service from his wife and the wife's duty to submit to her husband's sexual needs. Women, it was presumed, had no sexual desires of their own.[16] Many women, of course, managed to take pleasure in sex relations even under these obligatory conditions. Others, however, found them at best a chore.

In the late '50s the Kinsey report broke through the curtain of ignorance about women's sexuality. This was followed in the '60s by the research of Masters and Johnson, which showed that women could not only be as orgasmic as men, but given the opportunity, more so.

Women began to expect, indeed to demand, sexual gratification. On the whole this has had a salutary effect on marriage. Modern marriage has become a reciprocal relationship in the sexual as well as in other aspects of the couple's lives. It approaches what Simone de Beauvoir[17] calls "a genuine moral erotic relation, [in which] there is a free assumption of desire and pleasure, or at least a moving struggle to regain liberty in the midst of sexuality . . . possibly only when the other is recognized as an individual, in love or in desire."

The newer knowledge about female sexuality and the greater openness about the sexual aspects of marriage have had many other beneficent effects on the marital relationship. Men have begun to expect more than an available, compliant wife. They want a responsive partner, one with whom they can share mutual pleasure in love-making. One man told me, "When I sense that Sue doesn't really want me but lets me take her, it turns me off. It makes me feel like a rapist, even though there's no unwillingness on her part." Another man expressed his delight when his ordinarily shy wife sometimes takes the initiative in the love-making. This greater mutuality in their sexual life makes it possible for a husband, though disappointed, to desist from making love to his wife if she is unwilling without feeling rejected or unloved; and for a tired wife to graciously accede to her husband's wish for sexual relations without feeling martyred or abused, and neither feels like a failure if one or the other falls short of ecstasy.

It has also had its baneful effect. For some people it has spawned an overconcern with sexual performance that not only robbed love-making of spontaneity and joy but burdened it with achievement goals that often doomed it to failure. Giving an orgasm to the female became an end in itself. "Did you, honey?" "You didn't?" "I'm so sorry, dear."[18] Women who heretofore had given little thought to their orgasmic abilities now flocked to sex therapists, with or without their husbands, to remedy their newly discovered handicap. Classes in masturbatory techniques guaranteed to produce orgasm sprang up here and there. Some of the furor over female orgasm of the '60s and '70s, I am happy to report, seems to have abated as knowledge about human sexuality has become more widespread and individual differences in these matters taken for granted.

Sex as Recreation

Sex play has always been fun. Even in the days when preachers ranted against the sinfulness of sex for any purpose other than procreation, when sexual repression and sexual taboos were rampant, men and women managed to take their sexual pleasures whenever they could find them. For the poor married man who could not afford other diversions, it was his chief recreation, his consolation at the end of a day's or week's struggle for existence. But always the Damoclean sword of an unwanted pregnancy hung over the sexual embrace. Efforts to prevent conception by coitus interruptus diminished the husband's pleasure and fear of pregnancy diminished the wife's. Other contraceptive methods were risky and often failed. With the advent of the Pill and other advances in contraception men and women have been able to foil Nature's plot to populate the earth while enjoying sex. It has made the marriage bed an arena of recreation rather than procreation until such time as the couple wanted children.

Sexual Candor

Greater sexual frankness in literature, the theater, and conversation has helped to exorcise many of the verbal taboos that made the topic of sex so forbidding — and so fascinating. Unfortunately, it has also tended to trivialize it. The common use of what the FCC calls "frank language" has defused the four-letter word, robbing it of its aphrodisiacal effect. The other day a truck driver sitting on a stool next to me in a diner called out quite casually to the waitress, "Hey, Maudie, give me some fuckin' bread." Without blinking an eye Maudie handed him a basket of rolls.

In marriage the greater sexual candor has made the voicing of sexual desire and sexual preferences somewhat easier than in earlier times. Of course the taboos of childhood are not so readily discarded. Many women, including feminists, have told me that they are still diffident about making direct, frank requests for certain pleasurable acts, settling for whatever the partner wants. (One benefit of sex therapy has been to help couples with sexual problems learn to speak openly about their sexual wishes.)

Lest one think that the sexual millennium has arrived, it must be said that deep-rooted attitudes about sex, particularly about male sexuality, persist. A number of my informants, for the most part older men and women (including a few active feminists), "confessed" that despite their awareness of current research studies and findings on human sexuality and even despite their expressed views, deep down they believe the sex drive in men is stronger and more urgent than in women, and that inherent in the marriage contract is the obligation of the wife to have sexual intercourse with her husband when he desires it. What, I asked the women, if they really didn't want to sometime? Most of them said they managed to "wriggle out of it" by claiming illness or fatigue, or by guile, like finding an excuse not to come to bed until after the husband fell asleep. Nearly all, however, said they felt guilty about such maneuvers. Apparently it takes a strong-minded, aggressive woman to say an outright No. And an unusually patient and understanding man not to feel offended.

Premarital Sex and Its Effect on Marriage

In my grandmother's day premarital chastity, at least for the female, was an avowed expectation. Today many young people, at least in colleges and urban centers, look upon this as an outmoded custom. Premarital sex has become a respectable standard.[19] Surveys among college students indicate that by the third year over half the men and slightly under half the women have engaged in sexual intercourse, many on a regular, ongoing basis with one partner. Among my own married informants between the ages of 20 and 40, nearly all said they had had sex relations with their spouse (or with others) before marriage. So, I might add, did the majority of the men and women over 40 whom I interviewed.

Increasingly young people are living together, sometimes for years, without benefit of clergy. Parents, who only ten years ago were in a dilemma over what to do about sleeping arrangements when their son or daughter brought a lover home for the weekend now shrug off their children's living arrangements with a member of the opposite sex as "standard operating procedure." A friend joshingly refers to her daugher's lover as "my sin-in-law," another to her son's companion as his "live-with friend." The other day I was introduced to a young man by an acquaintance who stated quite casually, "This is Jim, my daughter Audrey's lover. They live around the corner."

In the long run I believe this trend is all to the good. It gives a young man and woman a chance to learn each other's ways and to test their own adaptability in living intimately with a member of the opposite sex. For those young people who are seriously involved with each other and contemplate marriage in the future, this can be a sort of "trial marriage" before assuming the social and institutional responsibilities of actual marriage. A poor choice of mate, one's unreadiness for marriage, or unrealistic expectations of the relationship can be rectified by separating without the legal entanglements of divorce. If this kind of "trial marriage" can help stem or postpone teen-age marriages — so often the result of infatuation, poor judgment, ignorance, and doomed to failure from the start — it will have served a useful social purpose, whatever its cost in temporary distress to the parents and disapproval by the community.[20]

Changing Attitude toward Divorce:
Its Effect on Marriage

A hundred years ago there was one divorce to every 34 marriages. Today there is one divorce to every three marriages.[21] While still a painful, often a heartbreaking experience to the participants, particularly the children, divorce is no longer considered a disgrace to the family or even a failure of the couple. We are always saddened upon hearing of the separation or divorce of a couple whose marriage we recall as the fruition of romantic love. We remember the youthful hopes of a long and happy life together, now smashed. But we accept divorce more readily than our forebears did as a solution to a burned-out or destructive relationship.

Today, as working wives feel more independent and husbands feel less responsible for their working wives, the possibility of divorce as a way out of an unhappy marriage is more readily entertained, whether or not it is acted upon. This is in marked contrast to the attitude toward divorce one or two generations earlier, as illustrated by an interview several years ago over the BBC of a Nova Scotian couple celebrating its golden wedding anniversary. "In your fifty years of marriage did you ever think of divorcing your husband?" the interviewer asked the wife. "Never!" she replied, "but I often thought of killing him."

By freeing a man or woman from a dead or life-destroying relationship, divorce, whatever its immediate cost in grief and pain, may in the long run be beneficent if it opens the way to a richer and more fulfilling life for both. Moreover, the changes that have taken place in recent years in the divorce process in most states — as, for example, the establishment of "no-fault" divorce and the mitigation of the harshness of some support and custody legislation[22] — has helped to lessen some of the bitterness and vengefulness that almost inevitably is spawned as a by-product of the traditional adversary system of divorce.

In general, this has been salutary for marriage. But not always. The readiness to turn to divorce as a solution to a troubled marriage sometimes leads to an unnecessary breakup of a family, unnecessary if the couple might have made the marriage work had they recognized their unrealistic expectations or each one's own contribution to the marital conflict (rather than only their spouse's deficiencies) or had they struggled harder with the inevitable frustrations and disappointments in all close relationships, especially the marital. Or had they sought professional help. In my work I have had quite a few men and women who suffered the rigors of divorce tell me that in hindsight they question the wisdom of their action now that they are faced with the loneliness, the hardships of single parenthood, and the painful disruptions in their own and their children's lives.

Changing Attitudes toward Extramarital Sex: Its Effect on Marriage

In civilized societies adultery has always been officially frowned upon. In the U.S. adultery was regarded as so heinous a transgression against marriage that it was grounds for divorce in every state in the Union.

Attitudes toward female and male adultery have differed among different social strata. Female adultery has always and everywhere been considered a moral, and in some quarters, a legal, offense.[23] Male adultery, on the other hand, has often been winked at, at least among certain privileged classes, so long as it was not flaunted and was kept at least nominally secret from the wife. A Hungarian count I once knew, upon observing our marital customs, exclaimed, "America is a funny country. You divorce on the first mistress!"

Although the numbers of married men in the U.S. who engage in extramarital sex is considerable — statistics range from 50 to 90 percent — most Americans, at least ostensibly, condemn it.[24]

Whatever the customs, infidelity of the spouse is nearly always distressing. Even "swingers," who exchange partners with other couples for sexual acrobatics, feel outraged and betrayed if the spouse has sex relations with someone outside the prescribed rules.

Nonetheless, with the greater sexual permissiveness of our age, adultery has become less onerous an offense; for some, less guilt-ridden an act. Though no less painful or humiliating to the spouse, it is more likely to be condoned, less likely to break up a marriage than in former times. I have known many a spouse who has turned a blind eye or shed a secret tear when the adultery was discovered. In some instances the knowledge was used as an excuse for his or her own sexual ventures outside the marriage bed.

A more notable change in our time has been the greater prevalence of extramarital sex among women. Whereas adultery was always the unacknowledged privilege of the male, today more married women are availing themselves of the same privilege than they did fifteen or twenty years ago.[25] What effect this trend — if it is a trend — will have on marriage, I do not know.

Changes in the Moral Climate — "Looking Out for Number One": Its Effect on Marriage

Other, more subtle, changes, less amenable to statistical documentation, have affected the structure of marriage today and have contributed to the breakdown of individual marriages. Perhaps the most glaring is what Christopher Lasch calls "the culture of narcissism."[26]

Narcissism is characterized by self-centeredness, an inability to form abiding relationships with other people, and an incapacity for empathy. The narcissist sees people largely in terms of how they can serve his or her needs.

Narcissism has always been considered a psychological problem. While acceding that narcissism has psychological roots, it is so widespread in our present-day culture that Lasch believes it has become a social problem. He points to the plethora of books, articles, and so-called therapies promising "self-realization," "self-fulfillment," and "self-assertiveness" as commercial catering to this growing social phenomenon. A prime example is Robert Ringer's book, *Looking Out for Number One*, which became an immediate best-seller. A full-page ad for *Glamour Magazine* announces "A young woman's first priority is herself." A new magazine addressed to women is appropriately called *Self*.

In marriage some compromise between the fulfillment of one's own needs and that of the partner is imperative if the marriage is to work well — indeed, if it is to work at all. This is not easy. Except perhaps in the first idyllic flush of romantic love, when pleasing the beloved is an unreserved joy, an unconscious struggle goes on within the psyche of each partner and also between the psyches of both partners in trying to gratify their divergent needs. This unconscious tug of war underlies much of the stresses and strains in all close relationships. The mature person, committed both to the partner and to the marriage, manages somehow to resolve these conflicts. The narcissistic person, committed only to himself, or herself, doesn't even try. There is no "scientific" way of knowing how much the prevalence of "the culture of narcissism" contributes to the high divorce rate. I would guess a whole lot.

The Rocky Road

There is little question that the revolutionary changes in the social and moral climate of today's society have threatened the stability of the marriage institution. They have created tensions and conflicts that many marriages have been unable to withstand. Some women, awakened to the opportunities for work and independence, have, like adolescents in the throes of feverish rebellion, too hastily and too violently cast off their traditional roles of wife and mother, which they viewed as oppressive.

Some men, unable to cope with the changing role of women, especially its threat to age-old dominance-submission marital patterns, have opted for escape from a situation they hadn't bargained for.

As in all revolutions, be they political, economic, or social, exaggerations of behavior, at least at the beginning, are inevitable. Similarly, as the goals of the revolution are approached and fervor abates, violence diminishes, social behavior moderates, and a new equilibrium occurs. So too, as new patterns of marriage emerge with husband and wife approaching a more equal partnership both in responsibilities and privileges, I see the institution of marriage and the family becoming once more a secure haven for its members. Women will once again find joy — and admit it — in nurturing children. They will discover that raising a family can be as gratifying as writing copy for perfume ads or climbing telephone poles or directing multinational conglomerates. Men, liberated from the shackles of machismo-ism, will find pleasure in fathering their young and in sharing with their wives the joy and sorrow of parenthood. Husband and wife will become not only more loving spouses but better friends.

PART TWO

The Seasons of Marriage

"To everything there is a season,
and a time to every purpose. . . ."
—Ecclesiastes 3:1

4

Introduction

"We cannot live the afternoon of life according to the program of life's morning, for what was great in the morning will be little at evening, and what in the morning was true, will at evening become a lie."
—Carl Gustav Jung

Like the cycle of life itself, which, in its inexorable march from birth to death, traverses a series of developmental stages — infancy, childhood, adolescence, young adulthood, middle age, and old age — so marriage passes through a succession of different, though overlapping, phases. Each phase has its unique characteristics, its specific life tasks to perform, its special problems and crises, and its developmental gains. Each phase has its own pleasures and its own pains.[1]

Consider the different faces of marriage during different phases: The early years, when parents are beset with the responsibilities of rearing young children, with struggles to make a living, with occupational strivings. The middle years when, the tasks of child rearing over and occupational goals reached, one is confronted with an aging body and its grim portents, with vague marital and other discontents. The later years, when retirement comes and one can "take it easy," but when old age and the specter of death is lurking around the corner.

Each marriage is unique in the timing of each phase, the nature and intensity of its critical periods, and particularly in the vicissitudes of life to which it is subjected and over which it has no control, such as accidents, unemployment, illness, and death.

Still, over the decades there have always been certain life events in connection with the marriage cycle, such as when to get married, have a child, reach the top of one's career, and retire, that were expected to occur at certain "normal" expectable ages. But in this era of rapid social change, traditional timetables have gone by the boards.

Even biological timing is different today from that of earlier generations. For females the menarche comes earlier, the menopause later. Better medical care, nutrition, and living conditions in the U.S. have lowered the mortality rate markedly in the last half century.

Not only do people live longer, but stereotypes and characteristics ascribed to people of a certain age no longer hold. When I was young my grandmother, at 70, though mentally vigorous, was a little, dried-up, bent-over, bespectacled white-haired "baba" pressing sweets on the grandchildren when we came to visit. Today some of our most glamorous actresses are grandmothers. My svelte friend Lois, 72, executive director of a social service agency, is a great-grandmother!

Social timing in connection with marriage and the family is different from that of earlier generations. While some men and women are postponing marriage and parenthood until their late 20s and 30s, nationwide statistics show that the majority of our population is marrying earlier, having the first child earlier, having fewer children, and having them closer together than did their parents and grandparents. Moreover, husbands and wives have more years together after the children leave home. Grandparenthood comes earlier, widowhood later.

The trend in our contemporary society is toward a more fluid, less "expectable" life cycle. A man of 60 may be a grandfather from his first marriage, the father of a preschooler in his second. Many women in their 30s and 40s are returning to school.[2] My friend Joan, 43, is in the same freshman class at Smith as her 17-year-old daughter.

Since chronological age has become less relevant to "expectable behaviors," I have not ascribed, except in a broad range, specific age norms for each phase of the marriage cycle. Moreover, in view of the enormous diversity of marriage patterns, to circumscribe so protean, so various, so complex a social institution as marriage within neat time boundaries would be a presumptuous, if not a foolhardy, undertaking. Nonetheless, in order to obtain some kind of overall perspective and make the subject manageable, I have arbitrarily divided the marriage cycle into four stages, represented symbolically by the four seasons. They parallel roughly the last three of Erikson's well-known eight psychosocial stages of the life cycle, which he calls Intimacy, Generativity, and Integrity.

CHAPTER
5

Spring

*"spring slattern of seasons you
have dirty legs and a muddy
petticoat, drowsy is your
mouth your eyes are sticky
with dreams. . . ."*
— E. E. Cummings

The springtime of marriage for most people coincides with the springtime of adulthood: the season of burgeoning, of creativity, of boundless energy; the season of hope and great expectations. This first phase of marriage, its greening, is the time before the children arrive, be it nine months, two years, or ten. It is said to be the period of greatest marital satisfaction.[1]

I wouldn't count on that. Of course, later on in marriage, after a hectic day with the kids, that child-free era may indeed seem to have been halcyon. Staying in bed till noon on Sunday — sleeping or making love or reading the comics — with no bawling infant clamoring to be fed. Taking in a midnight movie or a vacation in Maine without complicated arrangements for child care and never free of worry. Making love any time, anywhere, with nary a thought about whether the kids were out or asleep. Buying him a cashmere sweater for Christmas, her a Vuitton bag instead of a snowsuit and flannel pajamas, size two. Fixing coquilles St-Jacques for dinner instead of spaghetti with meat balls and chocolate milk. In nostalgic retrospect those *were* the good old days.

"Rough Winds Do Shake the Darling Buds of May"

The raptures of early married life[2] — and I do not for a moment minimize them — are by no means unalloyed. Sooner or later they are marred by the imperative adjustments required to live a shared life. The kite of fantasies, unrealistic hopes and expectations that each partner brings to the wedding ceremony — and this is true even of couples who have been living together — is sooner or later brought to earth by the harsh winds of reality.

Some disenchantment is inevitable. No matter how well you think you know your mate, you are in for a few surprises. In courtship we put our best foot forward. Once married we let down our hair — and often our manners. Unattractive traits of the beloved, brushed aside in the urgency of desire, are highlighted by the intimacies of married life. She uses his razor to shave her legs. Forgets to fill the ice trays. Laughs too raucously at parties. Burns his toast. He starts to eat without her. Wolfs his food. Leaves a ring around the bathtub. Farts in bed. Petty quarrels break out. In those early months there are many times when we reconsider the wisdom of our commitment and wonder whether the marriage was a mistake.

Conflicts in early marriage may arise from differences in personal habits that stem from differences in family background. When two people love each other, these can generally be worked out as each tries to accommodate his or her behavior to the temperament and wishes of the other.

Eloise, 22, a secretary, and John, 24, a law clerk, have been married ten months. Eloise, one of six children, comes from an easygoing, closely knit, "blue-collar" Catholic family. Her father and two older brothers are construction workers. John is an only child who was raised by his widowed Wasp mother after his father, a lawyer, died when John was 12. His mother has two great sources of pride: being a member of the DAR and her son's splendid scholastic record. She was unhappy about his marriage to a "common shanty-Irish girl" but is trying to make the best of it.

Both Eloise and John had lived in their family homes until marriage. They now occupy a rather cramped studio apartment. They share the housekeeping chores. Eloise does the shopping and cooking and John helps with the cleaning and laundry.

Eloise and John had known each other for three years before marriage, the last two as lovers. Except for a few secret weekends and an occasional overnight stay in a motel, they never lived together until after the wedding. "One thing that bothered me about Eloise after we were married," confided John, "was her sloppiness. Like when we come home late from a movie or party, she just drops her clothes on a chair and crawls into bed without even brushing her teeth or washing her face! What tees me off most, though, is the way she leaves her cigarette butts in every ashtray in the house. Smeared with lipstick. It makes me feel like a servant, always going around and emptying them just to get those filthy butts out of my sight." (John, I need hardly add, is a non-smoker.)

Eloise has a different bill of complaints. "John stays in that bathroom for an hour getting ready for work in the morning. That leaves me about fifteen minutes to get washed and put my make-up on before I have to dash for the bus. What the hell takes him so long? It never took my brothers more than five or ten minutes to get shaved. And did you ever hear of anyone taking a bath *and* a shower every morning? It drives me nuts waiting to get in there. I don't care if the next apartment we get doesn't have a kitchen. It's going to have two bathrooms, believe me."

Fortunately, these two young people of radically different backgrounds have many positive assets going for them, like love and admiration for each other and enough trust to voice their complaints to each other. Most of all they have a deep wish to make the marriage work. Both are trying to modify their habits to spare the mate annoyance. "But every time I remind myself to shut those dresser drawers tight, and put the cap on the toothpaste," Eloise slyly whispered to me, "under my breath I cuss him out, him and his damn fussy mother."

Then there are the traits that were endearing in courtship but turn sour when they interfere with the mundane side of married life.

Janet, who had grown up in a parsimonious household and tended toward frugality herself, relished Harry's lavish gifts during their courting days, the elegant dinners at expensive restaurants to celebrate, say, the first snowfall or the Giants' victory or the weekly "anniversary" of their first encounter. She was thrilled by his nightly telephone calls from Rome to say "I love you" when he was there on business for a few days.

Janet knew Harry's expenses must have been very great, what with the upkeep of his penthouse overlooking the river and his awesome alimony and child-support payments. But since he assured her that he earned "pots of money" (though he never said how much) as a manufacturer, she reveled in his cavalier gestures and when they were married she thanked God she would never have to be "saving" like her penny-pinching mother.

After marriage she moved into his apartment and took over the management of the household. She soon found herself besieged with harassing telephone calls and dunning letters from collection agencies. Stacks of unpaid bills were lying around. Harry did indeed earn a six-figure salary but it was not commensurate with his extravagant ways. His expansive, openhanded personality, which had so delighted her before, now seemed self-indulgent, impulsive, megalomanic. Before long she found herself in a role she had despised in her mother, that of a stinting, complaining, scolding nag.

The choice of a person's mate is often incomprehensible to the outsider, since it answers some unconscious need that the observer (and the participants as well) cannot know about. "I wonder what he sees in her?" we say, as we note the marriage of, say, an eminent scholar to a cocktail waitress.

Many of us tend to choose a mate who gratifies some unconscious wish that we may consciously disapprove of and that we defend ourself against by behaving in the opposite way. The mate serves us by acting out our unconscious wish for us. We can then blame or berate the mate for this disapproved behavior, reinforcing our own defenses against it. Thus Harry's prodigal ways, which the provident Janet condemned, gratified her own unconscious wish to live recklessly, with no care for the morrow, a most sinful attitude that her mother constantly preached against but that was a never-ending source of fascination to Janet. In scolding Harry, she became her mother — and her conscience — scolding herself for her "bad" wishes.

Family Matters

Why is it, I am frequently asked, that two people who have lived together for months or years and presumably know each other inside out sometimes "break up" soon after the marriage? A couple I know who "went together" for five years broke up within six months of the marriage.

There is something about *publicly* committing ourselves to each other in wedlock, be it in a formal church wedding followed by a grand reception or in a simple civil ceremony before a justice of the peace, that changes the relationship, however subtly, at once. By legalizing the union, you have made a public statement. You have declared your willingness to assume certain social obligations that were avoided when living together out of wedlock. You have said to the world, "This is my spouse."

Along with your new role in life — husband or wife — you have gained another, often an ambivalent, even grudging, role — that of in-law. Unless you've married a waif, you've acquired a gaggle of in-laws and other kin, and with them responsibility for certain expected social behavior. This may entail merely a family get-together at Christmas or sending your father-in-law a tie for his birthday. On the other hand it may mean (depending upon geography and, even more important, the emotional ties of your spouse and yourself to your original families) close contact between the families: expected visits to your home or theirs; Sunday dinners, made-to-order opportunities, while serving the roast chicken and broccoli, for oversolicitous inquiries as to how you are getting along, and for the almost irresistible temptation for the "old folks" to offer free advice on how to conduct your affairs.

Mother-in-law: Mothers-in-law in particular seem to bear the brunt of whatever ambivalence the bride or groom may feel toward the family of the spouse, and, if truth were told, probably toward the spouse as well. I know few brides, including those who honestly like their husband's mother, who do not feel some discomfort in her presence, at least at the beginning. One recently married woman told me, "My mother-in-law makes me feel as though I robbed her of her prized possession." A friend of mine, married twenty-five years, said, "Whenever my mother-in-law comes to visit, she looks at my husband, shakes her head, and says sadly, 'Irving don't look too good.' In the last year she's added a new refrain: 'How come Irving's baldy already? Even his father isn't baldy. When Irving lived home he had so much hair! Maybe he worries too much.'" Fortunately, my friend has a sense of humor and takes a benign view of her mother-in-law's foibles.

True, there are exceptions. I know many mothers-in-law who are good friends with their child's spouse; mothers-in-law who feel their child was fortunate in choice of spouse; mothers-in-law who tend to side with the in-law in domestic quarrels. But the ubiquitous mother-in-law jokes are not without substance.

Parents: Less obvious than any "in-law" problems in the early adjustment to married life, but much more important, is each partner's relationship to his or her own parents. Getting married signifies a person's readiness to assume the responsibilities of adulthood, to stand on one's own feet, apart from one's parents, and set up one's own family. The Biblical injunction, "Therefore shall a man leave his father and his mother, and shall cleave unto his wife," is rooted, I believe, in this law of nature.

In the course of growing up we go through a gradual process of individuation and separation from infancy through childhood and youth until we reach our own adulthood. Much of the adolescent's struggles with his own family, which we're all familiar with, is to free himself from his emotional dependence on his parents and establish his own identity. Only after having achieved this successfully is he able to reach what Erikson calls the next crisis in the life cycle — Intimacy — i.e., readiness for marriage.

Getting married does not put an end to our relationship with our parents. Indeed, we may become better friends, more appreciative of them. What marriages does is reshape our relationship to them, give it a different quality. The original family can give the newlyweds welcome social, moral, and even financial, support while the couple is "trying out the dream." But they are now two separate family units, though forever connected by affection and blood.

This doesn't necessarily happen smoothly, or in some cases, happen at all. Sometimes the emotional independence from parents may be more apparent than real. Some married men and women, though they may have left the family home long ago, may nonetheless still be emotionally tied to one or another parent, enough so to make trouble for the new family unit, especially in the early stage of marriage. There is the only son of a widowed mother who has her join him and his wife for dinner twice a week because "she's so alone." There is the woman who visits her mother several times a week because "she's getting old and needs me." There is the young wife who telephones her mother every day for "advice" on what to cook, what furnishings to buy, how to deal with her in-laws. These may well be legitimate reasons for maintaining close contact with one's parents and may indicate a real concern. On the other hand, they may indicate an incomplete and unconscious emotional clinging to the parents that may interfere with the successful establishment of a true husband-wife relationship.

Money

Studies on sources of serious conflicts in marriage show that arguments over money matters rank very high. (A matrimonial lawyer told me that disagreements about money and sex — in that order — are the most common causes of divorce.) These days, when many wives as well as husbands are gainfully employed, money problems do not loom as large in this first stage of marriage as they do after the children arrive. To the childless couples I interviewed money was not a critical problem. All but one of the women who worked outside the home said they expected to continue to do so at least until they "started a family."

Most of my younger informants said they discussed their financial arrangements before marriage. One practical-minded couple decided that instead of pooling their earnings, they would each manage their own. They wrote down who was to pay for what in their joint expenses, as well as who was to do what in running the household. They took the unromantic but sober-eyed view that "if the marriage doesn't work out at least there won't be any money hassles."

Despite less need for penny-pinching with two incomes available, many couples admitted that disputes arose over differences in attitude toward money and in the way the partner handled their finances. Lisa, of old Yankee stock, believed in putting aside a specific amount from each pay check toward the eventual purchase of a home, though this meant foregoing some pleasures, like dining out or subscriptions to concerts. Pleasure-loving Jerry, on the other hand, felt they had plenty of time to save for their mythical house after he got that promised raise or after his rich old uncle Angus died and left him an inheritance. This bred friction. However, determined to make the marriage work, Lisa agreed to settle for a smaller amount of savings from their pay checks and Jerry to leaner expenditures for entertainment.

Quarrels over money may be a symbol for other unspoken needs. A patient who wanted a child but feared to ask her husband to impregnate her because he had declared before marriage that he wanted no children until he had reached a certain income level, salted away some of the household money each week in a secret savings account. At the same time she would complain to her husband that he was stingy and never gave her enough money for her needs. When arguments over finances persist and become a chronic source of strife (unless one partner is a compulsive gambler or spendthrift or miser), one can suspect that the conflict may be an overt substitute for some covert resentment.

Sex in Spring

In the long-ago-and-far-away, when sexual intercourse was postponed until after the wedding bells had rung, one reason — sometimes an urgent one — to get married was to enjoy regular bed and board with a chosen partner. Today, when premarital bedding down with a person of the opposite sex is standard operating procedure, a regularized sex life is the last reason for "getting hitched."

However, most of the young married couples I interviewed who had had premarital sexual relations with each other reported that their sex life took on a special glow after they became man and wife. Making love was "better than before," Jay said. "To come home to Jeannie after a rugged day at work, to see her lovely face, watch her walk across the room as she totes the lamb chops from the kitchen to the table — sometimes I say to hell with the lamb chops and we take off to bed." This is no perennially aroused youngster on his honeymoon speaking. Jay is 33, a fashion photographer who works with some of the highest-paid models in the fashion industry. (He can have — and has had — his pick of the most beautiful women around.) When he made that statement he and Jeanne had been married fifteen months. The emotional security that comes from the assurance of the mate's love, their commitment to each other, enriches the entire relationship, including, needless to say, its sexual component.

For the young married couple who has had little premarital experience, this is not necessarily a time of pure joy. Indeed, the sexual relationship may be a source of unanticipated misery. The seemingly emancipated but sexually inhibited young woman who went to bed a few times with her young man before marriage may have done so to be obliging or because it was expected of her — "the thing to do" — with no pleasure in the sexual act itself. The young man with little sex experience may be clumsy, impatient, find the "honeymoon" period a fiasco. Getting attuned to each other's sexual needs, giving and getting pleasure in the sexual relationship, takes time, experience, and often patience. Love is not always enough.

Nor is it always wine and roses for the more experienced couple. Friction may arise over differences in desire for sexual relations. The young woman who could hardly wait to hop into bed with her lover before marriage may be less than eager once she is caught up in the routine of married life. She may be "too tired" or claim a headache when his lordship is ready for "a rub and a tickle." He may find the woman in bed beside him with greased face less than appealing, and he may well turn his back on her when she feels amorous. These skirmishes usually resolve themselves, after some temporary annoyance or resentment, with little residual trauma to the marriage.

Each partner brings to the marriage not only the dregs of his or her childhood upbringing, instilled standards and values, sexual and other life experiences, but also fantasies and expectations of what marriage will be like. They can in no wise match the other's. It takes a period of adjustment — sometimes a long period — to accommodate one's expectations to the realities of living day in and day out with the mate.

Generally in time they adapt to each other. Sometimes they do not. The large numbers of young married people who attend sex therapy clinics attest to that.

Children? If and When

More serious are the conflicts, often unspoken, over the procreative aspects of sex. Implicit in the decision of most men and women to marry is the assumption that eventually they will raise a family. (Estimates ranging from 5 to 10 percent of the men and women getting married these days claim they do not plan to have children. Some of them will change their minds when they grow older, as past experience has shown.) Most of the newly married persons I interviewed reported that they had come to some general agreement before the marriage ceremony on when and how many children they would like to have.

Social, economic, or other circumstances after marriage may change the feelings of one mate about having a child when the other is ready for it. When George and Marie were married he suggested they save enough money from their joint salaries to make a down payment on a house before having a child. Marie, herself one of a large, happy family, would have liked to quit her job as secretary and raise a brood of children as soon as possible. However, she accepted the practical wisdom of George's plan and went along with it. After four years, when they were ready to buy a house, George lost his job. He then decided to return to law school, which he had quit after one year to take a well-paying job and get married. This meant that Marie would have to continue working and postpone motherhood for a few more years. Not wanting to stand in the way of George's career, she agreed, though she resented having always to subordinate her needs to his. Soon after, she "accidentally" became pregnant. He begged her to have an abortion. How could they manage with a baby, with him in law school and no income, at least for the many months of the child's infancy? She underwent the abortion. But unconsciously she was bitter and angry about it. She developed gynecological troubles, notably a vaginismus. The relationship deteriorated. The couple is now separated.

The Sunny Side of the Street

Lest I have scared off anyone contemplating marriage by my description of its early pitfalls, let me assure you that the joys of this first stage generally far outweigh its pains. Whatever may be the flaws of later married life, this period is for most couples by and large a happy one, some say the happiest. There is something about making a commitment to each other, anticipating building a life together, that infuses the relationship with a richer quality and marks a new stage of development.

A *Sense of Belonging:* "What do you like best about being married?" I asked Susan, 23, an office worker, married to Joe, 26, an insurance broker, with whom she'd "gone steady" since finishing high school at 18. "Knowing Joe is coming home to me every night," she replies. "I get home around five-thirty and prepare dinner. Then I wait for him to come home around seven. Sometimes it's not until eight. If he's talking to a customer you can't tell when he'll get home. I watch the seven o'clock news on TV, but all the time I'm waiting for Joe. When I hear his key in the door my heart starts beating fast. Even Zsa-Zsa, our cat, gets excited when she hears his step in the hall. She jumps up on the console in the foyer to wait for him."

"What else do you like about being married?" I pursue. "That he's mine," she declares. She blushes and amends her statement. "I don't mean we have to be together all the time, like, you know, smother each other. We have our own friends from before. Tuesday nights I play bridge with three of my old girl friends; they're married too. We take turns meeting at each other's homes. And Sunday morning Joe goes bowling with the fellas. What I mean is that we know we belong to each other and that feels good. Like I know if I need something I can ask Joe because I'm his wife. I like the idea of him being my husband, not just my boy friend, and me being his wife. It's like we're two people and one person at the same time."

I keep prying. "Anything else?" She thinks a while, then says, "Yeah. I think what I love most is when we're lying together in bed and we talk about our future. About having kids and what kind they'll be and how many and what names we'll give them. And about someday getting a house in the country. Things like that."

She makes no mention of making love. So I do. "Is it better, as good, or not as good as before you were married?" And I add, "Some people say that after you've been married for a couple of years it's more like a duty than a pleasure." "Oh no," she protests. "It's much better than before." She reveals that in the two years they had premarital sex relations she had never experienced orgasm or had she enjoyed coitus. "What I liked about it was lying in bed with Joe and having him hold me. The other I did just for him." Although she had been "on the Pill," she was never free of the fear of pregnancy in those days. A Catholic, she knew she would not have an abortion should she conceive. "I knew Joe would marry me if I got pregnant. But I would be ashamed before my family if I had a baby five or six months after the wedding. It happened to my friend Sally. She told everybody the baby was premature, but everybody knew she had to get married. I would hate to have people talk about me like that. Now I can relax and enjoy it." She laughs. "So now if I get pregnant, so what? We want to have kids someday anyway."

I asked Joe what he liked about being married. Joe answers in Sue's almost exact words. "It's great to come home and know she's there waiting for me. You know, she works only a few blocks from my office, and sometimes we meet for lunch. When I see her walking down the street to meet me, I feel good. She looks so pretty and I think to myself, 'She's my wife. She's mine.' It's a good feeling."

"Any regrets?" I asked. "No. It was the best thing I ever did," he replied. He laughs and adds, "Except that I gained twenty pounds that first year. Sue makes better lasagna than my mom and she ain't even Italian. I think being married is great."

Raised Self-image: Marriage is a symbol of maturity (whether or not it has indeed been attained) — a new status not only in the eyes of others but in one's own. I sometimes attend class reunions of a women's college where I teach. Almost invariably when I ask alumnae, "liberated women" all, most of whom are working in a professional capacity, what they are doing, their immediate reply is "I'm married" and, if mothers, they tell me about their children. Only afterward do they add that they are a lawyer, a doctor, an architect, a teacher.

I suppose I should not have been surprised, since women have always defined themselves as wives and mothers. But I had half expected that under the impact of the women's movement, the active feminists might have moved from that traditional stance. But wife- and motherhood still mean, at least to most women, the achievement of a giant step in their passage to maturity.

Not only is this passage true for women. The other day, while shopping at the supermarket, I bumped into a neatly dressed, clean-shaven, tweed-jacketed young man who looked vaguely familiar. As we turned toward each other mumbling apologies I recognized him as Freddy, the kid who had worked for us one summer about five years ago as a handyman. At that time he was a long-haired, bearded, scraggly youth, a college dropout, who worked only enough to meet the needs of his rather chaotic, though abstemious way of life.

"What's happened to you, Freddy?" I inquired. I needn't have asked as I spied the broad gold band on the fourth finger of his left hand.

"I'm married," he crowed, jutting out his chest in mock pride. Only after he had sung the praises of his bride of six months and described their apartment did he tell me that he had returned to the university to obtain a graduate degree and was now an apprentice architect with a prestigious firm. For men, too, it seems, the role of married man adds stature to their self-image.

A Place of One's Own: In my interviews with newly married couples, many of them, the men as well as the women, mentioned the furnishing of their home as one of the challenging concrete aspects of their new status as husband and wife.

"I didn't feel like I was really married," confessed Dotty G, "until George went with me to Sloane's and we picked out a dinette set for our breakfast nook in the kitchen."

It is customary, especially in urban centers, for young people to move out of the family home once they are earning enough money to support themselves. They generally move into a place by themselves or with friends, which they furnish with oddments from their parents' attic or their room at home, homemade furniture or something from the Salvation Army stores. If they lose their job or run short of cash they can always go "home," meaning under the parental roof. To paraphrase Robert Frost, home is where, if you want to go, they have to take you in.

To furnish a home with one's mate, even if it is the very place in which one has been living, takes on a new and even exciting aspect.

"One thing I hadn't expected," reported Jerry W, "was the kick I got out of furnishing the apartment with Karen." One of four boys, Jerry grew up in a ramshackle house in a small New Jersey town. After college he moved into a roach-ridden basement apartment in Greenwich Village with an ex-college roommate. It served primarily as a place to sleep, shower, and change clothes. "We ate out most of the time. Or we'd bring stuff in from the deli or pizza parlor. A woman came in once a week to clean the place. When Karen and I got married and we rented our first apartment, Karen expected me to go with her to pick out the furniture and stuff. I'd never been in a furniture store before. I was surprised how much I enjoyed it, picking out fabrics, deciding on colors, where to put what. I found I had a real flair for decorating. Back in college I did the sets for the theatricals and for awhile there I thought of becoming a scenic designer, but I soon gave up the idea because I heard it's a tough field to crack. [Jerry is a computer analyst] I also like to help Karen with the cooking and entertaining. I get home from work before she does and sometimes I surprise her with some crazy concoction I cook up. You know what Karen gave me for my birthday? Julia Child's *Mastering the Art of French Cooking!*"

I asked Jerry about his father's participation in the household. "My father? He wouldn't be found dead in the kitchen. Except maybe to get himself a beer from the fridge. That is, if my mother wasn't around to get it for him. He sits on his duff and expects to be waited on hand and foot by my mother. She waited on all us boys too. Of course my mother stayed home, so that's all she had to do. Karen works, so the situation is different."

Forced Marriage

"For what is wedlock forced, but a hell,
An age of discord and continual strife?"

So Shakespeare described the not uncommon plight of a "forced" marriage. The "honeymoon" period of a marriage precipitated by an unwanted or accidental pregnancy is already blighted, in many instances by the man's resentment at being obliged to marry before he felt ready, and the woman's feelings of unworthiness and low self-esteem at having obligated him to "do right by her."

Burdened with the responsibility of child rearing before they have an opportunity to adjust to each other's needs, the couple may falter under the strain and the marriage fall apart.

This is particularly true of teen-age marriages. When one considers that six out of ten teen-age females are already pregnant at the time they "pledge their troth," when they can scarcely look after themselves adequately, let alone an infant, it is no wonder that the divorce statistics are heavily weighted by these early misbegotten unions.

One might expect that with the legalization of abortion the frequency of such marriages has decreased. Statistics do not show this. Logic falls easy victim to the urgency of sexual desire in the adolescent, culminating all too often in pregnancy. All too often, also, romantic fantasies about babies and motherhood eventuate in an ill-advised marriage, unready parenthood, marital strife, and, nine times out of ten, divorce.

Let me add that I have known a number of adolescent marriages that turned out well, although they took place a few months before or shortly after the birth of a child. In each case, however, the couple had a deep love relationship.

Pregnancy[3]

"We're going to have a baby!" Mary and Jack's announcement is almost universally greeted by family and friends with congratulations — social recognition that they are about to join that special company of humankind known as parents. Even people weighed down with heavy cares of child rearing tend to respond to the couple's news with smiles of approval.

Pregnancy is a transitional stage in the marriage cycle between the seasons of spring and summer. It is a critical phase of development in the life cycle of each partner. How it is met and dealt with depends on what has gone before; that is, on the relationship between husband and wife before the pregnancy, and on the life experiences of each partner, particularly the pregnancies and births in their original families.

Stages of Pregnancy
and the Marital Relationship

Each stage in the development of the fetus has a different effect psychologically as well as physically upon the pregnant woman and consequently upon the relationship between husband and wife.

Early in gestation there may be physical discomforts — swollen breasts, "morning sickness," fatigue, drowsiness. The prospective mother tends to turn inward from the moment she knows there is a living being in her womb. "I felt myself wrapped up in my own little universe," said Liza, 22, even though she was busily working as a secretary in a large office.

In the woman's absorption with herself and the fetus, the husband is likely to feel excluded and even neglected. He may well be. In her fantasy of herself as "mother," he is seldom in the picture. Moreover, in her changed physiological condition she is languid and tired at the end of the day, especially if she works, and may not be as attentive to his needs as before. Her desire to make love is noticeably diminished. Yet during pregnancy her husband is more important to her than ever, since only if she feels secure in his protection and support can she invest herself contentedly in her altered state.

Most women report that the second trimester is the best time during their pregnancy. By the fourth month the initial physical symptoms have disappeared. The expectant mother is imbued with renewed vigor and enthusiasm. The husband, who had been "faded out" earlier, is now allowed to join the magic circle of mother and child. He shares the thrill of feeling his unborn infant's kick. One man said that his greatest pleasure during his wife's pregnancy was to lie on her distended belly and feel the new life within.

Husband and wife's joint concern for the growing fetus strengthens the bond between them. They refer to it by nickname, enjoy fantasying together about its sex, its appearance, its aptitudes, its future role in their life. Sexual activity, which may have been scuttled earlier because of the wife's discomfort, is now resumed.

The third trimester is generally a wearisome time for both husband and wife. Her increased weight, awkward balance, and fatigue make it difficult for her to carry on chores at the very time when she needs to make additional preparations for the expected newcomer. The husband is generally called on for extra household responsibilities which he may do willingly, reluctantly, or not at all. In addition, the strain of the last burdensome weeks is intensified if, as in many instances, the physician advises abstention from sexual intercourse.

As parturition approaches, the woman is flooded with mixed emotions. On the one hand, she is eager to get rid of this incubus; on the other, she is sad about giving up this very special union with her creation. Fears invade her thoughts about the possibility of death in childbirth. Worries about the baby's normality plague her. The joints she smoked or the pills she popped before she knew she was pregnant, did they damage the fetus? And what about heredity? There's Jack's retarded nephew and her own peculiar Aunt Lucy. . . .

These are universal concerns as delivery nears. Not until the new mother hears the infant's squall, gazes on its ugly red face with wonder and elation, are her fears allayed. At last she can rest easy.

The Expectant Mother

Pregnancy, particularly the first pregnancy, is a profound experience in the life of a woman, with deep repercussions in her psyche as well as in her body. It is a rite of passage, a "normal crisis of growth"[4] releasing her from whatever strands of emotional dependence upon her parents have remained. For the "normal" woman it changes, generally for the better, her relationship to her mother. Early conflicts are more or less resolved. A patient who spent a lot of her time in treatment proclaiming her hatred for her mother reported after she became pregnant that for the first time she began to "understand" and sympathize with her.

Every woman reacts to becoming pregnant in her own way. To the woman who has dreamed all her life of having children — to whom maternity has been a central definition of womanhood — bearing a child imbues her with a deep sense of fulfillment of her femininity.[5] She takes pride even in the gross distortions of her body — the swollen breasts, the thickened waist, the expanding belly. Annie G, 30, who had to wait five years before her husband felt they could afford a child, began to walk with her stomach jutted out in her tenth week of pregnancy. Julia, mother of four, said, "When I'm pregnant I love everybody."

I have known even neurotic women whose pregnancy allayed, if only temporarily, their distressing emotional symptoms. An anxiety-ridden patient with low self-esteem, who had grave doubts about her femininity because of her hirsutism, broadboned figure, and alto voice, was "cured" of her self-loathing when she became pregnant. She announced her condition not, as one might have expected, by saying she was pregnant, but thus: "I'm going to be a mother!"

On the other hand, the woman who is unconsciously ambivalent about her procreative functions, or is still struggling with unresolved dependency needs from childhood or because of external circumstances, is in conflict about being pregnant — such a woman may have a hard time dealing with this new stage of life. Her conflictual feelings may express themselves in disabling physical symptoms. A narcissistic patient who became pregnant because "one is supposed to have a child" suffered severe nausea and vomiting well into the second trimester. In her fantasy the child was "eating up my insides." She also feared it was draining her of calcium and she would lose her teeth. In her fifth month she suffered a miscarriage.

To an insecure woman her increased helplessness and dependence upon her husband as the pregnancy advances can arouse deep childhood fears of abandonment. A patient whose father had deserted the family when she was four years old became increasingly anxious and depressed as the pregnancy advanced. She was convinced that her husband was repelled by her shapeless body and would leave her for a more desirable woman, a groundless fear in her case, I might add.

While the possibility of dying in childbirth crosses the

mind of most women as parturition nears — a not entirely irrational thought in view of the maternal mortality statistics — some women are overly preoccupied with fears of death. A patient who "accidentally" became pregnant for the first time at 42 suffered throughout the pregnancy with severe functional respiratory and cardiac symptoms. One could see the terror on her face when she thought of what awaited her as she gasped for breath month after month. A Caesarian section was performed at the earliest possible moment, which immediately relieved her of her distressing symptoms. Other fears may beset a conflicted pregnant woman. Rebecca L, 25, an obsessive, "uptight" woman with unattainable high goals, who had always striven for "perfection" in her work, worried throughout the pregnancy that she might turn out to be a "bad" mother, like her own.

In general, one might say that the greater the conflict about motherhood, the greater the likelihood of physical or mental symptoms during pregnancy.

The Expectant Father

In the drama of pregnancy the expectant father is the forgotten man. Yet his emotions during his wife's gestation may be quite as deep — and as mixed — as hers. Perhaps even more so, since he is in a sense an outsider — he does not have the benefit of the mystical tie between mother and fetus growing inside her body.

How a man responds to this new phase in his life depends, like the woman, on his maturity and on the emotional baggage he carries with him.

Most men survive their wives' pregnancy without much *Sturm und Drang*. On the positive side is the pride a man takes in this manifest proof of his virility. There is also the imminent realization of fantasies he may have nourished in boyhood of someday himself becoming a father like or better than, his own, and of sharing with his offspring his own pleasures, traditions, and ideals.

Concerns about his future added financial and social responsibilities are to be expected. And most men share with their wives not only the hopes and expectations but the anxieties, fears, ambivalences, and restrictions that her pregnant state engenders. However, there are some men who become very emotionally upset by their wife's pregnancy. For example, there is the immature man who becomes frightened by the looming changes of his impending new role, especially if it has been thrust upon him by chance. There is the man who never resolved his sibling rivalry and in whom childhood feelings of jealousy or hostility are stirred up by the unborn child. Or the man who is unduly dependent upon his wife-as-mother, who fears he will be displaced in her affection or concerns by the unwelcome intruder. An occasional man becomes so depressed or otherwise mentally ill during his wife's pregnancy that he must be hospitalized.[6]

Some authorities claim that during their wives' pregnancy many men experience "womb envy," which may adversely affect their emotional equilibrium. I have had no experience with this phenomenon. However, in my work with pre-school children I have heard many a little boy pretend to be pregnant and claim he is going to have a baby.

Pregnancy and the Marriage Bond

In conclusion, one can say that if husband and wife are secure in their identities as responsible adults; if they feel truly committed to each other and to making the marriage work; if they are not too "hung up" struggling with unresolved conflicts from childhood; and if external realities of their lives are not too harsh, the wife's pregnancy, whether *planned or unplanned*, can advance their maturity and enrich the marriage bond.

CHAPTER

6

Summer

"It was the best of times, it was the worst of times. . . ."
— *Charles Dickens*

Early Summer

The Parenting Years:[1] Nothing changes your marriage so drastically as does the arrival of your first child. Overnight, from a twosome you've become a threesome. Yesterday you were concerned with your own needs. Today they must be swept aside in order to minister to this third party, this red, howling creature whose very survival depends on you.

However you may have fantasied yourself in the role of parent, the reality is ruder than you had imagined. No one, even after attending pre-natal workshops, heeding counsel of mothers and friends, and reading Spock, is prepared for the upheaval in your life that your first child creates.

A first baby is an awesome thing. A torrent of jumbled emotions inundate you as you gaze at your infant asleep in its crib — pride, joy, wonder, mingled with fears and anxiety about your responsibility for its care. The parents' emotional investment in the infant as well as the assumption of responsibility for its nurturing brings about a new developmental stage — the psychosocial stage in the life cycle that Erikson calls Generativity.[2] Awaiting you are new tasks, new challenges, new risks, new joys, new pains.

° 84 °

A New Role

The first baby adds a new dimension to your life. You have now assumed an additional, and irrevocable, role — that of *parent*. You have taken on, willy-nilly, a social, emotional, and economic responsibility to bring up a new member of society until it reaches adulthood. You have forged a link in the chain of humankind.

At the beginning both of you, as parents, tend to be more interested in the child than in each other. All your conversation centers around its every move. "She only drank half her bottle at the four-o'clock feeding. I wonder if the formula is right." "His stool is loose and kind of greenish. Do you think I should call the pediatrician?" "Look, he's smiling at me! I bet he knows I'm his dad." "Don't be silly. At his age it's only gas."

It's not only your conversation that changes. Even your sex life is affected. "One thing I hadn't figured on," confided Emmy Lou, "is that a baby sure knocks hell out of your love life. I'm so damn tired at the end of the day, the last thing I'm interested in is making love. All I want to do is sleep." Most husbands will abstain, graciously or grudgingly, from sexual intercourse, if so advised by the obstetrician, during the last weeks of pregnancy and the first weeks following parturition. But it takes the patience of a saint to put up with the wife's disinclination or reluctant acquiescence to make love weeks and sometimes months after the baby's arrival. Like Emmy Lou, the new mother, if she has no household help, is often physically exhausted not only from the delivery but from the never-ending care of the infant. Moreover, much of her emotional energy is bound up in an almost mystical union with the newborn (whom she'd been nurturing inside herself for nine months), leaving little libido for her husband, a situation he may find hard to understand.

This discordance in sexual needs at this time can create unexpected tension between the couple, which may express itself in domestic matters quite removed from its real source. The husband complains about the torn sock, the missing button from his shirt, the weak coffee, the overdone hamburger, the mother-in-law's interference. (In one instance I know, he blamed his wife for the poor reception on the television!) What he's really miffed about is his wife's sexual disinterest.

The wife feels harried, sometimes guilty toward him. She cries a lot. This state of sexual frustration is generally short-lived. Indeed, many couples report that, after some rocky weeks, sharing the new experience of parenthood bonded them more strongly and enriched their sexual union.

Hazards

Parenthood, even when ostensibly desired, is not always salutary to marriage. For some men the birth of a baby revives early feelings of sibling rivalry when his own younger brother was born. Although they may intellectually "understand" the wife's preoccupation with the infant, deep down they resent it. They feel displaced in her affection by the intruder. Most new fathers repress such feelings by their genuine love for the child and pride in their creation. They may sublimate them, as siblings do, by participating in its care. They may deny them by staying away longer at work, with the rationalization that they must earn more or get ahead faster now that there's a baby to support.

Some men who have never resolved their original attachment to their mother may lose sexual interest in their wife after she becomes a mother. In her new role she turns into a mother figure for himself as well, stirring up early childhood incestuous fantasies and their attendant guilt feelings. Without ceasing to "love" his wife, these feelings disturb or inhibit his sexual response to her, so that he may become impotent or otherwise sexually dysfunctional with her.[3] Such men may become infidelitous at this time, turning to "women of easy virtue" (as contrasted to their "pure" mother-wife) for sexual gratification.

Some men on whom the mantle of fatherhood fits poorly may turn to other women at this time to hold on to the image of themselves as still "free and unfettered." A patient whose wife bore their first child against his wishes went on a rampage of promiscuity. Like the rebellious adolescent that emotionally he still was despite his twenty-four years, he declared, "I won't let her turn me into a 'daddykin'!"

By and large most men manage to transmute whatever primitive emotions crop up from childhood into parental feelings of protectiveness and loving care not only for the helpless infant but for the wife as well. They become "fathers."

Parenthood is not without its psychological hazards for women. After childbirth a considerable number of women become depressed for weeks, sometimes for months. It is commonly called "the baby blues." An occasional woman develops a postpartum psychosis requiring hospitalization.

While some of the "normal" depression may be due to physiological factors, such as hormonal changes, not to mention fatigue, psychological factors play an important part in that reaction. A lot depends on the personality of the new mother. If she tends to be an anxious, insecure person with feelings of inadequacy, she may well feel uncertain about herself as a mother and get depressed at the prospect of being responsible for a helpless infant. A patient who suffered from deep feelings of inferiority and unworthiness delivered a healthy infant that, to her joy, she was able to breast-feed. However, the baby developed colic and the mother went into a depression, sure that her milk was "bad."

By and large, however, most women report that giving birth fulfills some deep, inchoate wish to bear a child. Many say they feel themselves enhanced by becoming "mommies." "That's what life's all about anyway," said Barbara W, 29, an ardent feminist, her face aglow as she showed off her first baby. A university professor on leave, Barbara plans to have one or two more children before she returns to her career full time.

The Hectic Years

The next five to ten years are the busiest in the lives of the couple. Hustling and bustling to raise the children, advance their careers, get settled in the community and perhaps involved in community activities, husband and wife have less time for each other in this stage of marriage than in any other. Moreover, they tend to relate to each other more in their parental than in their marital roles. The woman, even though she may be a wage earner, at this stage sees herself primarily as mother, the nurturer and caretaker of the family; the man, as father, the family's provider and protector.

Both are busy coping with the everyday needs of the children: taking the kids to the park, the dentist, the museum; attending PTA meetings; helping with homework; coaching Sonny's Little League team; being a den mother; ferrying them to music lesson, library, dancing class. Husband and wife have little time left for their own companionship. They're too busy with the kids.

Other external demands absorb their time and energy. The man (and, increasingly, the woman) is busy establishing himself in his career. The working woman has her hands full not only with the housekeeping chores in her "free" time but with the ever-worrisome problem of getting adequate care for the children while she is on her job — and guilt over not looking after them herself.

If she does not work outside the home there is, in these days of runaway inflation, always the problem of making ends meet on one pay check. Cutting down on household expenses takes more time — shopping around for "bargains" — there's a "special" on chunky peanut butter at Pathmark this week but the chopped meat is cheaper at the A & P; sewing the kids' clothes instead of getting readymades; baking cookies instead of buying them; preparing three meals a day, week in week out with seldom a reprieve.

There's the self-same boring daily routine: cooking and serving meals, clearing the table, putting the dishes in the dishwasher and taking them out again; dusting and sweeping and making beds, only to do it again tomorrow and the next day and the next. And never a respite from the kids, even dragging them along when you cart the dirty clothes to the

Laundromat because there's no one to leave them with. "I can hardly wait until Timmy goes off to nursery school," one young mother said. "Maybe I'll have time to sit down and read a book." No matter how much a mother loves her little children, being cooped up with them all the time can "get on your nerves." As one mother puts it, "Sometimes I long for a conversation with someone who is over three feet tall. Someone who doesn't say 'Why, Mommy?' to every word I utter." No wonder many young mothers dream of a free and unencumbered life [4] and a few actually take off.

On the other side of the ledger, most parents at this stage are still full of youthful vitality, able to bounce back from hardships, disappointments, and travail with optimism and vigor. Their future, still ahead, looks rosy.

They may be dashing around all day doing the world's work. But there are the nights together — the shared hours in which husband and wife can find surcease from the day's cares in their embrace. Many women report that they were more sexually responsive to their husbands after they became mothers. Whether this was due to some physiological or psychological maturation, to their enhanced self-esteem or to their increased confidence in their spouse, I am not prepared to say. Some men, I might add, report a similar reaction after having become fathers.

All in all, for most married men and women in the summer season of marriage, this is a sunny, if sometimes gusty, time of life.

Late Summer

The Hazardous Years: "Little children, little troubles; big children, big troubles," so goes the old saying. Most parents of growing children will heartily agree. As the children find new interests outside the family and spend more time away from home, parents begin to have more time for themselves and each other. But concerns about the growing children multiply as we see them being bombarded by all kinds of outside influences, pressures, and expectations, some of them harmful, which we are neither able, nor know how, to counteract.

This becomes an increasing dilemma for parents as the children reach the "teen" years. There are times when teenagers are a lot of fun for parents. Other times, perhaps more often than we care to admit, they are a pain in the neck. In their push toward adulthood, one important developmental task for adolescents is to establish their own identity apart from their parents. They need to free themselves from their emotional dependence upon the parents. To do so most, if not all, of them find it necessary to discount their parents, run them down.

It takes a lot of patience, forbearance, and a sense of humor to put up with their often aggravating behavior during this difficult stage in their development — often more than we have. To listen to their carping criticism of our values, our politics, our behavior, even our appearance, can be irritating, to say the least. To cope with their sudden mood swings — on top of cloud nine one moment, in the pits the next — can be bewildering. To deal with their erratic efforts, often misguided, at being "grown up" — their experimentation with drugs and sex, their scorn of our way of life, their defiance of our "old-fashioned" standards — can be maddening. To stand by helplessly as they flounder around, sometimes in a self-destructive way, in their attempts to separate from family and "make like" self-sufficient adults, can be most painful of all.

The very physical presence of adolescents in the house can be unsettling to some parents. Your daughter's full bosom, the sprouting hairs on your son's cheeks, their unceasing preoccupation with the opposite sex, are constant reminders that the kids are growing up and you're not getting any younger. Don't look now, but middle age is just around the corner.

Most people accept this inevitable bit of reality with a shrug or a sigh — "that's how it is." They take pleasure in their children's approaching adulthood, enjoy their achievements, their strength, their beauty, and their expanding intellect. Relieved of many earlier parental responsibilities, these parents are grateful for the new-found time to pursue their own interests.

Others find this phase of life disturbing. In our youth-oriented culture, expecially with the media's ubiquitous insistence upon the desirability of soft skin, silky mane, lithe young body, some men and women find themselves depressed at signs of aging. "Mirror, mirror, on the wall, Who's the fairest of them all?" asks the former beauty queen, already knowing it's her daughter, not she. Once the belle of the ball, she's now asked by her daughter to be the chaperon at the school dance. For an emotionally immature woman this is a bitter pill to swallow.

It is not only women who are distressed by physical evidence of getting older. It hits men too. I sometimes think men may be more disturbed by the specter of middle age than are their wives. After all, women have the advantage of creams, cosmetics, hair dyes, even face lifts and other plastic surgery to fend off or disguise the ravages of time. Relatively few men as yet resort to these beauty aids. To counter his thinning hair, the coarsening skin, the hint of a protruding belly, the man who fears aging may drive himself to perform heroic feats on the tennis court, the running path, and in bed, often not his own. Occasional impotence or failure to maintain an erection, a phenomenon that occurs at one time or another to nearly every male at this stage of life, devastates this man, especially when he imagines his punk son having ten orgasms a night.

Adolescents May Be Dangerous to Your Mental Health

Every stage in a child's development stirs up buried feelings and memories from one's own early years, none more so than the stormy adolescent ones. Overidentification with one's adolescent child (often accompanied by overpermissiveness), whatever its unconscious roots, may set off "acting-out" behavior in the parent that is alien to the person's standards or ideals.

Ted R, age 40, upon discovering that his 17-year-old

son was sleeping with a girl friend, found himself entering into a compulsive, risky affair with the sexually precocious and seductive 15-year-old daughter of his business partner. Recognizing and dismayed by the "drivenness" of his behavior, since he felt little real affection for the girl, yet unable to put an end to the affair, he entered treatment. Only after he gained insight into both his identification and rivalry with his son, which he was acting out in his unseemly relationship, was he able to stop what he called "this crazy business."

Sometimes a parent, in his (or her) need to deny or repress stirred-up sexual feelings, may become unduly harsh to the adolescent. In a family therapy session with the Gs, Sally, 15, reported that her father had beaten her severely the previous night, when she came into the house around midnight. "I was just hanging out with the kids on the block," she said. "We weren't doing nothing bad. We had only one joint for the five of us. We was just horsing around havin' fun."

Her father said he was sorry about hitting her. "I was damn mad. Those kids in the neighborhood are wild. They bum from school. They smoke pot, maybe worse, I don't know. I told Sally a hundred times I don't want her hanging out with them." The weary mother added, "I tell Sally to be in by eleven but she never pays any attention to me."

In a private interview with Mr. G he admitted that the sight of Sally, already a fully developed woman, with her ample, unbrassiered bosom half hanging out of her blouse, her tight jeans outlining every curve of her buttocks, her face flushed and hair awry, had roused him to a violent fury. He had wondered whether she was "already screwing the boys." This thought, he admitted, "drove me crazy and I started hitting her."

Sexual feelings stirred up in the parent by constant exposure to the adolescent's sexual "aura" may take its toll in physical symptoms. Alex R, a teacher of seventh-grade boys in a private school and father of a 14-year-old daughter and 16-year-old son, came into treatment after his internist could find no organic basis for his gastrointestinal symptoms, severe headaches, and insomnia. Tranquilizers offered little relief. In the first interview he reported a growing distaste for his work, which he had previously liked, overwhelming anxiety before he entered the classroom, and an almost uncontrollable irritability at home with his wife and children. Further interviews revealed that in the previous year he had become obsessed with fantasies and dreams of homosexual activity. He had had a few brief homosexual encounters with classmates during his early adolescence and one sustained relationship with a male friend during his last year at college, which ceased when he became involved with the woman who subsequently became his wife. The sexual "hothouse" atmosphere in which he was inundated both at school and at home had apparently triggered off homosexual feelings he had managed to keep repressed until now.

Adolescents May Also Be Dangerous to Your Marriage

Adolescents in the house can sometimes have an insidious effect on the husband-wife relationship, insidious because parents are generally unaware of any connection between the child's stage of development and their own marital discord. Fights between parents about the children are common. Unable to cope with their adolescent's exasperating behavior, they tend to blame each other. "You're too easy on him," father berates mother when they learn that 13-year-old Tim has been bumming from school. "You're too hard on her," mother complains to father when he won't let Annie go to a rock concert with her friends on a school night after she brought home a failing report card. These quarrels tend to blow over (unless they are a cover for more serious conflicts), and in the long run have little adverse effect on the marital relationship.

Sometimes, however, the adolescent's presence arouses such deep conflictual feelings in one or the other parent that the marital relationship is seriously disturbed. Few parents weather this turbulent and unstable period in their child's development without some disturbance in their own equilibrium and, as a by-product, in their relationship to the spouse.

Gertrude G, 42, a housewife and mother of Judy, 13, and Rick, 11, came into treatment because of her uncontrollable rages against her husband. She was afraid she was "going crazy" like her mother did at the menopause. Gertrude's list of complaints against her husband was long. "He's all wrapped up in his work. He stays in his office till nine or ten and when he gets home he won't eat the supper I kept hot for him because he ate already, he says." She was vaguely suspicious that he came home late because he had another woman, but she admitted she had no proof. "Our sex life is zilch," she said, in response to my inquiry. "It was good until the kids came. Since then it's been downhill all the way. It gets a breath of life in the summer when the kids are off to camp. But most of the time, forget it."

About the relationship to the children, she said, "He's always picking on Rick. But everything Judy does is perfect." Her jealousy of her daughter was patent. "She can twist him around her little finger," she said angrily. She also resented his "horsing around" with the girl. "He doesn't seem to realize she's practically a grown woman already. She's been menstruating for almost two years."

Her fierce anger seemed out of proportion to these not uncommon situations in family life. Its source, one suspected, lay elsewhere. Her history revealed the following:

Mrs. G was a twin. At birth her sister weighed 7½ pounds, she weighed under 5. Throughout their childhood, and to the present, her sister was bigger, stronger, and prettier than she. Moreover, Mrs. G was plagued with allergies and suffered from attacks of asthma until she went off to college. Her sister "was never sick a day in her life." Mrs. G did not marry until she was 28. Her sister was married soon after graduating from high school and has four children, all grown, and a grandchild. "We're good friends now," Mrs. G volunteered, "but when we were kids I hated her."

Mrs. G said that her sister was her father's favorite. When asked how she felt about this, at first she said she didn't mind because she was her mother's favorite and also her teachers'. "I was smarter than my sister and got much better grades." A little probing, however, unleashed a flood of tears as she poured out her grief. "My father loved her more because she was prettier. What used to hurt me terribly was that when my father would make house calls [he was a small-town doctor] he would sometimes take my sister along. He never took me. When I'd ask him, he'd say 'Next time.' But next time never came, I suppose because he considered me sickly and weak." In the third interview she reported an incident from her adolescence, the memory of which pains her to the present day. "I was thirteen or fourteen. My father had to make an overnight trip to the city. My sister was going along with him. My grandmother lived there and I wanted to see her. I begged my father to take me too and he said he would. That night I had an asthma attack. My father gave me an injection and I fell asleep. When I woke up I found that my father and sister had already gone. I can't tell you how it hurt me. I cried about it for a long, long time."

It took no great psychological acumen to see how her husband's loving relationship to Judy revived those painful feelings of jealousy and rejection buried so many years, and now projected onto her present family drama.

Fortunately adolescents eventually grow into adults — if we are lucky, responsible adults. They gradually stop "bugging" us. Sometimes they even begin, grudgingly, to admire us, to consider us not so stupid after all.

7

Autumn

"But at my back I always hear
Time's wingèd chariot hurrying near;
And yonder all before us lie
Deserts of vast eternity."
— Andrew Marvell

Early Autumn

There is a critical time in the life of every man and woman that marks the transition from early adult maturity to middle age. It has aptly been called "the mid-life crisis." It is a time when our delusion of indestructibility is forever punctured by undeniable physical evidence of the passing years — our first gray hairs, the letters getting smaller on the page, the lines around the eyes that cosmetics cannot completely hide, the huffing and puffing after three sets of tennis. It is our first confrontation with our own mortality, the recognition that death is a reality even for oneself. "To enter middle age," writes Dr. Morris I. Stein, "is to cross a threshold into an unknown world. It is exciting for some, a source of apprehensiveness for others."[1]

    Its intensity varies from person to person. Some choose to ignore it or deny it.[2] They may even begin to work harder, dash around more, dress more flashily, go to or give more parties, as though to prove to themselves and the world that they are stronger, more vigorous, more attractive than ever. Others, of a hypochondriacal bent, become morbidly concerned about their health, read disaster in every falling hair, every passing ache. They try every new diet, every new exercise regimen that seems to promise everlasting health.

The time of its appearance also varies from person to person. It can occur as early as the 30s, as late as the 50s. It seems to strike women earlier than men, perhaps because the approaching end of their procreative years is so concretely in sight. Most commonly, according to Nature's design, the mid-life crisis rears its head around forty.

There is something about one's 40th birthday that marks a special milestone in people's lives. Up to then we are busy advancing a career, raising a family, building a house. By 40 the children, busy with their own lives, seem to need us less and less. No matter how young we look or feel, our almost-grown children are constant reminders that our youth is behind us. We are forced to think about this new turn in our lives.

The mid-life crisis is characterized by a general dissatisfaction with one's life, one's spouse, one's children, one's work; by moodiness and unrest. We feel hemmed in by life, want to break out. A mild depression pervades our spirit without our knowing why. "After thirty," Emerson wrote, "a man wakes up sad every morning . . . until the day of his death." (This was written a hundred years ago, when the life span was much shorter than it is today.)

The psychoanalyst Edmund Bergler calls this critical period "an emotional second adolescence."[3] But unlike adolescence, when all the world seems to be opening up before us, now it seems to be closing in. We no longer have the luxury of dreaming about what we'll be when we grow up. One day it suddenly strikes us that we are already grown up and "this is it." A depressed patient told me that the most painful reality he had to come to grips with when he turned 45 was the realization that "my future is behind me."

Some of us — the fighters, the doers — take fate in our hands and change the course of our lives at this juncture. Fred M was such a person.

At 47, Fred gave up a highly lucrative business career and a twenty-four-year marriage to devote himself full time to painting.

"What got me thinking about my life," Fred told me, in trying to explain his decision, "was a telephone call from my brother. He told me that my best friend, Phil, dropped dead in his office of a heart attack. At forty-five! Phil and I grew up together in Canarsie. We got married the same year. When our kids were small we shared a summer cottage at Long Beach.

"Phil was strong as a horse. Could beat me at squash. Dead! It suddenly struck me that I could drop dead too. Here I was with my life half over and I hadn't really begun to live, if living meant doing what *you* wanted to do with your life, not what other people expected of you. Here I was, a clothing manufacturer, true, making lots of money, having all the so-called best things in life. But what I really wanted, always wanted, was to be a painter. Before I was married I took classes at the Art Students League. I was pretty good. These pictures in my office [pointing to several landscapes in oil] I painted when I was still a student. My teachers encouraged me. Said I showed real talent.

"Well, when I finished college Dad wanted me to go into his business. I never liked business, especially the rag trade. But Sue and I were going together and she was pushing me to get married. All her friends were getting married. When I'd come over to her house her mother would hint in not too subtle a way about when we were getting married. So we got married and I went in with my dad. I told myself I could paint weekends and vacations. And I did for awhile. But you know how those things go. After a year Timmie came, then Jennie. Then ten years ago Dad had a heart attack and I took on more and more responsibility for running the business. Five years ago he retired and I became president. I was good at it, mind you, but my heart was never really in it. By then my stomach was giving me trouble. All the worry and trouble with the unions, my competitors, figuring out next year's styles and fabrics and sometimes guessing wrong — they were giving me ulcers, all the work and worry.

"I had given up the painting bug long ago. But I never lost my interest in art. Had a lot of artist friends, loved to go to openings. Never gave up reading *Art News*. After the *Wall Street Journal* and *Women's Wear Daily*, of course," he added self-mockingly. "Well, when this happened to Phil it shook me up terribly. I began to take stock of my life. Dammit, I was going to do what I wanted before I conked out. And what I wanted was to be a painter. There was enough income from my share of the business so that Timmie could finish medical school and the family could live comfortably. Besides, Sue was earning a fat salary as an interior designer, so I didn't have to worry about her. She was so wrapped up in her work I didn't see much of her anyway. We hardly ever had dinner together except on weekends. Our sex life by this time wasn't anything to write home about either. So I turned over the business to my brother, rented a studio in Soho, and here I am. Living my own life at last."

(What Fred did not tell me, but I knew, was that he was sharing the loft with a female sculptor with whom he'd been having an affair for about a year before he moved out of the family apartment. I have noticed that it often takes the spur of a compulsive love affair or some other shocking external event, like the loss of a long-held job or, as in Fred's case, the death of a friend, to propel one into radically changing the direction of one's life at this critical juncture of development.)

Most of us, having neither Fred's money nor his courage, reconcile ourselves to our unfulfilled dreams, our wrong choices, the opportunities passed by. Whether out of loyalty and concern for others, out of fear or apathy, or out of just plain habit, we eventually settle for what we have. Arthur G once hoped to make great documentary films of social significance. He makes a living as a distributor of foreign art films. He contents himself with taking moving pictures of his wife descending the steps of the Parthenon and photographing wedding parties of their friends' children.

Marriage and Mid-Life Crisis

I know few, if any, marriages — the best as well as the worst — that have not gone through stormy times during these early middle-age years. Some founder. But most marriages manage to keep afloat during the turbulence, though they may be left with loose caulking, a bent rudder, a rotted plank, a leaky bottom — ravages, usually reparable, of the tempest they have weathered.

The emotional changes each partner is undergoing at this critical period of his or her life put a great strain on the relationship. He feels bored, trapped, discontented with his marriage, his family, and, most of all, himself. He may blame his wife, openly or to himself, for his unhappiness. She's dull, stupid, gotten fat, lost her looks. (In one of his short stories[4] John Updike writes perceptively of the effect of the passage of time on the appearance of suburban wives in early middle age: ". . . he had seen their beauty pass from the smooth bodily complacence of young motherhood to the angular self-possession, slightly grey and wry, of veteran wives.")

He picks at her, runs her down. She is hurt by his criticism, strikes back at his vulnerable spots. Tempers flare. They tell each other off. Or he withdraws, is silent, and when she asks him what's the matter, says "Nothing," since often he doesn't know himself what's bothering him. She feels denied, unloved. She wonders if he has another woman. She becomes depressed.

Let's admit it. Marriage, whatever its compensations, knocks hell out of our dreams. It is easy to blame marriage and the spouse for our boredom, our frustrations, our discontent. We dream of all we might have accomplished if only we had been unencumbered with family responsibilities. "If I hadn't married Louise at twenty-two and been saddled with three ungrateful brats, I would have gone to Paris and written the great American novel," muses the TV newscaster. In the fantasy his six-figure salary, the condominium in the East

Seventies, the house in the Hamptons, the Piper Cub, become insignificant baubles compared to the acclaim he would have received had he been free to fulfill his promise as a writer. Louise dreams of the great musical career she might have had, had she not been foolish enough to have married at 20. Never mind that their talents were mediocre, that the most he might have accomplished would have been three unpublished short stories and an unfinished novel, she a week's unpaid engagement at a neighborhood night club. The dream persists. Marriage becomes the villain.

The sex life of the couple at this critical period often goes downhill. No one expects the sexual relationship to remain as ecstatic after fifteen or twenty years of repetitive lovemaking as in its first flower. The marital bond may be stronger, the concern for each other deeper. But availability, regularity, habit, and the implied imperative of doing one's marital duty with the same partner year after year, often in the same way — hallmarks of long-married sex — can hardly inspire epic passion. Custom may not have staled Cleopatra's infinite variety, but she had the advantage over poor Octavia by being Antony's mistress, not his wife.

Sexual desire for the spouse does flare up from time to time — on vacation, in a new setting, away from the kids, on a train, under the harvest moon. The Ws, who live in a suburb of New York, revitalize their sexual relationship once in a while by getting away from the children to spend a weekend in the city. "I get a kick out of checking in at the Plaza with Grace even though it's all on the up and up," Mr. W said. "It reminds me of the days before we were married when Grace used to come down from Schenectady to spend a weekend with me — she was supposed to be visiting a girl friend in Brooklyn — and we'd hole up in some little hotel — we couldn't afford the Plaza in those days — make love all day and see the sights at night." These occasional weekends assure them that neither their love nor the former magnetism of their bodies has faded; they were merely anaesthetized by life's daily grind.

Infidelity and the Mid-Life Crisis: The Twenty-Year Itch

Studies show that married men and women are most vulnerable to infidelity at this phase of married life. All too commonly the "happily married man" falls in love with his secretary or his neighbor's wife. The hitherto fidelitous wife starts an affair with her husband's tennis partner — or a man she meets at a cocktail party.[5] There is nothing like an illicit romance to raise a person's spirits. It relieves a man's restlessness and boredom, assuages a woman's depression, and reassures both of their youth and attractiveness.

According to Kinsey and other authorities, the peak of women's extramarital activity occurs in their late 30s and early 40s. There seems to be something about approaching 40 that drives some women into a frenzy of erotic behavior. It is as though they need to assure themselves of their continued sexual attractiveness despite any biological changes, especially if they think their husband's sexual interest in them is waning. "I could be wearing a gas mask for all Hal notices me," Annie complained. Then, confiding her infidelity, she gushed, "Joe makes me feel beautiful and young — and interesting."

Sexual unrest, emotional turmoil, and erotic fantasies beset the man or woman in the mid-life crisis, whether or not there is physical infidelity. One has only to pick up almost any novel by our foremost contemporary novelists to know how pervasive are these sexual preoccupations at this time of life. Here is Allen Wheelis's middle-aged hero describing his "upsurge in lecherous preoccupation": "Desire for my wife had decreased and desire for every other woman had increased. There was nothing carefree about this. I had been beset with an intense and indiscriminate lust, a hunger for a variety and possession and penetration that would gather up and devour all the women of the world. I had not acted on these impulses but they had transformed my inner life into a venereal phantasmagoria."[6] (Shades of prurient adolescence!)

Not only are men beset with lustful fantasies. Women

also have their share. Mrs. R, in her early 40s, an "ordinary" suburban housewife, a faithful spouse and devoted mother, came to me for help because she was plagued with persistent erotic fantasies about her son's high school advisor, a young man in his 20s whom she had met only once at a conference about her son's work during open school week. She wondered if she was going crazy. "It's so unnatural," she cried.

Many very "proper" women nurture similar fantasies while remaining fidelitous wives. In my work I have come across many monogamous women (and occasionally a man) who are overwhelmed with guilt over errant sexual fantasies — the price we pay for the suppression of our unregenerate libidinal desires that is demanded by civilization in general and monogamy in particular.

It is my belief that one of the factors (among many) that propels some men in early middle age into extramarital affairs is the fear of waning sexual prowess and the dread specter of impotence. There is scarcely a man in his 40s (or 30s, for that matter) who has not at some time or other suffered the humiliation of a failed erection with his wife. She may brush it off as "just one of those things." He seldom does. To save his self-esteem he may blame the failure on her. She was unwilling or uncooperative or too aggressive. Or smelly. Some men, whose sexual life with their wives hasn't been too good anyway, may then approach her less and less frequently. Fatigue, illness, overwork serve as legitimate excuses for turning their backs on their mates. Small wonder if, in some incidental sexual encounter, finding themselves "full of beans" again, they blame their wives or the staleness of marriage for their sexual troubles at home. (And to the extent that the novelty and excitement of a fresh, illicit, sexual encounter is an aphrodisiac, they are right. No long marriage is a match for that.)

Whatever the precipitating causes, in general persons in mid-life — especially men — feel under greater stress than at almost any other time of life. Physicians tell us this is a critical time for the first signs of high blood pressure, coronary attack, ulcers, and sexual dysfunction. One psychiatrist suggests that "accidents, traumatic neuroses, illnesses, drug addiction, alcoholism, mild or severe depression, suicide, and other self-destructive behavior in mid-years may be symptomatic of an inability to work through mid-life crisis."[7]

I am always astonished by the hordes of well-dressed, obviously successful men in their early or middle forties crowding the bars around Grand Central and Penn Stations in New York after the day's work and before getting on the commuter trains taking them home to Westchester, Rockland, or Nassau counties.

On the Bright Side

It's not all disenchantment. On the other side of the ledger, there is an upsurge in psychic energy at this time of life. For many men and women, the 40s is a period of great productivity. Unless he is bogged down by a dead-end job, by now a man has reached, or is in sight of, his occupational goals. He may achieve more later on, receive more acclaim, wield more power, make more money, but at this stage he is in many ways in his prime. He still retains much of his youthful vigor at the same time that he is beginning to assume the power and authority of the "older generation." The same is more or less true for the career or professional woman.

For the housewife too this can be a critical time. As her role of nurturing parent recedes and her housekeeping tasks lessen, she may find herself with more time on her hands than before. Moreover, with the children busy with their own affairs and her husband spending more time at work or otherwise involved with advancing his career, she may feel less needed. She also finds herself more often alone. It is a time to re-evaluate her life situation, perhaps take steps to alter it.[8]

Under the impact of the women's liberation movement many women whose lives were bound up in their husband and children are beginning to see themselves as persons apart from their roles as wife and mother and to give expression to their own needs and preferences. It is a well-known observation that, the women's movement aside, many women become more self-assertive as they reach middle age. (One misogynist suggested that, no longer able to push the children around, they start on their husbands. My own theory leans toward a psychobiological explanation.)

The less adventurous housewife may settle for redecorating the home, taking a trip across country without her husband to visit friends or relatives, becoming active in politics or community affairs. More and more housewives are returning to school to prepare for a career or to complete their education cut short by marriage and child rearing. Many are discovering creative talents that give them joy and a new outlook on life.

A surprising number of housewives in their 40s and even 50s have ventured out into the world of commerce and, from the many reports I get, are delighted to be earning money, even though the job itself may involve little more than filing in an insurance office or selling housewares at Macy's.

"The best thing that ever happened to Joyce," my lawyer told me, "was taking a job as a saleslady at Saks. The kids were driving her nuts with their everlasting problems, their everlasting demands, their everlasting fights with her. And she was driving me nuts complaining about them the minute I got in the door. She found some joints in Teddy's jeans when she was putting them in the wash. What was *I* going to do about it? She learned that Susie was sleeping with her boy friend. What was *I* going to do about it? Jim said he was quitting school and driving out West on his motorcycle. What was *I* going to do about it? What the hell *could* I do about it at this stage of the game? Next thing you know we're yelling at each other, blaming each other for the kids' getting out of hand. It was getting so I hated to go home.

"Since she's working she's become a new woman. She looks absolutely great. She's always been pretty but now she's elegant. She's been promoted to assistant buyer and she loves it. She's not only happy in her work, she keeps us in stitches at dinner telling us about the funny things that happen at the store each day. Before she went to work dinner used to be a drag. As soon as we sat down she'd begin to scold the kids about something they did or something they didn't do that they were supposed to and before you knew it, there'd be a fight and dinner would end up with one or the other of the kids leaving the table in a huff.

"And hey, it's not so bad, her bringing in the green stuff, what with outrageous taxes and inflation. With the extra money she's earning we not only can send the kids to camp, but Joyce and I are going to Europe for our vacation, something we've wanted to do since our honeymoon in France twenty years ago."

Joyce confirmed her husband's report on the improvement in their home life and in their marital relationship. "I feel great," she said. "One of the best things about my working is the new respect the kids have for me. 'Our ma's a working gal,' they tell their friends proudly. And they've even begun to help around the house! Another thing that's great is having my own money. Ted's always been very generous with me, but you know how it is if you have to ask your husband for money every time you want to buy a dress. Half the time you buy something you don't really care for because it's cheaper than what you really would like. Now if I want to pay two hundred and fifty dollars for a pair of Gucci boots, well, it's my business. I can go ahead and be extravagant and not have to apologize to anyone."

There are other gratifications in family life at this stage of the game. For all their orneriness, their ambivalences, their sudden mood swings, their assertion of independence one moment, their childish dependence the next, our adolescent children can, and often do, grant us small joys to relish: Hal has been elected president of his junior class in high school; Mandy won a scholarship to the university; Jimmy has a summer job as camp counselor.

We see them growing up almost overnight: Hal shaving those few almost invisible hairs off his cheeks; Mandy looking like Aphrodite in her bikini; Jimmie towering over his father. We stand by with sympathy and fear (and a touch of nostalgia) as we watch them struggle with the same problems we (and probably our ancestors) struggled with during our own green years: with dating and infatuation and love and sex and acne and heartbreak and ecstasy and clothes and indecision about our future; with indignation over injustice and exploitation and the evils of capitalism and the stupidity and cupidity of our leaders; with exasperation over the ignorance and lack of understanding of our elders. And let's not forget the philosophic discussion as to whether there is a God. We try to keep hands off, telling ourselves they must handle their problems in their own way. But we seldom are able to exercise such heroic self-control. We find ourselves proffering our unwanted and often scorned counsel in a futile attempt to save them from making "mistakes."

We watch them leaving home one by one — to go off to college or take an apartment with three friends in their need to try themselves out as adults, coming home now and again for a good meal or to borrow a few bucks.

The children's growing up saddens and gladdens us. We are saddened that they no longer need us, replacing us with friends and lovers.[9] Saddened by the reality that as their strength and power waxes ours is beginning to wane. Gladdened to know we have done a job, for better or worse, in raising a new generation to adulthood to carry on the world's work.

The children departed, husband and wife are faced with a new stage in marriage — a twosome once more.

Late Autumn

The last child has left home. A new era in the marriage cycle has arrived. "There is hope for the disgruntled or disappointed parent," writes the psychologist Angus Campbell. ". . . Wait 17 or so years until you are all alone with your spouse again. Your satisfaction with life and your all-around good mood will return to where it was before you had kids. . . . Couples settled back in the 'empty nest' reported feelings of companionship and mutual understanding even higher than they felt as newlyweds."[10]

An exaggeration, of course, if applied to all marriages. What happens now depends largely upon how the relationship fared during the preceding rough years they had lived through with the children. I found, both in my observations and interviews, and my clinical work, that where it had been a "good enough" marriage, Campbell's comment is, by and large, true. Most of my informants in their 50s and 60s who had been married for several decades and weathered the storms of the mid-life crisis reported that this phase of the marriage cycle was "the best."

"Tell me what's so good about it?" I asked my middle-aged informants. "More companionship" was a frequent answer. "It's given us a new lease on life," said one woman in her late 40s. "Joe and I can do our own thing without always having to think if it's good or bad for the kids." "I feel like Martin Luther King, Jr.," joked one man, "free, free at last! Free of bills for orthodontia and tuition and ski boots and car repairs. Free of their criticism, of telling me I'm an old dodo because I think marijuana's harmful or that young people should at least be engaged before they hop into bed together." "Free of pots and pans and picking up clothes," added his wife, an ever-reluctant homemaker. "And of their complaints about my cooking and how I look."

The career woman is relieved at last of worry about her children while she's at work. Is the babysitter taking care of them? Did Johnny's fever go down? Is Mary bringing her boy friend into the house, though I warned her not to? She now finds time to take on new projects, enhance her career. The toil-worn woman who had to earn money to augment the family income can now work part time or quit her job altogether and enjoy domesticity. If she feels like it, she can make new curtains, convert Jamie's room to a den, cook gourmet dishes for her husband. She can take classes in belly dancing, jazz, ballet, or yoga; study French, take a course in psychology, get a degree. She can visit the sick, become a volunteer in a "golden age" center, teach reading to retarded children.

The "Empty Nest"

To some people it doesn't come easy, this renewed enjoyment of being a couple again. (In unhappy marriages it may never come.) Like all transitions from one phase of life to another, some emotional disturbance is "normal." Sooner or later most parents adjust to this new life situation. They find new interests, take pride in their offsprings' accomplishments, and, best of all, are now able to spend more time together.

Martha, a loving, devoted mother, telephoned me the other day, bursting with pleasure. "Hallelujah!" she shouted, "Josh [her youngest] just moved out. He's gone to live with friends in Soho. First thing Bill and I are going to do is take that trip to Italy we've been putting off for twenty years. And when we get back I'm taking that job I was offered in the D.A.'s office."

Some women find the departure of their children to lead their own lives a serious emotional wrench. The woman who had been wrapped up in her children, whose total identity lay in her role as devoted, self-sacrificing mother, whose self-esteem was derived from the achievements of her children, understandably is likely to suffer a deep sense of loss at their absence. She has lost not only her job of "mothering" (one of my child patients called it "smothering") but her very purpose in life. Should her son or daughter fall in love, God forbid, with some "stranger," she feels betrayed. Only yesterday she was Petey's adored mama. Now he hovers over some flibbertigibbet without a care for her. Such a mother's sense of loss may be severe enough to precipitate a depression. Therapists are kept busy with middle-aged women suffering from what is commonly called the "empty nest" syndrome.

Men seem to have an easier time adjusting to this new

phase of marriage, probably because their identity is less dependent upon their role as father than on their occupational or social status. However, some men also get depressed when their children leave home. This is not, I believe, so much a reaction to the children's absence as it is to its symbolic significance, indicating the end of their role as paterfamilias.

Many parents find it very hard to let go of their children even after they've left home: the mother who telephones her married daughter every day to make sure she's all right; insists that her son mail his laundry home from college and sends him packages of food every week so he won't go hungry. The father who tries to direct his son's vocational choice, who keeps the young man financially dependent upon him as long as he can.

With the children gone, a poor marital relationship may worsen. Cracks in the relationship successfully hidden even from themselves by parental concerns about the children are now exposed. Over time each may have developed separate interests, divergent ideas and attitudes they did not share. Occupied with the children's affairs while they were home, the couple perhaps had not realized how far apart they had drifted. Now they find themselves with little in common — nothing to say to each other beyond the ritualized conversation of two people domiciled together who have long stopped talking to each other in any meaningful way.

The woman who could gratify her need for power by bossing the children, deprived of that ready outlet, may turn to the next handy object — her husband. "I used to hate my mother for trying to push my father around," a middle-aged woman in a troubled marriage said. "Now that the kids are gone I find myself doing the same thing." Quarrels arise, sometimes seemingly out of nowhere, as her aggressive drives seek expression.

The man who appreciated his wife's job as a mother may now confront himself with her lacks as a wife. Her physical and intellectual deficits, as compared, say, with some idealized woman, are more glaring now. "She's lost her figure," he notes with dismay. Or, "She's so boring I wish she'd shut up," he thinks to himself as he half listens to her saga of shopping for new clothes. Somehow he hadn't been so aware of her dullness when they talked about the children. Her sexual restrictions or ineptitude that he had put up with now anger him.

These critical periods in marriage, as in life itself, more often than not work themselves out. Habit, fear of change, and most of all, the marital bond, that mysterious cement that binds a man and woman, despite their ambivalences, in time help them ride out these rough seas into smoother waters.

Psychological Changes

By late middle age the emotional turbulence of the mid-life crisis has abated. The pulls in a hundred different directions have slackened. Tormenting decisions about work, marriage, the course of our lives, have been, if not necessarily happily, resolved.

It is a time of stocktaking. We look beady-eyed at our spouse, our children, our work. We tote up our achievements. No matter how well we've done, we feel we might have done better. We recall our mistakes, the wrong choices, the ventures turned down, the opportunities passed by. A joylessness, a kind of malaise, pervades our spirit. We go through what a psychiatrist might call a "normal" depression of middle age, a kind of unconscious mourning for the loss of our youth, the approach of old age. And death.

Here is a graphic description of a "normal" middle-age depression by a gynecologist: "Achievements, if any, have lost their luster. . . . The spouse is observed as aging, less attractive, full of idiosyncracies and mannerisms that are barely tolerable. The initial flush of sex, which in some cases may be prolonged, fades. Even the erotic seems banal. . . . Sons and daughters are reviewed with an objectivity proper to a microscopic specimen. What is often seen is a magnification of our faults and a repetition of our errors. . . . Your friends and their wives in sailing, boating, tennis, and golf sometimes seem asinine; sport is juvenile, jogging is overexertion, walk in fair not foul weather. In Florida and Caribbean vacations, you find only a hotter sun. . . . Europe is crowded and inconvenient and rife with gouging. Mexico and South America are dirty. Home is dull. Ocean cruises are crowded with widows." [11]

Intimations of Mortality

"I grow old . . . I grow old . . .
I shall wear the bottoms of my trousers rolled.
Shall I part my hair behind? Do I dare to eat a peach?
. . . .
I have heard the mermaids singing, each to each.

I do not think that they will sing to me."
                                        — *T. S. Eliot*

Late middle age rubs our noses in our mortality.[12] A decade earlier we could brush the thought from our mind when the death of a friend or relative in the prime of life reminded us of our own vulnerability. Now, though we assure ourselves we're in splendid health, the illness or death of a contemporary shakes our equanimity. Somewhere in the back of our head there remains a nagging worry about that occasional pain in the chest. Indigestion, we comfort ourselves as we reach for the Alka-Seltzer. Shouldn't have eaten that duck à l'orange. We become preoccupied with our physical well-being. We watch our diet, keep tabs on our cholesterol level, switch to low-tar cigarettes or give them up altogether. We start to jog, join a health club.

We are disconcerted by irrefutable signs of aging: the belly muscles no longer taut despite the daily push-ups; the gray head that calls for hair dye; the sagging breasts; the skin changes that creams can no longer allay. Underlying the middle-aged person's preoccupation with physical signs of aging is the unspoken fear of waning sexual powers in the man, of waning sexual attractiveness in the woman. (A good-looking friend of mine in her middle fifties, a radical feminist, shamefacedly confessed that she is secretly pleased when men turn around to look at her in the street or when she is "propositioned" by the handsome man seated next to her at a dinner party.)

There are natural physiological changes in the male sexual response cycle as a result of the aging process — the slower erection, the prolonged plateau phase, the shorter period of ejaculation during orgasm, the diminished seminal fluid. These changes in no way need detract from a man's orgasmic response nor lessen his pleasure in the sexual act. Indeed, an experienced older man, in better control of his ejaculation, can be a more gratifying sexual partner than he was in his youthful, impetuous years. Nonetheless, the changes can be a source of distress to some men.

As for the postmenopausal woman, the physiological changes resulting from hormonal deficits need in no way interfere with her orgasmic response. (Diminished lubricity can easily be remedied.) But for some women the concrete evidence of the end of her procreativity, even though she may not want more children, has serious psychological repercussions. A childless woman who had enjoyed an active sex life became inorgasmic and depressed after the menopause. Moreover, though she "did her marital duty," i.e., engaged in sexual intercourse, she would no longer permit any foreplay. This so upset her husband that he insisted she enter therapy. In treatment she revealed that in her girlhood she had had an illegal abortion. After marriage she had several spontaneous abortions, but as long as she was menstruating she "felt like a woman," since there was always the possibility of having a child. Once the menses ceased, she felt "castrated," "sexless." Guilt, long repressed, over that early abortion, which she blamed for her inability to carry a pregnancy to term, now overwhelmed her. As "punishment" she could not permit herself any sexual pleasure.

Another woman, who, except for a brief affair early in marriage when her husband was away at war in Korea, was a fidelitous wife (although her husband was a notorious womanchaser), went on a rampage of promiscuous sex when her menses ceased. In her fantasy she was now "like a man" and therefore had the male's prerogative of extramarital sex.

The Pluses

In time, as mature persons, we resolve our grief over our lost youth, accept our limitations, and adapt to our present stage of life. We smile at the oldsters who refuse to "act their age" — the man of 60 still "chasing the young chicks," the woman on the shady side of 50 flirting with her son's classmates. We take pleasure in quieter pursuits — good talk with old friends; the aroma of fine wine; the taste of exquisite cuisine; long walks in the countryside; listening to our favorite records; collecting antiques. We still play tennis, swim, sail, jog, but without the heroics of youth. The love affair, no longer a threat to one's marriage, if continued, is conducted discreetly.

Generally by now the couple is better off financially than ever before. The man (and in many cases the woman) is holding a high-ranking and well-paying job. As a professional or in business he is near the top of his earning power. With the children on their own, some of the economic burdens have been eased.

Women "of a certain age" are more fashionably dressed, have more money to spend in beauty salons and on cosmetic aids, and are often more attractive than they had been in their younger years. (Sometimes more attractive than their daughters.) They are more secure in their taste, less dependent on the opinion of others for their self-esteem, have a better sense of who they are and what they want.

The same can be said of the middle-aged man. By now he has reached the zenith of his productivity and power in his work. While there is always the threat of being displaced by a younger man at this stage of his life, his position of responsibility and influence endows him with greater self-assurance, an air of authority. Whatever fears he may feel at being "pushed upstairs," he keeps them well in check.

Husband and wife are able to devote more time to community matters now that they are free of the children's activities. The wife who is not employed outside the home keeps busy with volunteer work. She may be running art shows or theater parties to raise funds for charitable enterprises, teaching handicapped children, manning the gift shop of a hospital, helping out in her grandson's nursery school. The husband is active in politics, serves on boards of social agencies, raises money for religious organizations, cultural foundations, or other "worthy causes." Both begin to get public recognition for their volunteer activities, find fulfillment as important members of the community.

"Joe and I have a lot more interesting things to talk about than when the kids were home," Cynthia said. "What we talked about then was mostly the kids' problems, my hassles with them, or his worries at the office, or his aches and pains."

Ada G, 52, a young grandmother, is teaching English to Russian immigrants. "I feel like a valuable person," she said. "I'm helping these people become Americans."

"I never knew Sylvia was such a hot shot," Max said admiringly when his wife was awarded a plaque for raising $25,000 for a charity.

Many of my informants in their fifties reported that their "love life" was "better than ever." They know each other's needs and preferences well. There is less emphasis on performance. Where tenderness and deep affection abide, just lying close together is pleasurable in itself. If one partner is disinclined to make love, the other no longer feels rejected or angry about it. "Sometimes we don't make it," one man confided, "but it doesn't seem like such a disaster anymore. So we'll make it next time." Another man said, "It takes longer, but it beats all that quickie stuff we did when we were kids."

Coming to Terms with Your Spouse

After twenty-five, thirty, or more years of marriage you've finally come to terms with your marital choice. You've lived through your disappointments with your spouse. You stop trying to change him or her to conform to your image of some fantasied person you would have liked as a mate. You make the best of what you have.

Esther R is a warm, lively, ebullient woman, still full of girlish enthusiasms about little events in her rather prosaic life — an interesting novel she read, a television "personality" she saw walking down the street, a conversation with a charming lady she met on the bus, a current art exhibit at the museum. She chatters away in her girlish voice like the proverbial magpie. She has been married for twenty-eight years to Harold, a botany professor, ten years her senior. He is a shy, reserved man, rather withdrawn and silent. They have three grown children, all married and living in distant places.

While the children were home Esther was busy looking after the household, tending to their needs and totally involved in their lives. Harold busied himself with his teaching, his books, and his hobby of growing rare species of orchids. When the children left, Esther found herself at loose ends, with little to occupy her time. She began taking extension courses at the university. She is now studying child psychology and English literature. While Harold fusses with his plants she does her homework.

"I'm a people lover," Esther explains. "Harold's afraid of people. He's only comfortable with plants and animals. I love to travel. He hates it." Except for one trip they made to South America several years ago to track down a rare species of orchid, he refuses to travel farther than their country house, where he is content to read and putter in the garden. "I get stir-crazy," Esther said. "I used to nag him to take trips on our vacation, but I don't anymore. When we were first married, we went to a few places, but he hated being away from home. He can't sleep in strange beds, doesn't like strange foods. Places I thought were fascinating he found dirty and uncomfortable. So now I go off for a week or two on those inexpensive charter tours with a girl friend — she's a widow. We go to all kinds of interesting places, Mexico, Guatemala, Yucatan, England, Italy" — she rattles off a list of foreign countries. "Harold doesn't mind. Sometimes I wonder if he knows I'm gone —"

Grandparenthood[13]

One of the unalloyed compensations of middle age is the arrival of grandchildren. "You get all the pleasure, none of the headaches," said Mrs. L, a 56-year-old grandmother, as she raves about the beauty and brilliance of her daughter's little ones, 5 and 3. (I remember well Mrs. L's "nervous breakdown" back in '68 when Linda at 17 ran off to Haight-Ashbury and was found by her distraught parents living in a roach-ridden basement with a black man, both unkempt, malnourished, hooked on drugs. All has long been forgotten in their pride and joy in the grandchildren Linda and her dentist husband have given them.)

I asked Mr. L how he feels about being a grandfather. "Great," he replied, then added, laughing, "though I don't like the idea of sleeping with a grandmother."

The relationship between grandparent and grandchild, especially during its young years, is generally a pleasantly loving one, without the ambivalence inherent in the parent-child tie. As Linda's mother explained, being a grandparent gives you emotional gratification without the concerns and worries of parenthood. You can indulge your grandchildren to your heart's content, and theirs — sometimes with the added pleasure of defying their parents. (As someone said, "You and the grandchildren have a common enemy.") In turn, the affection you receive from the grandchildren makes you feel loved, needed, "like a good parent."

There are other compensations. Grandparents can relive the early phase of their own parenting experience as they watch the development of the grandchildren. I have known many instances where mother and daughter who had always had a rather "distant" relationship with each other became close after the daughter had bestowed this new status on the mother. I have also seen rifts between parent and child, often over the latter marrying out of the faith, patched up upon the birth of a grandchild. Finally, the role of grandparent is as yet unsullied by derision or contempt.

CHAPTER

8

Winter

"Therefore my age is as a lusty winter,
Frosty, but kindly."
   — Shakespeare, *As You Like It*

Early Old Age[1]

Most people slide into early old age imperceptibly. On turning 60 one is not nearly so sharply aware of "time's winged chariot" as on reaching 40, even though one is by two decades nearer to one's demise. These days most people at 60 or 65 are still active, given reasonably good health, and looking forward to years of productive life. Unless they are confronted by some new ailment or the death or serious illness of a friend or relative, they are less preoccupied with monitoring their "innards" than they were in middle age. By now they have more or less come to terms with their aging bodies.

Retirement

For many, the shock of recognition that they are regarded as old by society (never mind that they consider themselves still in the prime of life) comes with mandatory retirement. It is a critical time. Retirement imposes a new way of life just when adaptation to change becomes increasingly hard to make. To the able-bodied, mentally alert person whose occupation was a central issue in his (or her) life and who is capable of working for many more years, arbitrary retirement can be a threat to mental health. Unless he (this is especially true for the male) finds other employment, paid or unpaid, he feels discarded by society as useless. In our culture, where work is so important to one's self-esteem, he may get depressed. Or he may develop physical symptoms, as though to justify his enforced idleness.

Other persons whose work was tedious, a boring or disliked means of livelihood, may look forward to retirement as a well-earned respite from a lifetime of labor, at long last a chance to rest, loaf, fish, putter around the house, go to a ball game or take a snooze in the middle of the afternoon. But even they, after the euphoria of endless leisure wears off, may find themselves at loose ends, time weighing heavily on their hands.

Retirement and Marriage

Retirement creates a new stage in marriage. The couple now spend more time together. Their interests become more centered in each other. They become more dependent on each other's company. If the relationship has been a good one, this enforced "togetherness" can have its pleasant and enriching aspect, even though, as one wife half-jestingly complained, "He's a nuisance, always under foot. I can't get my work done." When Gerald Ford retired from the presidency, Betty Ford, asked how she felt about his retirement, is alleged to have said, "I just don't want him home for lunch."

The couple who had grown apart during the years and had divergent interests may find they have little in common now that they are thrown together. "We've nothing to talk about," one man told me. The wife may resent his disrupting her accustomed activities. He may sense her annoyance, though it may be unspoken, and feel unwanted, irritable, or depressed.

Eventually a modus vivendi is worked out. Perhaps he begins to busy himself with community activities to fill his days, spending more time away from home. She begins to modify her routine to adjust to her husband's new pattern of life. I have seen couples who had grown apart during those busy years when she was raising the children and he earning a livelihood develop joint interests that brought them closer together in their later years. One such couple — he had been a traveling salesman, she a suburban housewife — began to study Hebrew together in preparation for a trip to Israel. Upon their return they joined a temple in their community and found themselves engaged in various cultural and fund-raising activities that served as a fruitful source of conversation and mutual enjoyment.

At this stage of marriage, having survived the vicissitudes of some thirty or forty years together, you have more or less reconciled your differences — differences of temperament, of opinion, of taste. You put up with each other's crotchets, avoid irritating the thin spots in your mate's skin, restrain yourself in the midst of an argument, no matter how tempting it may be, from throwing up the other's failings (and his or her forebears, for good measure). You resign yourself to the other's habits, like leaving him to watch the Cards beat the Giants on the TV on a lovely autumn afternoon when you would like to go for a stroll; or accompanying her to a boring concert when you'd rather stay home and read a book.

As the couple adapts their way of life to this new circumstance of retirement, the marriage can become enriched. Through the accumulation of experiences together in a long, "satisfactory" marriage — the hard as well as the good times they've gone through together, the children they brought forth and reared together, the troubles as well as the pleasures they shared together — the marriage bond becomes inextricably entwined. They have indeed become "one flesh." Have you ever wondered why couples married a long time come to look alike?

The Lion in Winter

"And still to love, though prest with ill,
In wintry age to feel no chill,
With me is to be lovely still . . ."
— *William Cowper*

Most of the elderly couples interviewed reported that their sex life was in some ways "better than ever," better, certainly, than in their hectic younger years when they were preoccupied with raising children and struggling to earn a living. Although the sex drive has diminished and coitus become less frequent, lovemaking, when two people care about each other, can be as gratifying in its own way at this stage as in youth.

Unfortunately many myths and misconceptions about sex and the aging abound, myths and misconceptions many older people are themselves taken in by. One such example is that men and women over, say, 65, are no longer interested in sex. This is nonsense. Though sexual prowess may diminish, interest in sex seldom does. When an older person who believes this myth finds himself or herself sexually excited and desiring sexual contact, he or she may think there is something shameful or perverse about it. Doctors report that common sexual dysfunctions, such as impotence or dyspareunia in the elderly is in many instances due not so much to any physical disability as to the notion that there is something wrong about "wanting sex at my age."

The Last-Chance Syndrome

Sometimes a man well on in years (less frequently, a woman), having fallen in love with someone, often considerably younger, in a desperate attempt to hang on to his youth, decides to leave his wife of thirty or forty years for his beloved. It is "a last chance at life," he feels. To end a long marriage, even a chronically unhappy one, takes not only passion — and defiance of public opinion and often one's own conscience — but the courage to inflict, as well as bear, pain. It takes almost superhuman strength and energy, something middle-aged men or women in their 40s, driven by need, still possess, but that in later years is tempered by time, blood pressure, and "common sense." However, a few older men and women do take that "last chance," as attested to by the number of divorces late in life.

Sometimes the decision to make so radical a move precipitates unexpected consequences.

Fred G, 62, one of the city's leading lawyers, had been married for 38 years to Alice, his childhood sweetheart. Their three children had blessed them with a bevy of adorable grandchildren who came to visit grandpa and grandma at Christmas and Easter. Alice, at 58, was still very pretty, had retained her youthful figure, was vivacious, "sweet," and sociable. She gave elegant dinner parties, was known as a great hostess, and regarded by his colleagues as "a perfect wife for Fred."

It was an "all right" marriage, although it had long ago grown humdrum to Fred. Handsome, debonair, successful, a connoisseur of fine wines and beautiful women, Fred had more than his share of affairs, none of which stirred a ripple in the even flow of his life at home. If Alice was aware of them, she turned a discreet back, assuming, correctly, that they would fade away when the next pretty girl he met had yielded to his blandishments.

What really sustained the marriage was an enduring love affair Fred secretly had been carrying on for the past ten years with Meredith, now 44 and mother of a fifteen-year-old son. She is a junior partner in his firm. From a passionate love affair it had gradually grown into a deeply meaningful friendship in which lovemaking had become an occasional, though no longer imperative, interlude. His dalliance with other women ceased. Their relationship did not jeopardize either marriage, since both respected and, in a lukewarm way, cared about their respective spouses. Neither wanted to disturb the stability of their conjugal lives.

One day Meredith's husband was killed in an automobile accident. Fred was expectedly helpful to Meredith and now, with good conscience, saw her more frequently and more openly than before. She began to lean on him for financial and professional counsel as well as for advice in coping with her adolescent son, who had become difficult to manage since his father's death. Before the year was out, Meredith was hinting about marriage. Hadn't he told her time and again that his was a marriage of conventional convenience? That had she been free he would have married her? Well, now she was free.

In the meantime Alice had become irritable and querulous. Whether it was due to post-menopausal changes or her growing suspicion of Fred's preoccupation with Meredith's family affairs, Alice became increasingly difficult to live with. What had been a tolerable marriage had turned into a chronic bickering. What a relief it was to escape from Alice's "paranoid" accusations to Meredith's soothing presence. To sit quietly in her penthouse apartment, sipping Napoleon brandy and discussing the Baake decision or Lévi-Strauss's structuralism theory. If only he didn't have to go home to Alice's nagging or to her boring talk about the sullenness of the cleaning woman. After all, he didn't have that many years of vigor left in which he could grasp happiness with Meredith. His father had died of a heart attack at 65. He would catch himself humming those lines "and the days dwindle down to a precious few. . . ."

But what about Alice? he would ruminate. What would happen to her if I left? Maybe she'd have a nervous breakdown. Commit suicide. No, she wouldn't do that. I'd give her everything. The condominium, the house in the country, the insurance, half my stocks, a most generous alimony. What would the children say? My friends? My colleagues? Would they think I'm a dog for leaving her? But must I sacrifice my remaining years just to protect her from facing reality — that

I don't love her and that I love Meredith? The conflict raged in his mind for months. He suffered from insomnia; his work deteriorated; he developed gastrointestinal symptoms.

One day over lunch at La Goulue with Meredith, he proposed marriage. He would ask Alice for a divorce that evening. He would do what had to be done to end his tormenting indecision. When they left the restaurant he felt elated, as though the weight of the earth had been lifted from his shoulders. He would call her, he assured Meredith, that very evening after he had his talk with Alice.

What followed was like something out of a Grade B movie. At 4 P.M. while preparing a brief he was to present before the U.S. Supreme Court the following month, he was stricken with a sharp pain in his upper abdomen. Was it the mousseline of salmon, he wondered, that gave him such distress? He didn't wonder long. The pain sharpened, grew intense, spread to his chest and shoulder. Two hours later he was in the coronary care unit of a nearby hospital, another m.i. case, as the charge nurse casually referred to his myocardial infarction.

Fred's recovery from his heart attack was uneventful. So was the recovery from his near divorce. An accident of Fate had settled the decision for him. Alice is the perfect wife for a man with a bad heart. She watches his diet meticulously, makes sure he gets enough rest and exercise, guards him against too much company. He plays only doubles at tennis these days, limits his jogging to fifteen minutes a day.

Meredith? There were, of course, the flowers sent to the hospital, the humorous notes during his convalescence, and once, after his return to work, a discreet dinner at a fashionable restaurant at which no mention of marriage was made by either. They meet at parties from time to time, kiss chastely, exchange pleasantries. The last I heard of Meredith she was off in Sicily with an Appellate Court judge whom she intends to marry on their return.

I have no idea how frequently such "near divorces" as

Fred's occur in the winter season of marriage. More frequently, probably, than we know.

Late Old Age

"An aged man is but a paltry thing,
A tattered coat upon a stick . . ."
— W. B. Yeats

Who is old? Winston Churchill coming out of retirement at 68 to become Britain's prime minister in wartime, and in his 70s write a definitive history of World War II? Eugene Ormandy at 80 conducting the Philadelphia Orchestra in Beethoven's Ninth Symphony? Arthur Rubinstein at 90 playing a Mozart piano concerto at Carnegie Hall? Golda Meir, the prime minister of Israel in her 70s? Ruth Stout in her nineties producing one of the finest vegetable gardens in Connecticut? George Meany at 85, the president of the AFL-CIO? Tito at 87 the leader of Yugoslavia?

The list of famous men and women in their 70s, 80s, and even 90s who are still active and productive is long. But by and large these are exceptional people, blessed by their genes, their abilities, and perhaps more important, their indomitable spirit, to continue a productive life long after their contemporaries are in wheelchairs, nursing homes, or the grave. Most of us, by the time we're 70, are ready, eagerly or reluctantly, to move to Florida to warm our arthritic bones in the sun, to take a back seat and let our children and grandchildren carry on the world's work.

"You are only as old as you feel," the cliché goes. It is a comforting anodyne to those oldsters who defy the calendar by going to work every day, play an eighteen-hole golf course, and sometimes even, God willing, like Charles Chaplin in his 70s and Bertrand Russell in his 80s, sire a child.

But two realities intrude into this consoling dream. One is a biological reality — the inexorable, however slow, waning of one's physical powers: the diminishing eyesight, some hearing loss, stiffening joints, hardening arteries, some memory impairment, other infirmities, large or small. The other is a cultural reality — the attitude of society toward the old.

The first can be relieved or mitigated by spectacles, hearing aid, vitamins, drugs, surgery, and other miracles of medicine. The second is much more difficult to remedy. In our youth-oriented culture, there seems to be something shameful about getting old. We dress up our devaluation of the elderly by such patronizing euphemisms as "senior citizens," "golden age" (like saying "body count" to mean the number of enemies killed or "bringing peace to the village" to mean burning it to the ground). The old themselves, accepting the conventional social definition of old age, cling to the illusion of youth, knowing that once they "give in" they will be relegated to the land of the superfluous.

In other cultures, such as India or pre-revolutionary China (I do not know how the old are treated in the present Republic), the old are treated with respect. They are regarded as repositories of knowledge and wisdom to be handed on to, and sought by, the next generations.

In the United States the young assume there is nothing to learn from the old. In these days of rapid technological advances, when satellites circling the globe are commonplace, colonies inhabiting outer space a likely possibility, babies conceived in a test tube no longer a figment of the imagination, the accumulated experience of the old is considered obsolete, their ideas out of date, their values old-fashioned. Useless, the old are discarded like Kleenex. The sense of historical continuity from one generation to the next is lost. On those rare occasions when the young man or woman comes to visit grandparents they are like two species from different planets making small gestures of affection as recognition of a few remaining strands of kinship. The wisdom of the older generation, accumulated over a lifetime, that could serve as guideposts to the young, is unwanted. Small wonder that many old people sink into depression.

Depression

The "melancholia" of old age is seen commonly in mental institutions where the old people sit, apathetic or dozing, before a TV screen. Often overlooked is the sub-clinical depression of elderly people at home. Their irritability, lack of libido, wish to withdraw from ordinary activity and contact with others — behavior that is dismaying or annoying to the spouse — are often symptoms of an unrecognized underlying depression.

It is understandable that the gradual waning of one's physical strength and the loss of near and dear ones by death or distance, may cause one to feel depressed. (Curiously, death itself is less feared by the old than by the aging.)

Most depressing, however, to many old people, especially those who have led active, independent lives, is the eventual necessity to surrender one's independence and accept the humiliation of dependence on others. True, most sick old people are quite willing to "lay down their weary load" and be looked after. But to the man or woman whose pride and self-esteem rested upon their self-sufficiency, this inevitability, if one lives long enough, is one of life's most bitter blows. Such a person may sink into despair. Others, perhaps of a more philosophical turn of mind, resign themselves to this inevitable situation and find some comfort in remembrance of things past. I often think that the serenity attributed to old age in nineteenth-century romantic poetry may, underneath, have been little more than resignation, patience, and, if one only knew, depression, as the old waited for release from earthly cares.

Compensations[2]

Lest I have given the impression that old age is "downhill all the way," let me add that it has many rewards and pleasures. There is the reward of having brought up a family to the best of one's ability; the reward of knowing one has led a useful and fulfilling life. There is the pleasure of reminiscing with a crony, or telling a grandchild about one's youth and "the good old days." There is the pleasure one can take in the accomplishments of one's children and grandchildren, through whom one's wish for immortality can be realized.

Finally, if the couple have been fortunate to have survived to old age together, there is the comfort of companionship. For many, this is richer, more fulfilling, more deeply gratifying, than in youth.

When I was a schoolgirl and, along with my classmates, donned the cloak of cynicism fashionable in my day, we snickered at those opening lines of Browning's "Rabbi Ben Ezra": "Grow old along with me! / The best is yet to be, / The last of life, for which the first was made." Corny, was our unvarnished verdict. When my green years passed and I began to work in a mental health facility with sick old people, those lines angered me. Seeing aged, disabled human beings, burdened with illness, poverty, and loneliness, shunted off into sterile mental hospitals, dreary nursing homes, or decrepit rooming houses, I regarded that poem as an outrageous fraud.

As I grew older I came to realize that the key words in those lines were *along with me*. To have a companion with whom you had shared the past, someone who remembered you when your hair was thick and black and curly, when you could dance together all night and watch the sun come up, someone who could look at you now and see, beneath the pudgy figure, the wrinkles, the arthritis, the fallen arches, the attractive person he or she had married a long time ago. (Corny? Yes, indeed. But unlike in my conformist youth, I am no longer afraid to be corny.)

To have a companion with whom you can kvetch about your respective aches and pains, whom you can entrust with your disappointments, your fears, your thoughts about death and dying, a companion to bicker and scold and disagree with — this is perhaps the greatest comfort of marriage in old age.

Most of all, companionship is a buffer against loneliness. Loneliness in youth is a painful thing, keen as a razor's cut. But there is also something exquisite, even enviable, about that pain, something you can revel in, write poetry about. Moreover, in youth loneliness is something that can be readily mitigated or ended when one gets bored with it. Loneliness in old age is a dull, constant ache, a comfortless solitude, a desolation. Men and women without close kin who have been widowed late in life tell me that loneliness, more than poverty or illness, is the hardest thing to bear. No wonder the suicide rate in this country is highest among the old, especially old men.

I have known elderly couples who have endured terrible marriages, ill-begotten unions that would have been best, so it seemed, for everyone, including the children, had they been dissolved long ago, but who remained tied together for whatever reasons — economic, social, religious, neurotic — and who achieved some kind of peace with each other in their waning years.

The room in which I write looks out on a bus stop. Every day at 4 P.M. I see a tiny lady, in her 70s, stand on the corner. I can always tell when the bus is approaching by her suddenly alerted stance, her anticipatory movements, the eager look that enlivens her face. The bus stops and an elderly white-haired gentleman alights. They kiss, she takes his arm, and they trot down the street, oblivious to everyone and everything (now that dog droppings no longer litter the sidewalks of New York) save each other's presence and each other's conversation. Their obvious pleasure in each other's company seems to me no less ardent than that of the young lovers I see embracing in the park on the street where I live. For all I know, this old couple may have gone through terrible times together when they were young. Perhaps they fought like cats and dogs, were infidelitous, jealous, tormented, or hated each other at one time or another, but who now in their ripe old age have found sanctuary in each other.

John Cheever, in one of his short stories, refers to "the sense of sanctuary that is the essence of love." I believe it is in

the last stage of marriage that the sense of sanctuary is keen-
est.

"Only — but this is rare —
When a beloved hand is laid in ours,
When, jaded with the rush and glare
Of the interminable hours,
Our eyes can in another's eyes read clear,
When our world-deafened ear
Is by the tones of a loved voice caressed —
A bolt is shot back somewhere in our breast,
And a lost pulse of feeling stirs again.
The eye sinks inward, and the heart lies plain,
And what we mean, we say, and what we would, we know. . . ."
                                              — Matthew Arnold

PART THREE

Family Life

CHAPTER

9

The Family as a Social Institution

"The trouble we take to arrange ourselves in some semblance of families is one of the most imperishable habits of the human race."

— Jane Howard

An Endangered Species?

Professional mourners for the imminent passing of the family have been as numerous, if not more so, as those for the end of marriage. Their gloom is not recent. In the twenties the eminent sociologist William Ogburn of the University of Chicago saw the assumption of traditional family functions by outside agencies as a sign of inevitable family disorganization. During the Great Depression of the thirties the passage of the Social Security Act and other social legislation recognizing the responsibility of the government for the social and economic welfare of its citizens was viewed by some social scientists as a dangerous chipping away of the very foundation of the family.* "The family as a sacred union of husband and wife, of parents and children will continue to disintegrate —

---

* The family is here defined as two or more persons related by blood, marriage, or adoption living in one household.

the main socio-cultural functions of the family will further decrease until the family becomes a mere overnight parking place mainly for sex relationship."[1]

In our own day jeremiads to the death of the family ring loud and clear. David Cooper already wrote its obituary in his book *The Death of the Family*. Urie Bronfenbrenner, professor of Human Development and Family Studies at Cornell University, while not going so far as Cooper, warned in an interview with the *New York Times* (4/23/78) that the family is "fast falling apart." Elsewhere he wrote: "It is most obvious that the family is breaking down, and this is common knowledge, although I don't think that people realize the extent to which this breakdown has occurred. It is probably one of the most radical changes in a basic institution in our society to have happened outside a national crisis."[2]

Barrington Moore, the noted political scientist, thought we could do away with the institution altogether. He wrote: ". . . . it [is] possible for the advanced industrial societies of the world to do away with the family and to substitute other social arrangements that impose fewer unnecessary and painful restrictions on humanity."[3]

The Church has always been worried about the American family. So, it seems, is everybody else these days. Even the politicians. Jimmy Carter, in his inaugural address, pledged himself to a strong pro-family policy and no sooner did he take office than he directed his staff to spend more time with their families. Ronald Reagan and his fellow Republicans in Congress lost no time in assuring the nation they would do something about "saving the American family." Jerry Falwell and his Moral Majority have been riding high on their so-called "pro-family" program (as though any opposing political group is "anti-family"), exhorting the public against legalized abortion, day care programs, and passage of the Equal Rights Amendment.

A White House Conference on Families was held in 1980, bringing delegates from all over the nation to consider ways of reviving that institution, and a proclamation was signed by the President declaring the last week of November of that year as National Family Week. Commissions, advisory panels, task forces, surveys, polls, researches studying one or another aspect of family life, have sprung up like dandelions in spring. Scarcely a week passes that I do not receive an invitation to attend some conference on such topics as "The Crisis in the Family," "The Declining Family," or "The Family: Does It Have a Future?"

The television industry has missed no opportunity to get into the act. It plies it viewers with countless programs on family life — not only family melodramas, soap operas, and "sit-coms," but with documentaries exploring the "crisis" of the American family.

Of course, the "traditional" American family has changed over time. I would wager that your children's family life is in many respects different from yours. In a democratic society like the U.S., where opportunities for educational and economic advancement are available, chances are the family life of your children is *materially* better than yours. They are likely to be better housed, better clothed, better fed. They also probably have more freedom of choice of occupation and even of social status than you did. Changing sexual modes, roles, attitudes, and behaviors that may make you uncomfortable, they take for granted.

The very physical boundaries of your children's world have expanded far beyond those in which you grew up. Already walking on the moon is old hat, flying to Paris on the Concorde in time for lunch a daily occurrence. Supersonic jets, nuclear power, computers, organ transplants, babies conceived in test tubes — these are a few of the scientific advances that are already a part of our children's daily lives.

The traditional nuclear family — mama, papa, and children — is undergoing other profound changes. Families are smaller. Relatives are fewer and often farther away. Divorces have become commonplace. Increasing numbers of children are being brought up by single parents. Or with stepparents. Many children are part of "blended" families whose biological parents have "custodial" (or "non-custodial") rights. Some are being reared in communes,[4] a few are being brought up in group marriages or by avowed homosexual partners. Perhaps most significant, parents are said to be increasingly "self-oriented"; that is, they consider their needs before those of their children.

The family is as old as the human species itself. It has always undergone changes in its form and functions, as it accommodates itself to the social, economic, and political conditions of society at a given time and place. In some periods of history changes have occurred more rapidly than in others.

Whatever the outward changes, the *task* of the family as a social institution has remained the same throughout time and history and across space and cultures. That task—aside from its primary purpose of procreating and nurturing the young — is to socialize the child: teach it what society expects of it. The family is society's emissary to transmit its standards, values, and traditions from one generation to the next in order to insure its continuity.

The family is the bedrock of society. It inculcates in the individual, through its mother's milk, figuratively speaking, that which society values and allows and that which society disapproves and forbids. It is in the bosom of the family that the individual learns its social — and sexual — role to be played out in the larger community. In a stable society the continuity of standards, values, and traditions from generation to generation keeps the family stable. In a period of social flux or upheaval that continuity is likely to be eroded or rejected and the stability of the family threatened.

A Historical Perspective[5]

To gain a better perspective on today's family let us take a brief look at the history of the family as a social institution in Western civilization (as exemplified in Britain and the U.S.) in the last five hundred years.

Before 1500 families were held together in large groups by kinship or clientage. The family unit included, beside the immediate family, relatives, servants, and slaves under one roof or nearby, all under the authority of one head.[6]

By the sixteenth century the nuclear family as we know it today — parents and children living in one household — was established. Marriages were based on property transactions, with no consideration of affection between the betrothed. Little affection was bestowed on children, the likelihood of whose death in infancy or early childhood being great. Those who survived were regarded as small adults, to be beaten for any infraction of rules. The husband and father was the sole authority in the household. His patriarchal rule extended not only over his wife but even over his grown sons.

In the early and middle seventeenth century Puritan attitudes pervaded family life. The sexual code was rigid. Sin was constantly warned and guarded against. The family was the stronghold of piety, with prayers and Bible reading in the family group a daily enterprise. Frugality, austerity, industry, and self-reliance, qualities that became the hallmarks of emerging bourgeois life, were virtues to be pursued.

By the end of the seventeenth century and through the eighteenth century, with the growing commercial prosperity of England, a change took place in the emotional bonding of families. They became a more affectionate group. Love, sexuality, and pleasurable pursuits became more openly permissible. Greater efforts were made to keep children alive. Wet-nursing, which had been common practice among the middle and upper classes, declined and was replaced by mothers breast-feeding their infants. A new spirit of "affective individualism" was a key feature of the eighteenth century's upper- and middle-class English family.

In the early nineteenth century the majority of American families lived on farms. They were, by and large, an economically productive unit, whose every member, including the young children, contributed their labor. Boys worked along with their fathers in the fields, the barns, the forge; girls with their mothers in the home, the garden, the yard, the hen-house. The family's comfort depended upon how much it could produce for itself.

By the mid-nineteenth century changes in the economy were taking place rapidly and with them, changes in family functions. Crops were sent to market and money became the medium of exchange. With the rise of industrialism family members went out to work in factories, mills, offices, and stores and they brought home wages to meet the family's expenses.

Work and family life became separate entities. The family became a shelter from the harsh, competitive world of commerce. Father went out into the world to earn a living for the family, while "the pure wife-and-mother stayed at home to protect the children's innocence against temptations and moral corruption of the threatening outside world."[7] This picture of family life pertained to the urban middle and upper class; it did not apply to the poor, whose women and children, as well as men, always had to work in order to eke out a subsistence, often for twelve or more hours a day under deplorable conditions.

During the late nineteenth century, and increasingly since, outside institutions, such as the school, the church, the law-enforcement agencies, and public and private health, welfare, and recreation agencies, began to encroach upon and eventually usurp many of the functions formerly provided by the family to its members, weakening the parental role. According to Christopher Lasch, although these institutions were meant to bolster and strengthen the family, in the long run this "invasion of the family" undermined its authority and "overthrew its integrity."[8]

1900 to the Present

In our own century perhaps the most radical change in the family as a social institution has been its transformation from a unit of *economic production* into a unit of *economic consumption*. Children, who used to contribute to the family exchequer, today are an enormous economic burden. In 1970 it was conservatively estimated that to a family of modest income the cost of supporting a child until he is eighteen was $35,000.[9] (Estimates today go as high as $100,000). This has meant that the years of child-rearing are the years of greatest financial hardship for most families. As a result, large numbers of women with school-age children must go to work outside the home.

The increased employment of married women with children (which began shortly before World War II) has undoubtedly been the most dramatic change in the family in the last half century.

Unlike any period in previous history, the average school-age child today has a working mother. The stereotyped image of Dad the breadwinner and Mom the homemaker putting up strawberry jam and Jane and Dick coming home from school to a glass of milk and some chocolate brownies Mom baked is fast becoming a nostalgic myth. More likely, the tiny tots are at grandma's or in day care; school children run into the house when class lets out to grab some potato chips and a Coke, then run out to play till Mom gets home from work, when she fries up some hamburgers or bakes a frozen pizza while Dad watches the six o'clock news.

Another drastic change in the family has been its decrease in size. With the option now available to have as many or as few children as one wishes, thanks to the efficacy of contraception, the average number of children per American family is 1.8 This decrease has made it possible for children to receive better care and have better social and educational opportunities than when there were many to look after. It has also, however, tended to intensify the emotional relationship between parents and children, and increase parental expectations of gratification from their children.

One dare not overlook the enormous influence — whether for good or ill, I am not prepared to say — of television on family life. It has been called "by far the most important new child-care arrangement of the century." It has been estimated that the average pre-school child spends 33 hours a week watching television. Whether television is in any way responsible for the increased violence in our society, as is claimed by some experts, I am inclined to doubt. What I am sure of, however, is that it is one of the most powerful tools of our capitalistic economy to increase desire for and consumption of goods. And it has changed the recreational habits of families more than we care to admit.

Do the changes that the family as an institution has been undergoing in the last half century indeed bode its erosion or decay? Are they not rather signs of its enduring viability, its resilience in the face of change?

The family is a living, flexible, social organism that adapts itself to social and economic influences while keeping intact its internal essence. I have little doubt that despite the assaults upon it, the family will continue to survive, as it has done since the dawn of history.

The Harvard research economist, Mary Jo Bane, believes so. In her book, *Here to Stay*, a comprehensive study of American families in the twentieth century, Bane not only refutes the notion that the family is declining; she concludes, on the basis of an impressive mass of statistical and other evidence, that there is more personal commitment to family life today than at any previous time in American history. She writes ". . . . the kinds of ties that are expressed in family life, between parents and children, between two adults making a long-term commitment to each other, are really important to our lives. There can't be any substitute for that institution. . . ."[10]

Bane found no decrease in parental watchfulness of children over the last three generations. ". . . the decline of the family's role in caring for children is more myth than fact." She found little change in the quantity or quality of mother-child interaction even when the mother worked full-time. Nor did she find a weakening of bonds between parents and children "despite changes in patterns of disruption" (i.e.

divorce). Children continue to live with one parent or the other rather than being sent to institutions or relatives, as happened frequently earlier in the century.

Other social scientists agree with Bane. "There is no better invention than the family, no super-substitute," says Sarane Boocock, sociologist at Rutgers U.[11] And that gray eminence, Talcott Parsons, writes "The family is more specialized than before but not in any general sense less important, because society is dependent more exclusively on it for the performance of certain of its various functions."[12]

Herbert Hendin, Director of Psychosocial Studies at the Center for Policy Research, while deploring the undermining of the American family by the divisive forces at work in our society, writes: "The evidence is overwhelming that the family is not disposable, that even the best alternatives do not equal a reasonably good family's power to raise responsible people."[13]

The Parents Speak

What do the parents themselves say and feel about the family? What are their views, their values, their concerns, their outlook on raising children in today's world? "Despite the long-term reduction in familial roles and functions, we believe that parents are still the world's greatest experts about the needs of their own children," writes Keniston.[14]

To investigate those questions, General Mills Consumer Center hired Yankelovich, Skelly and White, Inc., a national market-research and public-opinion organization, to learn how the 23 million American families with children under thirteen are raising their children in a period of rapid social change. Their findings have been reported in a comprehensive survey entitled *Raising Children in a Changing Society, 1976–77.*

The survey revealed that there was a general mood of optimism among the parents.[15] On the whole they felt they were doing a good job. The majority of the families interviewed found satisfaction in their family life, had confidence in the way they were handling their problems, the amount of enjoyment they had together, and the way the family worked together. They indicated a strong sense of confidence in their future.

True, none of the parents denied that this was a difficult time in which to raise children, and some indicated "a gnawing uncertainty" about how well they were raising their children. Still, when asked if they had it to do over again, would they choose to have children, 90 percent of the parents said "yes."

CHAPTER

10

The Blood Knot:
The Family and the Individual

"But there's no vocabulary
For love within a family, love that's lived in
But not looked at, love within the light of which
All else is seen, the love within which
All other love finds speech.
This love is silent."

— *T. S. Eliot*

How does the family serve the individual?

We are all born into families. Practically all of us grow up in them. Eventually nearly all of us produce families of our own. The family is our first and most important social environment. It leaves its imprint on our being forever. No matter how hard we try, we can never altogether erase it.

The psychoanalyst Leslie Farber defines the family as "that irreducible unit of willed and unwilled . . . connections whose reality lies entirely outside our inclination and whose inescapability is absolute. . . . You may revile it, renounce it, reject it . . . but you cannot resign from it. You are born into it, and it lives with you and through you to the end of your days."[1]

In recent times the family has served as the whipping boy for almost every psychological ill besetting man.[2] Books and articles bemoaning the irrevocable harm wrought by papa and mama on the tender psyches of their hapless young roll off the presses in an endless stream.

The family has been blamed for psychoses and neuroses, for criminality, homosexuality, bed-wetting, stuttering and overweight. Scratch a neurotic, a delinquent, a drug addict, a transvestite, a prostitute, a killer, and what do you find? A cruel stepparent, a drunken father, a neurotic mother, a broken home — or so some authorities assert.

"No wonder I'm all screwed up," wails the patient on the couch. "Look at my overpossessive [or rejecting] mother, my superior [or inferior] brother, my preferred [or scorned] sister." A young man I know demanded that his mother pay for his psychoanalysis because "she caused my neurosis." Blaming the family for the deficiencies of its members was carried to a ludicrous extreme a few years ago when a twenty-four-year-old Colorado drifter sued his parents for $350,000, charging that his failure in life was their fault.[3]

In the meantime penitent parents writhe in guilt and beat their breasts in self-reproach. They read books and attend lectures to learn what to do about their children; crowd the waiting rooms of therapists to seek advice on how to mend their errant ways.[4]

There is little doubt that the family is the breeding ground for many emotional ills. We all know people — perhaps even ourselves — whose lives have been hurt by destructive experiences within their families. From our knowledge of human development we know it is in our "first attachments" the first few months and years of the parent-child relationship — that the groundwork is laid for our developing character and personality. If these first attachments are loving and secure, chances are we'll develop a sense of basic trust, grow up to be loving, caring individuals. If these are warped or distorted in other ways, we may grow up to be troubled, alienated, or hollow adults, unable to commit ourselves to others or to fulfill the ordinary obligations of work, friendship, marriage, or child rearing.

But the family is also the breeding ground for all that is richest and most worthwhile in life. It is within the bosom of the family that we learn to be loved — and to love. Here we develop the capacity to form enduring human relationships — relationships that give us joy, that sustain us through life's exigencies, and that in black hours save us from despair. Here we learn our sexual roles and establish our identities. And here too we learn to deal with aggression — our own as well as others' — and where our attitude toward authority is molded. Here our character is shaped.

It is in the family, also, that we learn to have concern for others outside our own group — for the poor, the downtrodden, the weak, and sick — for the family of Man. Where we develop our capacity for indignation over injustice and exploitation and the will to take up arms against them.

"The family," states *I-Ching*, "is the native soil on which performance of moral duty is made easy through natural affection so that within a small circle a basis of moral practice is created, and then is widened to include human relationships in general."

And here is John Cheever in an interview with John Hersey: "One has gotten to be defensive about the enormous pleasures and diversity, the richness of life in a family . . . it's taken us . . . nearly two centuries to be candid about the enormous pleasures we take in one another and the enormous richness in our relationships."[5]

Haven in a Heartless World

For many of us, our family serves as a "haven in a heartless world," to borrow Lasch's felicitous title of his book on "the family besieged." Buffeted all day in our industrialized, computerized, success-oriented society by the ambitions and competitiveness of our colleagues, not to mention our own, at our workplace, where we must be on good behavior, contain our anger, swallow the guff from our superiors if we want to "get ahead" or just hang on to our jobs, we seek, and if we are lucky, find, refuge in our family at the day's end. Here we can shuck off our deferential manners along with our shoes. We can let down our hair, fight with our spouse, yell at the kids, kick the dog, holler and scream if we feel like it. We can also, if we feel like it, make love with our spouse, play ball with the kids, dandle the baby on our knee, cut our toenails, watch television, take a snooze on the couch. Here in our fortress we gather strength for tomorrow's skirmishes.

Intimate Relations

Perhaps the greatest value of the family to the individual is that it is here that we learn the true meaning of intimacy. Never, not even in the most passionate embrace of lovers, will we be as emotionally entwined with others as we are in our childhood with our parents and our brothers and sisters. We are privy to their every hidden wart as they are to ours. Sometimes, in moments of anger or cruelty, we may taunt them with our knowledge; but before strangers we close ranks and guard their secrets, as they do ours. It is a sacred trust.

Brothers and sisters who have grown up in the same family household are bonded together forever, though they may seldom or never see each other after they've left the family home — yes, even though they may hate each other or wish the other ill.

They are bound, among other things, by family rituals, jokes, secrets, by shared family history and experiences uniquely theirs: a gambling father; a mother who surreptitiously nipped the bottle; Uncle Willie who went to jail for "bothering little girls"; cousin Carrie who "had" to get married. There are the shared sad times: father out of work; mother in the hospital; brother Fred killed in action. And the shared happy times: family picnics, riding two hours on the subway from the Bronx to Coney Island, where, making room for ourselves among the sweaty, naked bodies trying to soak up the sun and succeeding only in getting burned, we spread our blanket and ate thick meat loaf sandwiches on pumpernickel bread, washed down with warmish lemonade Mama brought in a Thermos that didn't work.

There is something about being "connected" with others with whom we share the same blood, the same forebears, the same heritage, the same traditions and rituals (though we may have long since abandoned them) that enriches our lives. We may bicker with them. We may be embarrassed or irritated or burdened by them. We may try to escape from them by geographic or emotional distance. But we never altogether succeed. Nor, deep down, do we altogether want to. No matter how independent or emancipated we are from our families, in one way or another we need them.

My oldest sister Jenny — she's fifteen years my senior — lives in Southern California and is a member of an evangelical sect. I see her rarely, since I do not often get to the West Coast. When I do visit her I scarcely cross her threshold before I want to flee, for she soon begins to proselytize me with Biblical exegeses in the futile hope of saving my unregenerate soul. But I find myself staying. For she is my blood, my kin, however vexing or exasperating I find her. The stuffed cabbage and *kasha varnishkes* (our mama's recipe, she assures me) are a temptation. But more irresistible are the shared reminiscences about our parents, long dead, and family happenings in that long-ago-and-far-away small Illinois town where I spent my childhood. She holds me fascinated with tales about our paternal grandparents, whom I never knew, and life in the Ukrainian shtetl before she and my parents emigrated to America. (How well I understand our little children begging us to tell them about "the old-time days when you were a little girl.") Forgotten are her unwanted exhortations from Corinthians II, or is it Revelations? I leave her presence a richer, even though more emotionally wrought-up, human being.

Thicker than Water

We Americans pride ourselves on our independence, especially our independence of family ties. To achieve emotional as well as physical separation from our original family ("the family of orientation") is a mark of adulthood and maturity, a goal of mental health. ("No wonder she's never married," we say of the aging spinster, "she's still tied to her family.") Yet it is those very family ties that we count on in times of sorrow and in times of joy. We expect the family to get together when a relative dies, or to celebrate a marriage, a bar mitzvah, or communion.

We feel obliged to rally round a family member in time of need. The other day my neighbor rushed in, a frantic note in her voice. Would I please look after her cat and her plants for a few days? Her son, a forest ranger in Wyoming, had just telephoned. His wife had gone into premature labor and was in the hospital. A devastating forest fire was raging and he had to be on duty day and night. There was no one to look after their four-year-old child. Could she come at once? My neighbor does not hesitate for a moment, though her precipitous departure means leaving husband, home, and job with scant notice.

Kinfolk

One of the losses to be chalked up against our small isolated nuclear family of today is the diminution of emotional support that individuals in earlier generations received from belonging to a large family, some with relatives usually in close proximity. We seek, and sometimes find, some sense of belonging with a circle of friends, in clubs, in political, religious, or social organizations or movements. But this is by no means the same.

Kinship makes its legitimate demands upon us that, except for close friends, no other association can claim. It's 2 A.M. I'm roused from sleep by the ringing of the telephone. A young, unfamiliar voice says, "This is Jeff. I'm at Kennedy airport. I just came in from Istanbul. Our charter home was canceled. Can I stay at your place overnight?" Jeff? Who the hell is Jeff? I wonder in my drowsy state. Then I remember. A California nephew — my younger brother's son — I hadn't seen since he was twelve. "Okay," I say, anxious to get back to sleep. "Aunt Edith," he says . . . then a pause. "Is it all right if I bring a friend?" What can I say? Around 4 A.M. three weary teen-agers stumble in. Two are bearded, long-haired youths, the third a bedraggled girl with lots of unkempt hair. All are glaringly in need of baths. As they unload their backpacks on my antique Kirman rug they regale me with tales of mishap, mostly about travel snafu, missed connections, and no money. The refrigerator is soon emptied of Cokes, beer, hamburger, and other edibles. Sleeping bags and potato chips bedeck the living-room floor. After three mad, confusing, laughter-filled days, while they await money from their families for plane fare home (their paid-in-advance charter flight from New York to California had apparently been a fraudulent deal), to save my sanity I give them bus fare back to Berkeley.

After they leave, the house seems empty. I miss their chatter and their noise. And Jeff has reminded me nostalgically of my brother when he was Jeff's age.

Did I feel angry at being so unceremoniously put upon by three self-centered (and penniless) adolescents? Yes, I did. But I also felt it was a family obligation I had to meet. I did not for a moment question Jeff's right — and apparently neither did he — to expect me to bed him and his friends down *because I was kin.* It is that sense of obligation to our fellow men that distinguishes us from other species — that makes us human.

Families Are Forever

Families will endure because we need them. We need them not only as an institution in which to raise children, and not only as society's emissary to pass on values, standards, and traditions from one generation to the next. We need them because in families we experience "connectedness" with others — a feeling of solidarity. "Human loving has to do with reciprocity of responsibility, obligation and dependency, as well as knowing when to let others alone. . . . There is no group in society more capable of nurturing the creative, loving spirit of human beings than the family. To flee from family is to abandon humanness."[6] We need families because they are a constant reminder of our humanity.

PART FOUR

Love and Sex
in and out of
Marriage

11

Love and Marriage

"Bind me as a seal upon thine arm. . . ."
— *Song of Solomon*

If that mythical man from Mars were to visit the United States today he would deduce, after listening to our popular songs, viewing our movies and television programs, surveying our newsstands, studying our advertisements, and reading our fiction, that our national occupation was LOVE.

He would not be far wrong. A recent book on happiness, analyzing surveys involving more than 100,000 people, shows that Americans consider love the single most important element in happiness.[1] Moreover, we insist that being "in love" should be the overriding consideration in the choice of a mate for life and the progenitor of our children.[2] We give three cheers for King Edward VIII when he gives up the British throne to marry "the woman I love." When we hear of a friend marrying for mundane considerations — for money or social "connections," say — we raise an eyebrow or feel a twinge of scorn (masking, perhaps, a twinge of envy for our friend's improved fortunes). We feel sorry for people, whether in fiction or real life, whom custom or circumstance forces into marriages of convenience. Our hearts break for poor Glencora, that vivacious beauty with her "gift for laughter," when she is compelled by her society to forsake her hand-

some, ne'er-do-well lover and marry the eminently respectable but eminently dull Lord Palliser. ("Indeed he prided
himself on his dullness," writes Trollope.)

Mini-History of Love in Marriage[3]

Our forebears would have been surprised at this emphasis on love as a sine qua non for marriage. For centuries
marriage was a practical arrangement for the breeding of children, the continuation of bloodlines, and the handing down
of property from one generation to the next. "Dowry is the
condiment of love," declared a seventeenth-century writer.

Love was all right in its place, but marriage was not one
of them. Marriage "infused with beauty and amorous desires"
could be troublesome, Montaigne, the sixteenth-century phi-
losopher, warned, and cautioned against it. He minced no
words about the reasons for marriage. "Men do not marry for
themselves," he wrote, "whatever they may say; they marry as
much, or more, for their posterity, their family. . . . Marriage
is a holy union, and any pleasure taken in it should be re-
strained, serious, and mixed with some severity."

Love has undoubtedly informed the imagination and
behavior of Homo sapiens since he first walked erect. I like to
think that Mr. Neanderthal carried off to his cave one particular female rather than another because he fancied her pert
bottom or her beguiling smile. Even in Biblical times love as
a motive for marriage was not unknown. Jacob labored seven
years for Laban that he might marry his "beautiful and well-
favored" daughter Rachel. The Song of Solomon was presumably written in praise of God, at least so my orthodox grandfather insists, but I prefer to believe it was inspired by some
sloe-eyed beauty whom Solomon took to wife. History and
legend are replete with tales of star-crossed lovers who pined
away or killed themselves because they were forbidden to
marry. Tristan and Isolde, Abélard and Héloise, Romeo and
Juliet come to mind. And there were courageous souls in
every period of history who defied social conventions. But by
and large these were the exceptions.

It was not until the early nineteenth century — less than two hundred years ago — that the right of a marriageable male or female to select a mate on the basis of personal preference was argued. Even then, judging from the literature of that period, it was hardly in common practice. The nineteenth-century French social theorist Proudhon declared that love should be eliminated from marriage. "All amorous conversation [in marriage] is unseemly," he wrote, ". . . it is destructive of domestic respect, love of work, and the performance of social duty." Other writers of the time agreed. Even Balzac, that connoisseur of love, considered love in marriage, "an absurdity."

In our own time the choice of a marital partner is by and large left to the young people themselves, and is dictated in large part by the real or fancied experience of being in love. Of course, they assume they will live happily ever after, since like Chaucer's prioress, we are taught to believe that "omnia amor vincit " [love conquers all]. Never mind that the divorce rate is highest during the first eight years of marriage. Each enamored newlywed couple is sure that *their* love will last forever.

What Is this Thing Called Love?

"You who know," asks the youth Cherubino in *The Marriage of Figaro*, "what is this thing love?" This thing love, which Euripedes called "the sweetest thing on earth and the bitterest," has mystified Man since he first felt its stirring in heart and groin. Even Henry Miller, that down-to-earth realist, was awed by this inexplicable phenomenon. "If there is anything that deserves to be called miraculous, is it not love? What other power, what other mysterious force is there which can invest life with such undeniable splendor? . . ."[4]

Cherubino's plaintive query has yet to be definitively answered. We can describe love's joys and miseries in poetry and prose. We can spell out its physical symptoms upon sight of the loved one — the quickened heart beat, the flush, the sweaty palms, the throbbing crotch. Yet its core eludes us.

Love and Sex

All of us at some time or other in our lives have been intrigued with Cherubino's question. Poets throughout the ages have mused on it.[5] Modern-day scientists have scrutinized it under a microscope.[6] Philosophers have pondered on it.[7] Psychoanalysts wrestle with it in their daily work as they are confronted with its manifestation of what they call "transference."[8] Freud, who doggedly worried the phenomenon of love throughout his long career and filled volumes on the subject, near the end of his life confessed, "We really know very little about love."[9]

Still, let us try, however elusive the quest, to comprehend this mysterious seizure of the human heart that turns an otherwise rational being into a dazed, blind, oft-times foolish creature — like Titania, touched by Puck's love potion, falling madly in love with the ass-headed Bottom. Let us attempt to lay bare its inner secrets, however reluctantly we do so.[10]

First, to clarify our use of the word "love": We are inclined to use it loosely in many different contexts. We speak, for example, of love of God and fellow man; love of parents and children; love of dogs, cats, and butterflies; love of nature, of mountains, plains, and rivers; love of sports; love of pizza, Camembert and Dom Perignon; love of justice and mercy; love of home, country, and flag.

The word "love" is also used as a euphemism for "lust." "I love you," declares the importunate lad to the hesitant maid. Driven by an undifferentiated lust to penetrate the female — at times any female — he may even believe his declaration, only to have the illusion of love disappear with the satiation of his desire. We say, "We made love" when what we mean, if caring or concern for the partner is lacking, is "we fucked."

While we have always accepted lust as a natural male prerogative, until recent times we tended to deny its existence in the female or to dress it up in sentimental garb. It was not until 1933 that the nine good men of the United States Supreme Court ruled it no longer illegal to publish *Ulysses* or, in 1959, *Lady Chatterley's Lover*. Until then Molly Bloom's erotic reveries or the explicit details of Lady Chatterley's amorous dalliances with her gamekeeper were deemed obscene. Times have changed. Today the female protagonists of many of our best-selling novels revel in lust and call it by its rightful name.

In this chapter we shall cast a cold eye upon the various kinds of love between a man and woman that find expression, separately and together, in marriage — passionate, romantic, and conjugal love. We shall also consider the inevitable transformations that love undergoes through the various stages of marriage. For despite Shakespeare's high-minded declaration that "love does not alter where it alteration finds," love does alter, for better or worse, in the course of married life.

Passionate Love: Most marriages in America begin in an amalgam of passionate and romantic love. As one writer put it, "We think the job [of marriage] can be done by turning people loose with stars in their eyes and sex on their minds."[11] Passionate love, like lust, is fired by the sex drive, which seeks to discharge sexual tension through copulation and orgasm, accompanied by intense physical pleasure. But unlike lust, which hunts for sexual gratification without regard for the other, in passionate love the sex drive is gentled by awareness of the partner. The passionate lover finds joy in giving as well as receiving sexual pleasure.

The psychiatrist Smiley Blanton defined passionate love as "the life-giving fluid of human existence . . . It is a profound urge to preserve and extend life by means of union with another living force, and it expresses itself through an exchange of energy that mutually strengthens and rejuvenates."[12]

Bertrand Russell saw passionate love as "something far more than desire for sexual intercourse. It is the principal means of escape from the loneliness which afflicts most men and women throughout the greater part of their lives . . . Passionate mutual love, while it lasts, puts an end to this feeling.

It breaks down the hard walls of the ego, producing a new being composed of two in one."[13]

Sooner or later the sexual component of passionate love loses its intensity. For passionate love battens on novelty, on anticipation, and on overcoming resistance and obstacles. Once sexual accessibility is a certainty, as in marriage, excitement diminishes and appetite is dulled.

Marriage tends to desexualize love. To be ignorant of this existential reality can cause distress and even havoc in a marriage. Husbands and wives may think something is wrong in the relationship if the rapture that emblazoned their premarital and early marital nights and days flickers or grows dim. They wonder if the marriage is foundering when making love becomes a duty. New or strange coital positions recommended by sex manuals may trigger orgasmic release. But it is a short-lived elation. Sexual calisthenics are a poor substitute for passionate desire.

The dwindling of desire for the spouse is not necessarily inevitable. Many couples married for two, three, or more decades have reported that their love-making, while neither as frequent or importunate as in youth, has improved with the years. As the bond between a loving husband and wife grows stronger, acceptance of the other deeper, and sharing of interests greater (particularly after the departure of the children), their feeling of "oneness" can find expression in greater sexual responsiveness. I dare say, however, that this is not the common experience of people married a long time.

Romantic Love: Fortunately for the institution of marriage, romantic love has more staying power than passionate love. Romantic love is the fusion of desire with tenderness and concern for the other that unites and exalts them both.[14]

In romantic love we tend to "overevaluate the object," to use a psychoanalytic term; that is, we idealize the loved one. We endow the beloved with qualities bred of our own fantasies and desires. These often becloud our judgment. Her hair, like ripe wheat in the wind, her voice, like the dulcet song of the dove, her breasts, like ripe melons (or whatever one's fancy in breasts) obliterate her vanity, her self-centeredness, her stupidity, her greed. (Someone said that to be in love is to forgive everything — bad manners, bad taste, even bad breath.)

"To believe in a woman," writes Honoré de Balzac, "to make her your religion, the fount of life, the secret luminary of all your least thoughts — is this not second birth?"

In an ephemeral world of uncertainty and doubt, romantic love gives us the illusion of certainty ("I have found the perfect one"), an ecstatic taste of the eternal ("Our love will never die"). Solomon expresses it thus: "for love is strong as death . . . Many waters cannot quench love, neither can floods drown it. . . ."

Conjugal Love — "*A different kind of affection*": "What happens to romantic love in the course of marriage?" This question was asked of a representative sample of American men and women in a Roper poll (1974) that undertook to study marital satisfaction in marriage. The majority of respondents replied that "romance" did not last in marriage but that it was replaced by "a different kind of affection."

Those of us who have been married more than a few years need no pollsters to tell us that the mystery and excitement of courtship and "newly wedded bliss" fade as the everyday jostlings of married life take over. We may not care to go so far as the essayist André de Missan, who wrote: "You study one another for three weeks, you love each other for three months, you fight for three years, and you tolerate the situation for thirty."[15] Nor would many of us declare as boldly as the eminent sociologist Willard Waller that "marriage is the cure for the disease of love."

But we would have to admit some disenchantment. Those idiosyncracies we found so endearing in courtship days can irritate us when we must put up with them day after day. Her dreamy, "faraway-princess" air that had delighted him now irks him when she forgets to send his shirts to the laundry or lets the roast burn while she's listening to Monteverdi on the gramophone. His masterly command of maitre d's, bartenders, cab drivers, and waiters that had aroused her admiration now seems like overbearing bossiness when he orders her around.

The daily chafings of domestic life also take their toll. The never-ending housework, the penny pinching, the intrusive relatives, the children's clawing demands, were never dreamed of the day John and Mary vowed to love, honor, and cherish each other all the years of their lives.

And let's not overlook the fights. Quarrels, disagreements, misunderstandings invade every marriage, the best as well as the worst. As newly-weds, quarrels are soon patched up under a shower of kisses, mea culpas, and avowals of eternal love. However, as time goes by, the illusions bred of romantic love wither away, transmuted, in a basically sound marriage, into another aspect of love. It is called conjugal love. Conjugal love is more calm, more settled, more comforting than romantic love. It may not inspire poetry. But it can inspire wonder — wonder at how it unites two disparate people in such a way, writes Pierre Teilhard de Chardin, "as to complete and fulfill them, for it alone takes them and joins them by what is deepest in themselves."

There is a quality in conjugal love that transcends romantic or passionate love, something akin to, but more intimate than, friendship. It is the quality of *affection*. "Sometimes I love Jane and sometimes I hate her," a friend confided to me about his wife of fifteen years, "but I always *like* her."

To like one's spouse is not as common as it sounds. It implies, aside from fondness, a respect for the other person's uniqueness, a good-humored acceptance, however grudging, of the mate's failings or weaknesses of character. It implies sharing a common vision. "Love," Saint-Exupéry wrote, "does not consist in gazing into each other's eyes, but in looking together in the same direction."

Those very aspects of conjugal love that some men and

women — people who need the excitement of the chase, the novelty of a variety of sexual partners — would find dull and oppressive others find comforting. They treasure security and even the sameness of the partner, the certainty that when they come home at night after a day's work their spouse is, or soon will be, there to greet them, to exchange experiences of the day, to listen to the children recount their activities, to settle their fights, put them to bed; and after the tumult and the shouting has subsided and the kids are asleep, to have a long drink together and watch the eleven o'clock news.

One such person is Eduardo, my hairdresser. I have followed Eduardo's career over some fifteen years — from the time he was a roving young bachelor working in a prestigious Fifth Avenue beauty salon, through the time he bought his own modest shop and married a quiet, shy schoolteacher, a friend of his sister, to the present, now the paterfamilias of four children, a girl of 8, a pair of twin boys, 5 years of age, and an infant. Eduardo is handsome, gracious, elegant, and Italian-born. His clientele include some lonely as well as some predatory women who would not be loath to enjoy more intimate attentions from their hairdresser than is available in the salon. I have seen Eduardo handle these sticky situations with dignity and grace and without hurting the sensitivities of the client.

"How do you like married life, Eduardo?" I asked for starters.

"I like it fine," he says. "What do you like about it?" I ask. (I try to keep my opening questions broad.)

"It's hard to say." Eduardo is not what you'd call an articulate fellow. I encourage him to go on. He fumbles with words, then says, "I guess I'm what you'd call a family man. I like family life. I like the responsibility of raising my kids. I like to see Maria at the door when I come home. I know she is glad to see me. And the kids come running and jump on me and say, 'Hello, Papa, what did you bring me?' I'll tell you something else, you'll think I'm nuts, I like the noise the kids make. I like to sit down at the table with the family and watch

Maria dish out the lasagna. She cooks better than my mother. My mother better not hear me say that. After supper I help Maria with the dishes. Then we sit on the couch in the living room and my little Anna plays the piano for us. Last night she played a new piece by Beethoven and it's called something like 'For Alice' and it is very pretty. You know something? I would rather listen to Anna play the piano than Vladimir Horowitz."

I ask him about their weekends. "You mean Sunday," he corrects me. "You know I'm at the shop on Saturday. Sunday is what I work for all week. Sunday we sleep late. Every morning Maria gets up at six to feed the baby. She stays up to get the kids dressed and fed and off to school and to serve me breakfast. But on Sunday morning, after she feeds the baby, she comes back to bed with me. Now that Anna's big, she makes Sunday breakfast and brings it to us on a tray. The kids stand around and watch us eat it. They think it's very funny, us in bed eating breakfast. Then Anna and the kids go to eleven-o'clock Mass. I generally stay home. I have the excuse I have to watch the baby. Every other Sunday we go either to Maria's mother's house for dinner or to mine, and the other Sundays they come to ours.

"The kids and I are making a garden in the back yard. I teach them how to grow radishes and beans. These things come up very fast, so they can see the results of their work right away. Sometimes we take a drive to the Bronx Zoo or Jones Beach. Sometimes I take them to a museum. Next summer I'm taking the family to Disneyland in Florida."

"Do you ever fight with Maria?" I ask. He laughs uproariously. "Sure. All the time." "I mean real bad fights," I say, then add, "Most people, even if they love each other, when they fight they hate each other. Do you know what I mean?" "Sure I know," he replied. "One night Maria got so mad at me, she took Anna — it was before the other kids were born — and went to her mother's house. 'The hell with you. I'm leaving for good,' she yelled. 'Good riddance,' I said back. But after a while the house got very quiet and empty like. After I got undressed and went to bed I began to feel terrible, like I was all alone in the world, so I got dressed, it must have been two o'clock in the morning, and I went to her mother's house and apologized and we both were crying and the next morning she came home. That was the only time she left." "What were you fighting about?" I asked. "What made her so mad?" Eduardo thought for a while, then grinned sheepishly. "You know," he said, "I can't remember."

"Do you ever think of the old days at Rudolfos?" I ask. "Do you miss them?" (The beauty salon was patronized largely by "show people.") "Sure I think of them. But I don't miss them. Remember Enzo, the guy who used to work on all them actresses? He's still there, still screwing around. He comes to my house once in a while. He sees me with my wife and my kids and he envies me. He says, 'Eduardo, you got the right idea. I think I'll get married and settle down.' But I think all them dames spoiled him for a nice, decent girl who would make him a good wife. Couple of times Maria invited him with different single friends of hers. But nothing ever happened. Maybe he thinks another Barbra Streisand will come along. I feel sorry for Enzo. If he doesn't watch out he'll turn into a lonely old bachelor with nobody to look after him but his mother out on the Island."

Corny? I guess it is. But when I think of the lives of many successful, sophisticated business and professional men I know — their preoccupation with getting ahead; working too hard in order to pay off the mortgage on their country homes; threatened with a coronary, if they've not already had one; paying large tuitions for their overindulged kids in private schools and, need I add, in therapy; constantly walking a tightrope between their discontented wives and insecure mistresses — I wonder if some of them might not envy my hairdresser, "a family man."

The Enemy Within

Have you ever wondered why, when a marriage is breaking up or already severed, a man and woman who had once loved each other passionately now spew hatred and loathing at the other? Anger, hurt, retaliation, revenge — these are feelings that can drive an emotionally injured person to behave in a mean, even vicious way. What surfaces when love is violated is its backside — hate.

A schizophrenic patient used to let me know in her bizarre language that she had engaged in perverse sexual practices with a man she disliked (but lusted for) by announcing, "I made hate last night." We need not go so far as schizophrenia to see hate's ugly countenance on the reverse side of love. We see and hear it loud and clear in little children. "I hate you! I hate you!" screams 3-year-old Johnny at his beloved mother when she denies him a desired piece of candy. At this moment rage and hate is all he feels.

Ambivalent feelings arise in early infancy. The child loves his mother when she gratifies his needs — caresses his skin, feeds him when he is hungry, changes his diaper when it is wet and cold. He hates her when she frustrates his demands — when she does not appear instantly at his cry, waits to feed him until "it's the right time," lets him lie in discomfort in a clammy, cold mess. In the normal course of emotional development, these opposite feelings are fused. The forceful aggressive feelings energize the loving ones, giving power to love that, as the poets say, transcends death.

Norman Mailer, no stranger to violent passions of love and hate, writes of "the whiff of murder just beyond every embrace of love." All intimate human relationships, be they between parent and child, husband and wife, or between lovers, friends, or siblings, harbor hateful as well as loving feelings. If our need or our concern for the other person is great enough, our hostile feelings are repressed or held in check. Sometimes they are projected onto some less meaningful person. Or sublimated in outrage at injustice or the violation of human rights. But they never entirely evaporate. They lie in wait in our unconscious, ready to spring forth when frustration of our primitive wishes becomes unendurable.

Freud (who was obviously fascinated by the phenomenon of these opposite feelings residing in the human breast at the same time, to judge from his voluminous writings on the subject) described it concretely in the case of "little Hans": "Hans deeply loved the father against whom he cherished . . . death wishes; and while his intellect demurred to such a contradiction, he could not help demonstrating the fact of its existence, by hitting his father and immediately after kissing the place he had hit."

Farther on in the same essay, Freud warns us against making a difficulty of such a contradiction. "The emotional life of a man is in general made up of pairs of contraries such as these . . . In the adult these pairs of contrary emotions do not as a rule become simultaneously conscious except at the climax of passionate love; at other times they usually go on suppressing each other until one of them succeeds in keeping the other altogether out of sight."[16]

It is an unsavory but adamant fact of life — ambivalence — our own toward others and theirs toward us. ". . . Every mind must face the unyielding rock of reality, of a truth that does not bend to our whim or fantasy," Thomas Aquinas wrote. This is one unyielding rock of reality, a truth we must accept if we want to understand, and reconcile ourselves to, our humanness.

We needn't despair. Like roses blooming in a dunghill, love can prosper among the weeds. Freud, that expert on love-hate relationships, wrote: "Nature, by making use of these twin opposites [love and hate] contrives to keep love ever vigilant and fresh, so as to guard it against the hate which lurks behind it. It might be said that we owe the fairest flower of our love life to the reaction against the hostile impulses which we divine in our breasts."[17]

CHAPTER

12

Sex in Our Time

"Sex is the most fun you can have without laughing."
— *Woody Allen*

Sex and Science

Poets, priests, philosophers, writers, and artists have been preoccupied with the mysteries of human sexuality throughout the ages. It was not, however, until the late nineteenth century that men of science, such as Krafft-Ebbing, Havelock Ellis, and Sigmund Freud, began to explore the subject scientifically. However, their findings were available primarily to an educated elite. Only in the late forties when Kinsey and his associates published the first of their two studies in human sexual behavior[1] was the public let in on what actually transpires in the sexual lives of their fellow human beings. Breaking through a wall of sexual ignorance, many of their findings were a surprise even to the scientifically sophisticated students of human behavior. For example, they found a marked difference in sexual practices among different socioeconomic groups and educational levels; a wide range of frequency and types of sexual "outlet" among the population; a difference in the extent of pre-marital and extramarital sex relations among different cultural groups, and a not inconsiderable amount of pre- and extramarital sex in earlier generations.

Then in 1955 along came Masters and Johnson's research in human sexual response.[2] With their ingenious photographic equipment and their compliant subjects, they were able to tell us precisely what goes on physiologically in the act of sexual intercourse. For the first time, minute details of the female orgasm, down to the last spasm, were documented. Among other findings, they corroborated what every orgastic female knew, that, given sufficient manual, oral, or genital stimulation, women were capable of multiple orgasms during the sexual act.

In 1976 the Hite Report was published.[3] It investigated the sex lives of 3,000 women ranging in age from 14 to 78 years, with particular scrutiny of their orgasms — their nature, frequency, and how obtained. Hite concluded that "female sexuality has a complex nature of its own . . . it is not a response to male sexuality." As proof she pointed out that many women have difficulty achieving orgasm in sexual intercourse but do achieve it through masturbation. According to the book jacket, Hite "explodes the myth that women should have orgasm automatically from sexual intercourse."

And now (1981) cometh the Kahn Report,[4] which enlightens us, on the basis of a questionnaire given to hundreds of men and women, listing 19 (!) coital positions, that the number one preference for both sexes is oral sex. The poor old missionary position has fallen to low estate. It ranked ninth.

These books, together with many spin-offs in inexpensive paperback editions, became widely available to the public. They could be bought in practically every bookstore, pharmacy, bus station, airport, five-and-dime, and candy store in the country and sold by the millions.

This sexual enlightenment of the population has, for the most part, been all to the good. It has brought light and air into the dank, subterranean cellar of many people's lives. It has swept away the shroud of secrecy around the coital act, demystifying and defusing an emotionally laden subject that, for far too long, has been overgrown with myth, guilt, and sin. It has led to a greater openness about sex and a greater tolerance of its vagaries. It has alleviated some of the sexual inhibitions inherited from our Puritan past and brought relief from anxiety and guilt to many men and women who learned that their sexual proclivities, fantasies, and practices, which had been regarded as perverse or bizarre, were shared by a large part of humankind.

Studies in human sexual behavior have brought about beneficial changes in child-rearing practices. They have also augmented the curriculum of many educational institutions. Courses in human sexuality are being taught along with analytical geometry, Spanish, and the *Cantos* of Ezra Pound.

This new spirit and new knowledge has had a sexual liberating effect upon marriage. Morton Hunt writes: ". . . the principal effect of sexual liberation upon American life has been to increase the freedom of husbands, and even more of wives, to explore and enjoy a wide range of gratifying sexual practices within the marital relationship. Most discussions of sexual liberation concentrate upon its meaning for the unmarried, the unfaithful, and the unconventional, but by far the largest number of people whose sexual behavior has been influenced by it are the faithful (or relatively faithful) husbands and wives."[5]

Side Effects

Like many life-saving drugs, this panacea has had some unsavory side effects. It has distorted the role of sex out of all proportion to its place in the whole fabric of living. It has placed a premium on performance in bed, so that lovemaking, instead of being a spontaneous union of a man and woman coming together out of love or desire or sexual urgency, becomes a challenge, a job to be accomplished. Should the man fail, as sometimes happens, it is chalked up as a minus point on a hypothetical scoreboard. Should the woman fall short of orgasm, she berates herself or the ineptness of her partner.

Our deification of sex has led us to burden it with undue responsibilities in marriage. "Sex is asked to provide all that religion, work, and the family once provided — something greater than oneself, a means of relief from worldly concerns, a way of getting out of oneself and onto a higher plane of existence. Instead, sex today does the reverse: the relief it offers from the world is only as great as one's physical stamina, nothing is more sharply calculated to remind one of human limitation, and the completion of no other act so quickly brings one back to reality. Perhaps nowhere is more asked of sex than in marriage, yet perhaps no other institution is less set up to deal with the modern sexual imagination. The ideal of the modern sexual imagination is variety and multiplicity. But in marriage — theoretically, at least — one person must serve where multitudes are forbidden."[6]

It is this insoluble paradox — the expectation from marriage of an intense, exciting erotic life along with an exclusive, permanent, stable relationship — that has brought some marriages to grief.

Kiss and Tell: That delicious secrecy about one's love life, once privately savored, is now scorned as prudishness, diffidence to talk about one's erotic fantasies, as inhibition. The current vogue to "tell all" by public figures, particularly those in the entertainment field,[7] has made those once-banned books by Frank Harris, Henry Miller, D. H. Lawrence, and James Joyce, which informed and excited an older generation, seem like Sunday-school tracts.

This rush into print is by no means confined to people in show business. Not long ago two female students at the Massachusetts Institute of Technology published an article in the school paper rating the sexual performance of 36 male students with whom they had had sexual intercourse in a period of two months.

Trivialization of Sex: Perhaps the most regrettable side effect of the so-called sexual revolution has been the trivialization of sex. "It's a fun way to spend an evening," my 19-year-old patient says in describing sexual encounters with casual partners she "dates" once or twice. The phallus, one of Nature's more astonishing masterpieces, in honor of which religions have been founded, temples built, epic poems sung, has been turned into a toy.

It is as if erotic encounters involve only thrashing bodies, not thinking, feeling, loving human beings. Sexual intercourse has been promoted as a device to lose weight (each coitus burns up 150 calories), calm the nerves, relax visceral tension. The *Ladies' Home Journal,* a "family magazine," prints an article entitled "Exersex"[8] in which the reader is instructed, with detailed illustrations, on how to keep the muscles efficient for "a more rewarding sex life." The pelvic tilt, for example, illustrated in both a sitting position and on all fours, is recommended as "increasing the skill and pleasure of lovemaking."

For some, sexual intercourse, even between marital partners, becomes a numbers game, the man's virility equated with the number of ejaculations during a hard day's night, the woman's sexual score rated according to the number of orgasms she can chalk up.

How-to Sex Literature

Books, magazine articles, and manuals on how to improve your sex life — like how to improve your golf score or your cooking with herbs — have proliferated. Like the manual that accompanies your Cuisinart or your outboard motor, which instruct the reader on how to use the equipment properly. They explain step by step the technical skills that must be mastered to be sure the studious couple will enjoy sex in the proper way. One author advised the engaged couple to study the diagram of the female genitals in his book and recommended that on the bridal night the husband should compare his wife's genital region with the diagram.

Many of these popular sex manuals sound like instructions for workers in a laboratory or shop. (Do we carry our work ethic into the bedroom to relieve our guilt about enjoying sex?) The historian Paul Robinson,[9] commenting on a passage in Masters and Johnson's *Human Sexual Response* in which the physiological details that precede orgasm are depicted, writes: "This sounds more like an account of child labor in nineteenth-century Manchester than an experience of erotic excitement. Sex here has become tortuous and alienated, much of it appropriately carried out in the presence of, or aided by, machines."

Some books, like Alex Comfort's best-selling *Joy of Sex* (subtitled, for whatever you wish to make of it, "A Gourmet's Guide to Sex") and David Reuben's syrupy, also best-selling *Any Woman Can*, have steered away from the performance principle and have stressed the pleasurable aspect of sex. They have opened up wider opportunities for sexual fun and games and perhaps have helped some couples revitalize sexual relations that had gone stale. They may even have encouraged some women to become more active partners in sex play, and helped to make sexual contact between two human beings a free and joyous encounter instead of an obligatory or compulsive act for the relief of anxiety or the discharge of sexual tension.

Whether their instructions have brought the reader joy — or *more* joy of sex, as Comfort's best-selling sequel to his original best seller is titled — is dubious, unless there is some caring relationship between the partners. Even those "liberated" men and women who regard the sexual act as a physiological function, like eating or defecating, or as a pleasurable exercise good for the health, often report that after the brief exhilaration of orgastic release feelings of emptiness and desolation pervade their being.

Sex as Big Business

Aside from the vast sums earned by purveyors of hardcore pornography, billions of dollars are spent yearly by the American public on the various media catering to its prurient interests. People stand in line before movie theaters, sometimes for hours, to view multimillion-dollar films depicting in vivid colors explicit sexual acts (simulated, I assume) by our most adulated movie stars. Magazines reporting the sex lives of rock, television, and film "personalities" sell by the millions. My respectable newsdealer does a thriving business in his tiny shop selling glossy as well as pulp magazines devoted to sexually oriented and profusely illustrated articles. These are on display. Under the counter he keeps the "dirty" ones for special customers. (It seems we still crave some secrets.) Publishers have become rich on novels, especially by women writers, that depict every itch of the crotch, every palpation of the genital.[10]

Yellow journalism has always battened on the insatiable curiosity of people about the sex lives of others, particularly the rich and famous. Today our most respected journals report the "irregular" sexual goings-on of public figures. The extramarital shenanigans of a political leader stir more interest among the citizenry than his accomplishments in world affairs. Whereas not so many years ago revelations of clandestine sex activities brought ignominy to the participants (remember the Profumo affair, in which a member of Parliament was brought down in disgrace, a physician committed suicide), today's sex scandals involving Congressmen and other high public officials serve primarily to increase newspaper readership and as conversation pieces over cocktails for a week or two.

Sex clinics, workshops, weekend encounters, and private therapists, all purporting to improve the sex life of their clients, have spawned without end. (There are said to be thousands of sex therapists in New York City alone. Practically everybody, it seems, is either receiving or dispensing sex therapy.) While many of these dispensers are professionally trained and indeed can, and do, relieve the sexual woes of their patients, others, untrained, self-anointed therapists by virtue of their delusional beliefs in their intuitive healing powers, can and oftentimes do, harm their patients. At the very least, they do little good. Still others go into the sex therapy business, as one cynical practitioner who advertises in the *Village Voice* told me, "to make a fast buck."

I do not wish to minimize the help accredited clinics and therapists give to thousands of men and women suffering from serious sexual dysfunction. I know marriages that were repaired by sex therapy of the couple. I wish only to call attention to any overemphasis on the discretely *physical* aspects of sexual disturbances, to be "cured" by prescribed exercises or massage, or special manual techniques, without taking sufficiently into account each patient's inordinately complicated mental and emotional make-up, of which the sexual symptoms reveal only a glimpse.

Female Orgasm

Until well into the nineteenth century only "a lascivious female of low moral character" was allowed to enjoy sex openly. Sexual desires in a well-bred woman were considered a curse, a manifestation of the devil's handiwork, to be eradicated by prayer and cold baths. As recently as the 1920s clitorectomies were performed in this country as a cure for this affliction.

Up to 1953, when Kinsey and his associates reported their findings on the sexual behavior of the female, relatively little attention was paid by the scientific community to the female sexual experience. It was a married woman's duty to accommodate her husband's sexual needs. If she found pleasure in his embraces, well and good. If she merely tolerated them as an obligatory task to fulfill the marital contract, she supposed she was no different from her friends and neighbors. Whatever sexual tension she may have felt was dissipated in household chores, the care of children, and good works in the community. If she could free herself of guilt, she might find relief through masturbation.

The Kinsey Report, with its wealth of information about women's sexual behavior, opened the way for the demythification of female sexuality. However, it was Masters and Johnson who cleared the fog that had cloaked any real knowledge about the female orgasm.

Some radical feminists hailed their documented evidence that women can be multi-orgasmic during one coital act as a discovery comparable to Newton's law of gravitation. Here was scientific proof that the female was sexually superior to the male since he, poor fellow, must rest after each ejaculation. "I told you so," they cried. They further utilized Masters and Johnson's findings to point up women's sexual, as well as social, economic, and political oppression in our patriarchal society, since women have traditionally been consigned to serve men's sexual needs. Now they demanded equal rights with the male to full sexual enjoyment. A woman's orgasm became not only a goal, it became her due.

The quest for the orgastic grail was on. If one couldn't "make it" with a man, there was always masturbation. Articles flooded the market on how to achieve orgasm via masturbation, including the directions on how to masturbate to garner a string of orgasms (the more the merrier). Some radical feminists advocated masturbation as the sex outlet of choice, since orgasm could be attained without the encumbrance of a male.

Whereas a generation ago physicians used to have difficulty eliciting information from a woman about her sexual functioning — should a physician be bold enough to inquire — now they were being inundated with couples who were distressed by the woman's inability to achieve orgasm with the man.

This emphasis on performance in bed, promulgated by a flood of discussion in print and over the air, has turned what could be an enjoyable experience (with or without female orgasm) into a grim job requiring technical skills performed by two individuals, each an observer as well as a participant, the result to be rated on its quality and quantity on a scale from one to ten. The irony is that to work at achieving orgasm defeats its very end, since female orgasm can occur only by evicting the watchman in her head and "letting go." Only when she abandons herself to her partner and to the overwhelming sensations kindled by the union can a woman revel in those Elysian fields that for so long have been the male's eminent domain.

The spectrum of female orgasm response is wide indeed. It ranges from totally nonorgasmic women, no matter how stimulated, at one end, to highly responsive women at the other.[11]

Each woman's sexual expression, like each man's, is unique. Here is Mailer's vivid description of the varieties of female orgasmic responses: ". . . yes, if there were women who came as if lightning bolts had flung their bodies across a bed, were there not also women who came with the gentlest squeeze of the deepest walls of the vagina, women who came every way, even women who seemed never to come yet claimed they did, and never seemed to suffer? yes, and women who purred as they came and women who screamed, women who came as if a finger had been tickling them down a mile-long street and women who arrived with the firm frank avowal of a gentleman shaking hands. . . ."[12] Moreover, a woman's sexual response may differ widely at times, depending on her physical condition, her mood, her stage in the menstrual cycle, her feelings about herself as well as about her husband at the moment.

Her sexual response may also undergo a change at different stages of life. In general most women grow more sexually responsive as they grow older. Some women discover increased pleasure in lovemaking and more intense orgasmic response after menopause, when all fear of pregnancy is removed. On the other hand, some post-menopausal women become inorgasmic precisely because they can no longer bear children and therefore unconsciously feel themselves not entitled to sexual pleasure.[13]

Too, a woman's sexual response, like a man's, may differ with different partners. Fantasy, it must be remembered, plays an inordinately important part in one's sexual life. To the unscaled eye of an objective observer, a certain man may appear to be a most ordinary fellow; to a woman in love with

him he assumes the guise of Robert Redford and Paul New-
man rolled into one.

The fixation on female orgasm has produced other unfortunate overtones. Here is Frank Caprio, M.D., on the subject: "Whenever a woman is incapable of achieving an orgasm
via coitus, provided her husband is an adequate partner, and
prefers clitoral stimulation to any other form of sexual activity, she can be regarded as suffering from frigidity and *requires
psychiatric assistance* (italics mine)."[14] Such a pronounce-
ment from an authority must have distressed many a woman
and, I should think, sent her, and probably her husband as
well, to a psychiatrist for help.

The fact of the matter is that many "normal," warm,
loving, responsive women find great pleasure in coitus without necessarily experiencing orgasm. They enjoy the closeness, the holding and being held; above all, they enjoy the
touching, the caressing, the feeling of being loved and desired
by their mate and of loving and gratifying him. As one woman
told me, "I love being filled up with him. When he's inside
me, I feel we're one person, whole and complete. If I have an
orgasm that's great. If not, it really doesn't matter to me. It's
the feeling of being joined with him I love most."

In my work with promiscuous teen-agers, none of
whom, incidentally, experienced orgasm except by manual or
oral stimulation, many told me they engaged in sexual intercourse primarily for the pleasure of being held. It was the only
way they knew to get the cuddling and closeness of a child by
its mother, something most of them had missed and still
longed for. All of us — grown, mature men and women — at
one time or another want to be "mothered," and it is in adult
love play — the touching, the caressing and holding — that
we seek and sometimes find it.

CHAPTER

13

Sex in Marriage

"Embraces are Cominglings even from the Head to the Feet."

— *William Blake*

Sex as Life Force

"Sex lies at the root of life and we can never learn to revere life until we learn how to understand sex," wrote Havelock Ellis.[1] It perpetuates all living kind and links our past with our future.

The functioning of the genitalia is only a part of human sexuality. Human sexuality embraces a wide range of bodily excitation and pleasure-seeking activities. It informs such diverse pleasures as the thumb-sucking of a child, the stroking of a beloved's hair, the fantasies of a lovelorn adolescent, the nursing of an infant, the touch of a woman's bottom.

Human sexuality in its many guises enriches our daily existence. It is contained in the sensuous enjoyment of the smell of baking bread or the taste of a wild strawberry chanced upon in the woods, the feel of a warm shower on our skin, the sight of Fonteyn dancing or of Michelangelo's *David* in the Piazza del Signoria, the sound of Louis Armstrong's trumpet or of Dylan Thomas's voice reading *Under Milk Wood*. Human sexuality is the unguent that soothes the inevitable cuts and bruises of daily life.

From the Beginning

The sex drive is present in the human species from birth. Freud outraged Viennese bourgeois society when he announced his theory of infantile sexuality in 1905. Yet for those who dared to observe as courageously as he, the evidence is clear: The suckling's orgastic bliss at its mother's breast; the infant's erection when fondled; the masturbatory activities of young children; their sexual curiosity; their play at "house" and "doctor" as an occasion to explore each other's bodies. And of course there are more subtle but no less compelling sexual manifestations of the Oedipus complex, which obtrudes itself around the age of three.

During latency, when the school-age child is avid to master skills — to read and write, to skate, jump rope, play ball, swim, do tricks, solve puzzles — the sex drive is said to go underground (hence the term "latency"). Recent observations of school-age children have brought this concept into question. The very eagerness to master skills during this stage of development is fueled by the sex drive, with which the aggressive drive is fused. Listen to the hilarious laughter of ten-year-olds as they tell "dirty" jokes. Watch their enjoyment of rough-and-tumble play during which they can experience bodily contact without guilt or reproach. The sexlessness of the latency child has turned out to be a myth.

Comes Puberty

The sex drive, blatant and undeniable, once again is "bustin' out all over." *With this crucial difference.* Now the pubescent girl and boy are physically ready, willing, able, and eager — often all too eager — to gratify *directly* their biological urges toward sexual union. Mother Nature, whose monomaniacal goal is procreation, now comes into her own.

At this point society stomps down on the young. To keep the adolescent's unruly sexual urges in check, society admonishes, prohibits, and even punishes. It was not so long ago that young people were warned that masturbation led to insanity or, short of this, growth of hair on one's palms as the telltale stigmata of sinfulness. Fornication is not only a moral but in some states a legal offense. The birth of a child out of wedlock is still considered something of a disgrace among "respectable folk" (although it does not prevent over a million adolescents in the U.S. from having illegitimate children every year).

While we have come a long way from our Puritan days when a Hester Prynne had to wear a scarlet letter on her bosom to publicly proclaim her shame, perhaps we are not as far as we like to think. Vestigial attitudes toward sex as somehow "dirty" persist. Even the young, in their exhibitionistic flaunting of convention, their insistence that parents accept and preferably applaud their premarital liaisons, bespeak in this very defiance a lingering uneasiness about their behavior. The warnings of our childhood, the sexual conflicts and anxieties of our youth, trail after us into our adulthood. Sometimes they follow us into the marriage bed.

Sexual Initiation

In the not-so-distant past, when female virginity was prized, the act of defloration on the wedding night was of monumental significance. In the Lithuanian village where my grandmother grew up the female elders of the community would appear the morning after the wedding to inspect the sheets for proof of the bride's chastity in maidenhood. Shame on the girl whose hymen had been prematurely or inadvertently ruptured. Before the wedding — sometimes only hours before — the bride's mother would inform her of her marital duty, often in language so euphemistic that the bride was left bewildered and apprehensive. The groom, it was presumed, was more knowledgeable about sexual matters and it behooved him to initiate his bride into their arcane mysteries. Often he was as ignorant and as anxious as she, and together they fumbled their way toward connubial bliss.

My grandmother told me that as a girl she knew sexual

intercourse took place on the wedding night — was not the purpose of marriage children and one's own family? — and that the genitals were somehow involved. But she had imagined coitus as a tender, gentle embrace in which entry would be made, unbeknown to her, while she was in a swoon. She was hardly prepared that first night in the nuptial bed for the thrust and pain of penetration and she ran crying from the bridal chamber to her mother in the next room. Her mother explained that it was her religious duty to serve her husband's sexual needs and bear his children. She had only to lie still and submit to his gyrations. "It won't hurt anymore," her mother reassured her, "and you'll soon get used to it." "And so I did," my grandmother added. I had wanted terribly much to ask her whether she had ever gotten to like it. But she was a reserved, formal little lady, my grandmother, and I feared the question might embarrass her. I wish I had had the chutzpah.

The adult who initiates a young girl or boy into the sex act, whether prior to or after marriage, always remains in a special relationship to the novice. This is particularly true for the female virgin, to whom the act of being penetrated assumes symbolic as well as physical significance. The nature of the initiation — whether it was pleasant or unpleasant, forced or acquiesced to, sought for or fought against — has colored many a woman's attitude toward the sex act throughout her life.

Today, when petting and prolonged sexual forays just short of "going all the way" are part of adolescent "dating" rituals, one would assume that the eventual capitulation of the female to the importunities of the male (I am assuming the traditional obligatory reluctance of the female to yield her favors readily) and the triumphant enterprise of the male would be something less than cataclysmic.

But from my experience with young people, "the first time" is still a "red letter" occasion.[2] To the young male it often takes on the aspects of an initiation rite admitting him to the company of men. To the young female, along with any feelings of guilt or fear, is a sense of exultation. "Now I am a woman!" A 17-year-old female patient who had dated a veritable battalion of boys and young men and who had petted to orgasm many times, telephoned me at 2 A.M. one morning to announce, in a pitch of excitement, "Mrs. A., Joe got it in!"

The female novitiate regards herself as "a different person now." She has been let in on The Secret of the adult world. Since the "revelation" often takes place hurriedly, clumsily, in the back seat of a car or a hallway or behind bushes in the park or in some other less than felicitous surroundings, she may well find the discovery a disappointing one. "Is that all?" she asks in dismay.

Premarital Sex and Marriage

The "wedding night" of the young couple of today is a far cry from my grandmother's. Surveys tell us that 90 percent of men and 60 percent of women have had sexual intercourse with one or more partners by the time of marriage and that most couples have already slept together, and in some instances openly lived together for months and even years before legalizing their union.

This may be all to the good for the marriage. To be aware of the sexual needs of the partner, familiar with his or her sexual tastes and proclivities, removes at least one stumbling block in those difficult early months of marriage when all manner of social, economic, and psychological adjustments are required if the marriage is to work. For most couples, at least for most women, whose goal in life (despite the heroic consciousness-raising efforts of the women's movement) is to get married and have a family, marriage brings a sense of security, surcease from uncertainty about oneself and one's future. One has only to glance at the glowing faces of honeymooners, who may have been lovers for years, to realize that their public declaration before the community of their commitment to each other has added an extra dimension both to their individual and their joined lives.

I believe that in general the greater openness about sex, the increasing equality between the sexes, the greater acceptance of sexual practices once labeled "deviant," and above all, the relative freedom from risk of pregnancy, have made for a more mutually pleasurable sexual relationship among today's "young marrieds" than in my grandmother's time.

Adolescent Marriage at Risk

Although early disillusionment can happen at any age, it is more likely to occur in marriages of teen-agers. For many youngsters, the illicitness, the risks, the guilt, the fears — as well as the defiance of parental authority and conventional codes of behavior — add a secret spice to their excitement that sharpens their ecstasy and confirms their belief that they were "made for each other." "How lucky we are that we found each other," they exclaim, marveling at this wonderful accident of Fate. Once married, their made-in-Heaven relationship, stripped of its forbidden-fruit aspect, is robbed of its illusionary perfection. All too soon the frailties of the partner are mercilessly exposed. Disappointment and regret set in.

The fact that 80 percent of teen-age girls are pregnant when they take their marriage vows doesn't help matters. Marriage is tough enough for mature people. For two fledglings, themselves still in need of parenting, to be burdened with the responsibility of caring for an infant before they have an opportunity to adapt to each other's needs and to the demands of married life, the ordeal may become too difficult to endure. The quarrels, resentments, and angers, precipitated by the social, emotional, and economic responsibilities that they cannot handle, before long adversely affect their sex lives. Once sex goes sour, on top of all their other unanticipated woes, there goes the marriage. The dissolution of teen-age marriages accounts for more than half the divorces in the United States.

Contraception and Marriage

The face of marriage has changed in many ways, but nowhere more radically than by the advances in almost fool-proof contraception and the liberalization of abortion laws. They have alleviated the fear of an unwanted pregnancy. Many women have told me that their watchfulness, especially if coitus interruptus was the contraception of choice, kept them from enjoying sexual intercourse. Many older women who did not enjoy coitus during their child-bearing years reported an increase in sexual desire and pleasure in lovemaking after the menopause. (The same is true for some women after a hysterectomy.)

To the married couple who did not want a large brood of children, yet had sexual intercourse regularly, there was always the likelihood of a pregnancy, no matter how "careful" they were. With the Pill they needed no longer fear the Damoclean sword of an unwanted pregnancy hanging over every act of love. Both could now relax and enjoy it.

Sexual Patterns in Marriage

Frequency: If one were to ask that mythical "man on the street" what he thought was the usual frequency pattern of sexual intercourse in marriage, he might reply something like this: "At the beginning, every day, maybe several times a day. After a year or so, about two or three times a week. In middle age it would gradually decline to about once a week, until in old age, say around sixty or seventy, it stopped altogether."

True? No. Oh, in some general statistical realm this broad, overall picture may apply to millions of married folk, but it is by no means characteristic of other millions. Frequency of sex activity varies enormously from couple to couple. It also varies enormously in the course of each marriage and may tend to decline with age. But this is too broad a generality. There are couples in their 20s who have sexual intercourse only occasionally and oldsters in their 70s who enjoy making love whenever the spirit moves them, be it once a month or once a day. Here is John F. Cuber, Professor of Sociology at Ohio State University, on the subject:

"The conventional assumption that youth and sex are associated and that early marriage has a strong sexual accent is probably true in the majority of cases, but there is an important counterpoint. A significant number of young people, whether married or unmarried, are not really much interested in sex. They devalue it in one way or another by very low frequency and, whether consciously intended or not, many among the more educated sublimate sexual activities to others associated with education, career, art, hobbies, and other time-consuming and, often, physically exhausting activities. I know of no careful research data which firmly establish the proportion of the American population which could be classified in terms of the above model, but in samples which have come to my attention it is well documented that this is not an inconsequential group of the population and that they are not necessarily people whose devaluation of sex causes them any discernible problems. . . .

"Another interesting and unexpected fact that parallels the general tendency of sex to decline in importance with passing years is a reverse syndrome, namely, a virtual discovery of sex after a dozen or more years of marriage. Sometimes this occurs through some extramarital experience, although not necessarily so. Particularly among women there appears to be some kind of delayed sexual reaction. I know of numerous instances in which wives who, although they participated in sex with pleasure, did not experience orgasm until some time in their 30s and then continued a vigorous sexual life. These were not necessarily women who had psychological problems with sex in the ordinary sense; they just didn't discover the pinnacles of sexual ecstasy until later in life."[3]

There is an ebb and flow in every viable marriage that is reflected in the couple's sexual life. There is scarcely a marriage, happy or unhappy, early or late, in which sexual activity does not dwindle or cease for a time and then resume its accustomed rhythm.[4] Countless factors, from the state of one's health to fantasies, wishes, expectations, and sudden feelings of love or hate can fire or dampen the biological urge for sexual union.

An all-too-common cause for the temporary cessation of sexual activity is depression in the male. Unlike the depressed female, the depressed male cannot feign enjoyment of the sex act. No libido, no erection. His only recourse is to claim fatigue and turn his back on his wife.

A professor, aged 60, who had expected to be appointed head of his department at the university when his chief retired, was passed over and a younger colleague given the post. He rationalized to himself that he was relieved by this turn of events, since the senior post would have entailed many administrative duties he disliked. But the slight rankled. He felt humiliated and wondered if his age had been held against him, since retirement was mandatory at 65. A vigorous physically active man who had enjoyed a lively sex life, he began to feel "old." He developed a bursitis in his shoulder and had to give up his weekly tennis game; he experienced some vague cardiac symptoms; and, for almost the first time, found himself impotent with his mistress as well as his wife. He became increasingly depressed and lost interest even in his work.

At Christmas he visited his only son and daughter-in-law and their three small children in Vermont, where his son was teaching in a university. While he was there, his son received notification that his application for the presidency of a small but prestigious college was approved by the board of trustees and that he would be expected in the fall. His identification with his son and his pride in the young man's achievement restored the father's self-esteem, which had been more deeply wounded than he could admit. His depression lifted. The noisy play of his grandchildren, which had given him a headache, now sounded like music to his ears. His potency returned.

Variety: Sexual practices are infinite in their variety. Mother Nature has generously bestowed upon men and women the blessings (or curses, if you are so inclined) of a ubiquitous sex drive, lustful appetites, abundant erogenous zones, hormonal secretions, and both the wish and capacity for experiencing exquisite physical pleasure, all for the purpose of fulfilling her one compelling goal — the perpetuation of the species. Man, with the aid of another of Nature's gifts, *imagination*, has ingeniously managed to devise myriad ways to savor that pleasure while foiling Nature's scheme.

Sexual practices range among married (and unmarried) people from the two-minute "wham-bam-thank-you-ma'am" maneuver to the hours-long languorous lovemaking in innumerable positions described in the *Kamasutra* and other erotic literature. (Some of the "how-to-make-love" books and magazines that have proliferated by the hundreds in the last few years carry this quest for sexual pleasure to what, to the writer's perhaps old-fashioned notions, seem rather ludicrous extremes, like smearing the penis or vulva or other erogenous parts with whipped cream, marmalade, or similar goodies to be licked off by the partner for the delectation of both.) Aphrodisiacs, from fabled oysters to the use of "dirty words," are employed by some couples to enhance sexual pleasure. (The best aphrodisiac, many women will tell you, is the whisper of those three words, "I love you.")

Some people must ply themselves with alcohol or other drugs before making love. Whether the imbibing of alcohol is to drown temporarily one's inhibitions or anxieties about one's performance or to help face the ordeal of making sexual contact with another person, or for some other reason, would depend on the individual's needs. The irony of using alcohol or drugs for sexual purposes is that while they do act as a stimulant at first, their eventual effect is that of a depressant. Men who drink heavily at parties may do so as a "legitimate" excuse for their inability to "perform."

Some couples, in their search for ever more titillating pleasures, resort to auxiliary gadgets like vibrators, ticklers, and gussied-up condoms to heighten sensation. Some seek participation of a third or fourth person or engage in group sex to add excitement to an otherwise dull sex routine. The *ménage à trois* is a not uncommon theme in literature. One need not resort to fiction to learn of the prevalence of this practice. Here is a not unusual ad from the eminently respectable *The New York Review of Books:* "Uninhibited, inventive NYC couple, early 40s, she vibrant, voluptuous, he tall, tender, wish to share their affair with sexy bi-lady in friendly, discreet, mostly week-day encounters." The popularity of "Sex palaces" like Plato's Retreat in New York City, or Sandstone in California, made famous by Gay Talese,[5] are public acknowledgment of the diversity of sex practices of both married, as well as unmarried, couples.

Ingenious are the variety of sadomasochistic practices whereby that ever-sought-for Nirvana, the orgasm, can be reached only by inflicting or receiving intense pain or by humiliating, or being humiliated by, the partner. That the numbers of men and women who obtain sexual gratification through sadistic or masochistic practices are not inconsiderable is attested to by the many clubs, "leather bars," restaurants, resorts, underground films, magazines, and newspapers that cater specifically to persons with esoteric tastes in sex.

Waning Sexual Activity in Marriage

"Why have I lost interest in sex?" This is a common plaint presented to physicians and marriage counselors. A little probing reveals the real question: "Why have I lost interest in sex *with my wife* [or my husband]?" This dwindling of sexual desire for one's spouse is a disturbing experience to husbands and wives who care for each other.

While lessening of sexual interest in the mate may indicate some erosion of the marriage, more likely it is the normal concomitant of the ongoing process of the marriage itself. It is a price one pays for the other aspects of a good marriage — its comforts and security, the intimacy and companionship with one's spouse, the regularization of one's life, the joys (and sorrows) of parenthood, the status of responsible householder in one's community. Exciting sex is a sacrifice on the altar of marriage.

Marriage is a many-dimensioned institution (for some lucky people a many-splendored one), of which sexual relations are an integral part — for some couples its core. To a man and woman in love, making love is by far the most gratifying way of expressing their feelings for each other.

Observe the newlyweds at a party holding hands, casting amorous looks at each other, stealing chaste kisses (perhaps because they think it is expected of them?). He is whispering in her delicious shell-pink ear, "Wait till I get you in bed!" She is smiling in secret conspiracy. But that physical magnetism that drew them to each other sooner or later loses its force. The explorations and discoveries of each other's bodies, minds, emotions, opinions, tastes (You love Bartok too!), so delightful in courtship, in marriage eventually come to an end. All secrets are revealed.

The novelty of making love at will wears off. Sex becomes routinized into a ritualized pattern of same words, same time, same place, same ways. That drive to possess or be possessed, that wish for reassurance that one is lovable and loved, which had earlier kindled passion and kept it aflame, is now gone.

Other activities necessary to making a life together engage the couple's energies: like buying furniture ("Do you think this lamp will look right on that end table?"), shopping for groceries after work ("There's a special on string beans today") and preparing dinner together, paying bills (where does the money all go?), giving a cocktail party and exchanging observations of the guests afterward in bed. All are new, and, in their own way, pleasurable shared activities that enrich the couple's joined lives. Putting up bookshelves or baking a carrot cake will never take the place of making love, but they have their own special pleasures in married life.

There are, I'm sure, free-spirited souls who will spontaneously decide to make love in the kitchen while preparing an omelet. But I imagine they are the exceptions. No matter how imperious is John Newlywed's desire for Jane while she's pouring the breakfast coffee, he (and undoubtedly she as well) has got to run to catch the 7:22 for the office. Lovemaking becomes relegated to bedtime, when both may be tired from the day's work, or to Saturday night because they can sleep late the next morning. As lovemaking gradually turns perfunctory, it is not surprising that it may also become less frequent. A gradual dissipation of those overwhelming joys of the early stage of marriage sets in. The erotic drive has been domesticated.

Parenthood

The arrival of *children*, the cornerstone of family life and the raison d'être for most marriages, is perhaps the greatest dampener of sexual ardor. A husband's tender feelings for his wife may be aroused at the sight of her pregnant belly, his pity stirred by her travail in labor, his grateful love overflowing by the miracle of her bringing forth the fruit of their union. But he is unlikely to be seized with passionate desire for her when she's wiping up the baby's vomit or, harassed and bedraggled after a physically exhausting day, she screams at the kids. The baby's crying in the night as they are about to make love is no aphrodisiac either.

Studies show that a deterioration of the sexual side of marriage sets in following the birth of the first child and that it becomes greater with each additional child. Many reasons, both obvious and subtle, account for this process.

Among the more obvious are the physical and financial drains. There is, however, a more subtle factor in the devitalization of the couple's sex life after the arrival of children. It is the shift in identity not only in themselves but toward each other. The lover, the husband, the wife, is now the PARENT. Unwittingly he has turned into "daddy," she into "mommy," not only to the children *but to each other*. How many times have we all heard a wife say, "Father, it's time to go home. We promised the baby sitter we'd be back by twelve." And the husband, "Mother, the baby's crying. Better go see what she wants."

In every marriage where love and tenderness abide, the multifaceted relationship of the mates carries within it elements of childhood family relationships — of parent and child, of brother and sister, for example. Every man at some time and under certain circumstances has paternal feelings toward his wife (and even on occasion, maternal ones, as when she's ill). And a woman's motherly feelings toward her husband are readily aroused, particularly if he happens to fall into a weak or helpless state. These feelings in no way vitiate the man-woman relationship—indeed, they may enrich and solidify it. But they also take their toll in the sexual side of the marital relationship.

Abnormal Loss of Sexual Interest in Spouse

In the foregoing description of waning sex in marriage, the sexual relations between husband and wife have become low-keyed or routine or less frequent, but they continue more or less unabated throughout the life of the marriage. However, there are some men and women for whom the legalization of the union throws a pall on the sexual relationship. For them, illicitness and secrecy are absolutely essential for sexual gratification.

Others can only enjoy sex with a partner whom they consider inferior or dissolute.[6] Freud described men who could admire and love virtuous women but never desire them, and who could enjoy sex only with a woman "who is more or less sexually discredited, whose fidelity and loyalty admit of some doubt."

A similar mechanism in women, called the "Saint or Sinner syndrome," is not uncommon. These women are sexually attracted only to "bad guys," profligate fellows who abuse or exploit them. (Literature is full of such women.)

These men and women disassociate love from sex, usually because of some disturbance in their very early psychosexual development. Once married, such a man unconsciously perceives the wife as the pure, sexually forbidden mother. Such a woman perceives the husband as the sexually forbidden father. In the sexual relations of these men and women the incest taboo looms up and strikes them dead, metaphorically speaking.

"I don't know what's wrong," reported Anna G, age 34, married six months. "Our lovemaking was fantastic before we were married. Now I can't stand to have Jim touch me." She and Jim had lived together for two years before the marriage. She had been reluctant to marry because her first brief marriage several years earlier had ended disastrously, and she didn't want to risk another failure. However, she wanted a child and time was getting short.

Jim was hardly the perfect choice for a husband. He was an unreliable fellow, a gambler and a rake, in debt for alimony and child support. But as she described him, "Jim was attractive as hell and marvelous in bed. Besides, I wanted a baby and I wasn't getting any younger."

Not long after the ceremony she experienced an abhorrence of sexual intercourse with him, though she still liked him. She developed a vaginismus, which prompted her to seek treatment.

In treatment it became apparent that by his willingness to marry her, Jim turned into "a good guy" like her father. What's more, whereas she had always perceived herself as a "bad girl" and hence could enjoy sex, once married and looking forward to motherhood, she fantasied herself like her mother, whom she regarded as "pure" and "sexless." (Though intelligent, sophisticated, and educated, Anna was convinced that her parents had sexual intercourse only twice — to conceive her and her brother.)

The Contented Sexless Marriage

One of the many varieties of enduring marital relationships, by no means as uncommon as one might suppose, is the sexless marriage. Discounting marriages of convenience maintained for social or economic reasons, in which love as well as sex is missing, and marriages in which the serious illness of a partner precludes sexual relations, there are marriages in which love and affection, tenderness, sympathy, and respect for the partner continue as deeply as ever though sex relations have ceased.

This is particularly true of older loving couples for whom sex in their earlier years, while enjoyable, was "not all that important" and who now accept its cessation as a final stage in Nature's timetable. For them the companionship, the greater physical intimacy sometimes necessitated by bodily infirmities, the sharing of memories of a long life together, sweeten their waning years and make the inevitable march toward extinction tolerable. To some older couples for whom sex relations were largely a conjugal duty, their discontinuance comes as a relief, especially if there had been occasional impotence and anxiety about performance. Often these elderly people turn to community activities with vigor and productivity or to the pursuit and even flowering of intellectual or artistic endeavors.

One of the best-known examples of a "happy sexless marriage," thanks to their son Nigel's biography, *Portrait of a Marriage,* is that of Virginia Sackville West and Harold Nicholson. Both avowed homosexuals before as well as after marriage, these two intellectual friends mated only for procreative purposes. After producing two sons, they returned to their homosexual lovers with the full knowledge of the other. According to their son, the pair were deeply devoted to each other. He considered the absence of sex between them as a positive element in their enduring love and happiness together.

The Virgin Wife

Some years ago an internist sent me one of his patients, a woman of 40, with acute and disabling cardiac symptoms for which no physical basis could be found. She refused to see a psychiatrist but with some urging consented to see a psychologist. When she came to my office I found a very pretty, petite, dainty woman who looked nearer 20 than 40. She had been married twenty-one years to a well-known writer of mystery stories, ten years her senior. They had no children.

Her cardiac symptoms developed about six months before referral and were apparently precipitated by her husband's impending departure for Spain to serve as a consultant on the filming of one of his novels, in which a world-famous actress was to star. She could not accompany him because her mother, who lived in Israel, was coming to visit her during the time of her husband's assignment.

In the first interview the matter of her childlessness arose. Had she wanted children? I asked. Yes, she said, but she had never conceived. Surprisingly, she had never consulted a gynecologist about her apparent sterility. Before proceeding further, I thought the couple's sterility problem should be investigated and I referred her to a gynecologist. To my astonishment the gynecologist reported that the patient was a virgin and that he had had to rupture the hymen surgically.

I then asked to see the husband. I had read several of his books, which were filled with scenes of lurid, explicit sex, some of it violent and perverse. I confess I was very surprised to meet an elegant, courtly, soft-spoken, and unusually shy gentleman. The wife had admitted to me that she was afraid her husband might "fall in love" with a movie starlet while he was parted from her. Her fears were groundless, he assured me. He then revealed that in the course of this twenty-one-year marriage to a virgin he had never had a mistress or even a casual love affair. He reported that early in the marriage they had attempted coitus several times but her fear of penetration was so great (fantasies of damage to her body, I later uncovered in treatment, were rife) that sexual intercourse short of rape proved impossible. A loving, kind, and considerate husband, he did not pursue entry. She did permit intracrural sex and in the course of time occasional clitoral stimulation to the point of orgasm. Since he was not my patient, I can only surmise that the husband's fear of sexual intercourse probably matched the wife's and that the fantasy of her as "child bride" fed the unconscious needs of both. As a postscript I should add that her illness served as an excuse for him to cancel his assignment abroad (and with it any danger from those seductive "starlets"). Two months after the hymen perforation, the patient conceived and was delivered in the course of time of twins. Since the birth of the children the couple have enjoyed an active sex life together.

Sex for Procreation

And God said, "Be fruitful and multiply."

It is a comment on our contemporary society that the procreational aspect of sex, which Nature intended and God commanded, is relegated to a few paragraphs of a chapter on Sex in Marriage.

In Puritan times (and among some fundamentalist sects even today), the purpose of sexual intercourse between spouses was for procreation. Preachers warned from the pulpit eternal fire and damnation for sinners who had sex relations solely for pleasure. Moreover, in those days having many children was an economic advantage. They could help on the farm or bring home pay from the mill, mine, or factory. They could be counted on as a source of security in one's old age. Besides, feminists are quick to point out, by keeping wives pregnant and tied down with the responsibilities of raising children, men could maintain their patriarchal power over the family.

Revolutionary changes in our social and economic life in the twentieth century as well as in our psychological attitudes have radically altered our perspective on the role of procreative sex in marriage. While nearly all the young men and women I interviewed said they married with the expectation of having children, very few mentioned having more than two. (1.8 children is the average number in today's American family, and some of them "accidents.") Nonetheless, men as well as women will tell you that the greatest joy in lovemaking is "when we're trying to make a baby." A childless friend of mine, in her late 30s telephoned me from across the continent late one night to announce that she was pregnant. "How long?" I asked. "About fifteen minutes," she said. When I asked her how she knew, she said that it was the greatest lovemaking she and her husband ever experienced. Nine months later she delivered a child.

"Good fucks," says Norman Mailer, "make good babies." Father of seven, he should know.

Coda

The role of sex in marriage is as varied, as diverse, as disparate as marriages themselves. No sooner do we arrive at some truism than a contradiction springs to mind. Take the self-evident "common sense" statements that 1) the degree of sexual compatibility between a husband and wife is a pretty good barometer of their general compatibility; and 2) that sexual joy in each other is an essential ingredient of a good marriage. And yet . . . and yet; — there are many good marriages — if by "good" one means a stable, enduring, loving relationship between a man and woman — in which the sexual aspect leaves much to be desired.

Conversely, there are many unhappy marriages, in which the husband or wife is alcoholic, cruel, promiscuous, unreliable, in which the mates make each other miserable and yet whose sexual relationship is good. Neurotic or perverse, one will say. Perhaps, especially if those characteristics we call "bad" are the very ones that gratify some unconscious need in the partner and hold the marriage together. In such marriages their gratifying sex life is no barometer of their happiness together. But there it undeniably is — a very good thing.

The vagaries, the unpredictability, the elusiveness, of sexual desire and lack of desire, of sexual attraction and repulsion, whether in marriage or outside it, is awe-inspiring. No one states that insoluble mystery better than Norman Mailer:

"... We all know that fucking is thus complex and contradictory that people who can hardly bear each other have sex in which is often by mutual consensus sensational, and couples wigged with pot, speed and the pill fly out on sheer bazass, 'great lovemaking, great!' whereas the nicest love of two fine minds in two fine bodies come to nothing via fornication — sex is capable of too many a variation, love to some and lust to others! sex can lead to conception and be as rewarding as cold piss — the world is not filled for nothing with people who have faces like cold piss! — sex can be no more than a transaction for passing mutual use, yet heaven can hit your hip; there is no telling, there is never any telling, which is why novelists are forever obsessed with the topic, it is an endless frontier. But such a chartless place!"[7]

14

Trouble in Paradise: Sexual Problems

"The rocks many couples run aground on are in bed."
— Tennessee Williams

Researchers tell us that over half the marriages in the U.S. suffer from serious sexual problems. In every marriage some minor sexual disequilibrium between husband and wife crops up from time to time. He's eager, she has a headache; she's eager, he's tired. He turns to her in bed for a loving embrace and is jabbed in the eye with a hair curler. He curses and moves away. She cuddles up to him and is repelled by the reek of stale sweat. She turns her back on him.

They've had a fight that evening over her request for more house money, or his flirtation with the neighbor, that sexy little number who came in to borrow a cup of sugar, Johnny's failure to pass fourth grade, Mary's staying out late, how often his relatives come to dinner (My God, they were just here last week!), her brother's irresponsibility, his sister's sluttishness — any one of a million things a husband and wife can find to argue about. Later, in bed, the fight long since forgotten by him, he seeks to make love to her. But she is still seething over his slurs about her family, her intelligence, her handling of money, her discipline of the children. She repulses the advances of this unfeeling, selfish male chauvinist pig who can think only of his own pleasure. She reprimands him or perhaps, enlisting woman's ever-dependable ally, starts to cry. On the other hand, she may submit to his sexual pursuit without protest; but she feels victimized, exploited as a

sex object, resentful that he can so lightly sweep his cruel
words from his mind.

These are the everyday scratches that irritate the sur-
face of a marriage, but do little or no serious damage to a
relationship that is essentially sound. These are not the problems the pollsters are counting.

There are also some sexual incompatibilities in marriage, like differences in the timing and frequency of desire
for sexual intercourse or differences in sexual tastes, that may
cause some ongoing distress to one or both partners but are
not seriously injurious to the marriage. These differences may
have a cultural origin or be a product of ignorance or super-
stition. Where there is genuine concern for the mate and no
deep underlying pathology in one or the other (or both), these
conflicts can generally be resolved or a compromise reached
through frank discussion with each other. If this isn't possible,
professional consultation can often be of help. One of the
benefits of psychotherapy is that it helps to open up communication between the partners as well as to clear away misunderstandings, myths, and misinformation.

Sexual Dysfunctions in Marriage[1]

There can, however, be sexual inadequacies or dysfunctions in one partner or both (eventually both are affected)
that may seriously injure the fabric of a marriage. Many couples remain together for a lifetime despite a history of chronic
sexual dissatisfaction. Often it is unadmitted, swept under the
rug or displaced onto more admissable arenas for marital
bouts, such as fights over money or children. However, sexual
problems have increasingly become an acknowledged symptom in the syndrome of marital complaints for which couples
seek professional help. Upon scrutiny, one often finds that the
couple's unhappy sex life is an outcome, rather than a cause,
of the couple's incompatibility.

One of the biggest culprits in sexual dysfunctions of
men and women is marital disharmony. It stands to reason

that sex in marriage, which is only one aspect of a complicated, emotion-laden relationship between two enmeshed
people, is bound sooner or later to be affected by the slings
and arrows of unresolved conflict between the adversaries. A
woman — or a man, for that matter — who harbors chronic
feelings of anger or resentment or bitterness toward the
spouse would hardly be eager (unless one were perverse or
neurotic) to make love. If sexual intercourse does take place
either out of conjugal duty or because of the partner's persua-
siveness or demands, what better way — indeed, what other
way — to express one's negative feelings than through some
sexual dysfunction? The body's language speaks louder than
words.

Female Sexual Dysfunctions: In these days, when one is all
too prone to attribute psychological causes for bodily ail-
ments, from backaches to cancer, physical conditions underlying sexual disorders are sometimes overlooked. Pelvic
pathology, such as malformations, cysts, tumors, and, most
commonly, infections, may cause or contribute to the sexual
dysfunction. Dryness of the vaginal tract, the inexorable leg-
acy of the postmenopause (an estrogen deficiency easily remedied) may cause pain in coitus, so that a woman, otherwise
loving and responsive, wants to avoid sexual intercourse. A
husband's ineptitude may be another reason for a woman's
apparent "frigidity."

Common wisdom tells us that a woman's reproductive
system, that complicated, mysterious machinery about which
all too many women — and men — are ignorant, may well be
affected by some emotional disturbance in her psychic organization. The common diagnosis of "hysteria," an emotional
disorder considered peculiar to females, is derived from the
Greek word meaning "womb."

In a male-dominated world, a woman's sexuality is her
trump card with which she can sometimes triumph over the
male's almost always winning hand. Like a small child whose
only weapon against his mother's power is his power to refuse

to be toilet-trained or to have a bowel movement in an appropriate place, so a woman's sexuality is her one powerful weapon with which, consciously or unconsciously, she can assert her "I-ness" and against which the male has no recourse.[2] A woman's lack of sexual responsiveness can unconsciously serve to denigrate a man, to say, in effect, "You do not [or cannot] please me." It may, unbeknown to her, be an expression of buried anger or chronic resentment for slights, psychic or physical, real or imagined. With vaginismus, the wife can literally shut out her husband as definitively as if she had shut a door in his face.

The most common female sexual dysfunction is inorgasmia. A generation ago it is unlikely that a section devoted to a woman's failure to achieve orgasm in sexual intercourse would have found a place in a book other than a medical text. So much brouhaha has been stirred up about the female's right to orgasm equal (preferably more equal) to that of the male that many a woman who enjoyed making love but was only occasionally orgasmic has begun to wonder if there was something wrong with her. Gynecologists report that the most frequent question asked by such women is whether they are "normal."

The fact is that the inorgasmic woman "may be warm and responsive with her partner, frequently reaching high levels of arousal, but remaining stuck at the plateau level. Rarely is such a woman impaired in her ability to exchange warmth and affection in a sustained and meaningful way."[3]

Many women fake orgasm out of concern for their husband's feelings. A patient said, "Joe would feel like a flop if I let him know I never 'come' with him," (she was orgastic with other men). "It would devastate him." One risk of such deception is that it not only sets up a false premise for their life together but that the truth is bound to come out sooner or later, perhaps in a moment of anger or retaliation, and could be infinitely more devastating to the husband's self-esteem than if he had come to terms with her inorgasmia initially.

Countless factors can contribute to a woman's so-called

"frigidity," that pejorative term implying a cold or unloving woman, used to describe in an overall way a woman's lack of response in sex relations.

There are, for example, psychiatric disorders, notably depression, which vitiate the sex drive. There is the ignorance or the rigidity about what is "dirty" and what is "proper," and the guilt of engaging in the former. There are the early parental prohibitions against sex, debris we drag along from childhood into our adulthood, and which, despite our "knowing better," bollix up our sex life with anxieties, guilt, and shame.

A not uncommon cause of orgasmic inhibition in women is fear of losing control. "If I let myself go," a meek, soft-spoken patient said, "I'm afraid I'd go crazy, fall apart, go wild." She refused to fellate her husband for fear of biting off his penis.

Some women fear penetration as a sadistic attack that will damage their insides. A patient reported that she enjoyed foreplay but would become tense upon entry to guard herself against the thrusting penis from "ripping my womb."

A woman's deprecatory feelings about herself may interfere with her enjoyment of sex. Lucy G, age 26, was married for three years when she and her husband decided to have their first child. They had a very good relationship and, only — and lonely — children themselves, were looking forward to having a large family. When she did not conceive after many months of trying, she consulted a gynecologist, who found she was sterile, the result of an old inflammation from a botched illegal abortion when she was eighteen. She became sexually anaesthetic. She believed that her sterility was God's punishment for having "taken the life of a baby." Since she couldn't have children, she felt she didn't "deserve" to enjoy sex.

Curiously, infidelity may precipitate sexual dysfunction. For thousands of years women, except for a privileged few, were expected — and expected themselves — to be fidelitous in marriage. While social as well as moral and religious prohibitions against adultery have been notably weakened in recent years, those centuries-old admonitions are ingrained in our conscience, and neither new "values" nor even the powerful force of lust or love can erase them without leaving some mark. I have known several women who became "frigid" with their husbands after they had entered into an extramarital affair. Some of these women, proclaiming their belief in the "single standard," justified their secret affair on the grounds that they had as much right to adultery as their infidelitous husbands. But gynecological symptoms ensued. What they failed to take into account was their conscience, which often makes a mockery of our intellectual convictions.

The accidental dredging up of some buried childhood experience, especially about incest, real or fantasied, can sometimes trigger sexual dysfunction.

Mrs. L, aged 35, married fifteen years, with three children, had a "good enough" marriage. She enjoyed making love with her husband, during which she often achieved orgasm, until one night, for no apparent reason, she developed a vaginismus. When it persisted for many months she finally went to a gynecologist. Medical examination revealed no physical basis for her symptom and she was referred for psychotherapy. Airing her hostile feelings toward her husband over an adulterous affair he had confessed to about a year before, which might have contributed to her problem, had no ameliorative effect.

Further exploration of events at the time of onset of the symptom revealed the following: Her husband, age 42, slender and boyish in figure and manner during most of their married life, gained over twenty pounds in the past year, grew a mustache, and was getting bald, thereby taking on an astonishing resemblance to her father. One day, when her sister remarked on the resemblance, she became very angry, calling the remark ridiculous. That very night she had a nasty fight with her fourteen-year-old daughter for staying out late, during which she called her a tramp and a whore.

Two incidents from her early adolescence, long forgotten, popped into her mind. In the first, she had entered her parent's bedroom one hot summer's day to get something for her mother. Her father was taking a nap. He was wearing a pair of shorts but they were open and his genitalia were exposed. She quickly withdrew from the room, but her curiosity to see more — she remembered her awe at the mass of pubic hair — drew her back to the ajar doorway, from which she peered guiltily at her father's exposed genitals. This time she saw "everything"; that is, his penis and scrotum. She felt she had committed some awful sin by having returned to look at her naked father (it was the first time she had seen adult male genitalia) and the sight haunted her for a very long time.

The second incident occurred not long after. One day she was "horsing around" with her father in the yard and in the tussle she felt his erection against her. She became very excited by this and that night masturbated with the fantasy of her father penetrating her. She felt terribly guilty and began to avoid any physical contact with him, even refusing to kiss him good night.

These incidents had no affect on her adolescent sexual development, which followed the usual course of progression for an attractive high school girl of her socio-economic class, from necking to petting to sexual forays short of coitus. No sexual problems of any significance transpired in her subsequent life until the night of her fight with her adolescent daughter. Her fantasies of the girl's sex activities stirred up her own guilt-ridden memories, which contaminated her sexual response to her husband.

Male Sexual Dysfunctions: There is an old saying that a man pursues a woman until she catches him. Whatever truth may lie in it, it has always been the prerogative of the male to initiate and, it is hoped, to bring sexual encounters to a successful conclusion. For centuries it has been taken for granted that sexual intercourse, aside from its procreative purpose, was for the man's gratification. If in the happening the submissive woman also found pleasure, that was so much lagniappe for both. But it was not an essential part of the transaction.

In recent years attitudes toward the traditional sex roles

of the male and female have shifted, particularly among better educated and more affluent classes. (The role of the male as cock of the walk, the female as little brown hen still persists in most cultures.) While the male's dominant status has automatically bestowed upon him many privileges, it has also placed upon him certain responsibilities, including, in recent years, that of seeing to it that his sex partner receives her fair share of pleasure. If, for whatever reason, she is not "pleasured," he feels himself at fault.[4]

Men have always taken pride in their virility. Boasts about "how many times," denoting their sexual prowess, have been the subject of countless legends, stories, and jokes. Many men who have lived by the "macho" stereotype — what the sociologists call "hypermasculine gender role" — have been discomfited by the new demands for gratification by the female, especially the increasingly prevalent aggressive female, and sometimes they find themselves unable to function at all. Ruth Moulton, M.D.,[5] in a study based on male patients in therapy, found that their sexual problems were precipitated in large part by the changes in attitudes toward sex-role stereotypes. Other psychiatrists have reported a notable increase in "secondary impotence," i.e., a retreat from sexual activity following failure with an assertive woman.

Men have been cursed with sexual problems long before Masters and Johnson came on the scene. Even Don Juan, so they say, had his troubles. In fact, his acclaimed promiscuity has been attributed to his frantic hunt for a girlie with whom he could, as our vernacular so aptly puts it, "make it." Nothing so deflates a man's ego, I am told, than to be stricken with a deflated penis while making love. Yet there is scarcely a man alive — or dead, for that matter — who hasn't found himself at one time or another in that humiliating position. For most men this is a passing embarrassment or inconvenience. For others, however, impotence is a chronic problem. It causes them, and often their wives, much grief. It can be devastating to a man's self-esteem.

Impotence is a very complex disturbance and its causes,

like those of female sexual dysfunctions, are infinite. Ruling out physical anomalies and illnesses,[6] impotence can be triggered by some psychiatric disorder, the most common of which, as with many sexually unresponsive women, is *depression*. A woman can disguise her disability. A depressed man has no such recourse. He stands exposed in his disablement.

External situational crises can adversely affect a man's potency. Losing his job or worry about losing it, for example, may not only preoccupy a man's thoughts but rob him of sexual energy. Although some men seek solace or refuge from their existential problems in sex, whether with their wives or others, most men, when bogged down with issues of survival or blows to their self-esteem, lose interest in sex, however temporary. If, compelled by a sense of duty or his wife's expectations, such a man attempts to make love, it is hardly surprising if he fails in the task.

Silver Threads Among the Gold: What about aging and potency? There are no ready answers to this question. With sexuality so largely "in the head" ("An odd place for it," said Robert Graves), much would depend on the man's attitude both toward aging and sex. Certainly a man's vigor diminishes with age and orgasm takes him longer to reach than for a young man. But gerontologists tell us that, barring physical disability or psychological barrier, there is no reason a man cannot continue to enjoy coitus into his 70s, 80s, or 90s. And, given a wife of child-bearing years, sire children.

Nonetheless, a not uncommon attitude that subtly pervades our culture and affects our thinking, the old as well as the young — a vestige of our Puritanical attitude toward sex that clings despite the so-called sexual revolution — is that by the time the children are grown and off on their own, and certainly by the time grandchildren arrive, old married folk should "put that sex stuff behind them." We call a man in his 70s with an appreciative eye for the women "a dirty old man." We snicker upon hearing that an older man has married a young woman.

Some years ago a friend came to me in great distress. His father, a retired widower of 69, was planning to marry a divorced woman of 38. He was even talking about raising a family with her! Did I think his father was getting senile to think of marriage and children at his age? Would I see the old man and evaluate his mental condition? I consented. I found a charming, intelligent, mentally alert man who was fortunate enough in his September years to find a splendid young woman with whom he fell in love and who was willing to marry him. After his wife's death five years earlier, he had lost all sexual desire, had no sexual relations, and took for granted that he was impotent. However, with his prospective bride he found himself fully potent and with exceptional sexual vigor. (When I asked him about future children he laughed and said he was only teasing his son — perhaps in this way boasting of his sexual potency; he felt he would be too old to raise young children.)

Not infrequently when a man in his 40s or 50s finds himself impotent in a sexual encounter he wonders, "Am I over the hill?" If the experience had been emotionally trau-matic he may fear failure again and avoid the possibility of its recurrence. Or he may decide he isn't interested in sex any-more, particularly if he was finding it routine and a bore, and may welcome the cessation with some relief. Here we see a kind of self-induced impotency.

But by far the overwhelming causes of potency distur-bances lie in the relationship with the partner. Earlier we called attention to the connection between the sexual dys-function and the pressure a man may feel from the expecta-tion of the female that he "give a good performance"; i.e. that he give her an orgasm. Once spontaneity and joy in the sexual union is tainted with anxiety, ambivalence, a sense of duty, or guilt (sometimes a man becomes impotent with his wife after becoming involved with another woman), anything can hap-pen. And often does. A man who had been passively resistant in his childhood to his mother's overwhelming power by ig-noring her demands upon him — and for whom passive resis-tance has become a way of life — may unconsciously utilize this defense to defeat what he feels to be his wife's excessive sexual demands.

Premature or Retarded Ejaculation: Other potency disturbances such as ejaculatory problems can be quite as distressing, embarrassing, and humiliating as erectile problems. One associates premature ejaculation with youth, with the uncontrolled, impatient eagerness of the young to discharge at once the intense sexual tension. And it is true that an older man is, in general, more experienced in controlling his desire to ejaculate in order to pleasure his partner. But premature ejaculation is a common problem with men of all ages, including the middle-aged and old. One often finds that, with men who suffer from premature ejaculation, anxiety is attached to the sexual act, which seeks immediate relief through physiological discharge.

Some men experience this dysfunction with their wives but not with other women. One patient, who functioned well with his wife premaritally developed this problem after they were married. He had married reluctantly, after the girl became pregnant and refused to have an abortion. One might readily assume that his sexual dysfunction was an expression of his anger at having been "railroaded" into marriage. It turned out, however, that what stirred up his greatest anxiety was having to make a commitment he felt himself incapable of fulfilling. Exploring his sexual history, one found that in all his previous relationships with women — and there were many — whenever the woman hinted at marriage or some other extended live-in arrangement, he developed this symptom, which served to end the relationship.

The reverse — premature ejaculation with a mistress but not with one's wife — is more common. The guilt attached to infidelity, the lies, the complications, the difficulties about arrangements, the fear of being found out, may arouse too much anxiety, offsetting the excitement of the illicitness, and produce this symptom. It can also serve as an excuse to put an end to the affair.

In a discussion of premature ejaculation with a psychoanalyst who had a great deal of experience with patients presenting this problem, he said that by and large these men had "good object relations," that is, they had a capacity for mature, loving relationships with others, but they also had a vivid imagination, an overrich fantasy life, which tended to screw up their sexual performance. Curiously, he found that many of them had been bed-wetters in their childhood. How, I asked, would this tie in with premature ejaculation? Their bed-wetting, he explained, elicited special concern and attention from their mothers centering around the product of their penis. For example, they would be picked up in their sleep during the night and put at the toilet or told to produce a stream before they went to bed. When they wet the bed they were fussed over by mother, perhaps scolded or shamed. Whatever mother's reaction, a big production was made over this involuntary behavior of his penis. (Many children think that in sexual intercourse the man urinates into the woman's vagina. Some little boys wet the bed when they dream of having sexual intercourse.) In the sex act, memories or fantasies of the mother's ministrations around their bed-wetting are evoked and trigger off premature ejaculation.

Retarded ejaculation is rarer. For those who like numbers, sex surveyors report that one out of 700 men suffer from this dysfunction. In this symptom (ruling out any physical cause) one can see more clearly perhaps than in its other Janus face, premature ejaculation, a connection with the husband's ambivalent relationship to his wife. Here he is unconsciously saying, in effect, "You do not give me ecstasy or even surcease from tension; this is work, not pleasure." Or "I won't part with what is mine." Or "I don't want to give you what you want."

This last is illustrated by the Bs. They had been married five years, in a relatively happy, sexually compatible relationship, when they decided to have a baby. Shortly afterward Mr. B developed this symptom. It took no great psychological insight for Mrs. B to interpret her husband's failure to release his sperm as his way of withholding "giving me a child." She felt angry, deprived, and eventually developed a dyspareunia which she attributed to the prolonged irritation of her by now dry, resentful vaginal tract. Sexual intercourse had turned into not only a chore but an undeclared battlefield.

This unhappy state of affairs brought them into treatment. It became apparent that despite his protestations that he wanted a child, he felt economically threatened by the advent of a dependent. Not only would his wife have to quit working, but his own employment — he was a college instructor without tenure — might dry up at any time. Then where would they be?

However, his economic insecurity was only partially the trouble. Further work with him revealed that he was the eldest of eight children, each born a little more than one year apart, in a poverty-ridden family. With the arrival of each additional sibling he felt, and indeed became, increasingly neglected. Now the prospect of an infant in his midst again aroused his old feelings of rivalry, neglect, and unhappiness. In his childhood he used to wish he could stop the brats from coming. Then he was powerless. Now he could gratify that wish.

Reciprocal Sexual Dysfunctions: Sexual dysfunction in one partner sooner or later almost inevitably affects the sexual functioning of the other. Masters and Johnson reported that over 43 percent of the couples referred to their Foundation for treatment presented sexual inadequacies in both. They wrote, "Isolating a husband and wife in therapy from his or her partner not only denies the concept that both partners are involved in their sexual inadequacy with which the marital relationship is contending, but also ignores the fundamental fact that the sexual response represents (either symbolically or in reality) interaction between people."[7]

As indicated earlier in this chapter, a woman's lack of sexual response (except in those cultural groups where the female is expected to be passive and receptive) may very well make a man feel inadequate as a lover and as a consequence he may develop some potency disturbance.

Potency disturbances in the husband may arouse anger

in the wife, particularly if she is a narcissistic woman, as though he is cheating her of her rightful due, and she may reciprocate unconsciously by becoming "frigid" or developing a vaginismus. In my experience, however, I have found that most mature women whose husbands are occasionally or even frequently impotent feel compassionate and sympathetic, sometimes even guilty, as though they are somehow responsible for his failure.

But whatever the sexual dysfunction, it need not be a fatal impediment to an otherwise sound marriage.

15

Forsaking All Others: The Question of Fidelity

"Wilt thou . . . forsaking all others, keep thee only
unto her [him], so long as ye both shall live?
                                                  — Book of Common Prayer

That awesome vow of fidelity[1] pledged by bride and groom in the traditional marriage ceremony has been more honored in the breach than the observance. Even in Biblical days, when adultery was punishable by death — ". . . he that committeth adultery with his neighbour's wife, the adulterer and the adulteress shall surely be put to death" — the proscription did not deter King David, enamored of Bathsheba, his neighbor's wife, from sending her husband to the front line of battle and certain death so that, forsaking his own wife, he might marry her.

There have been legal as well as religious prohibitions against adultery throughout the ages. To this very day adultery is punishable by fines and jail terms in several states. Until not so long ago, when its divorce laws were modified, in the great state of New York the only grounds for divorce (aside from desertion of long standing) was — not wife-beating or criminality or non-support or insanity, but adultery. (Some years ago, before the New York law was modified, I gave a dinner party for a "man of distinction" who had to leave at 11 P.M. in order to get into bed in a hotel room with an unknown woman hired for the occasion by his attorney, so that his wife, from whom he had been separated for ten years, and her witnesses might break in by prearrangement and obtain evidence of flagrante delicto, so that she could procure a divorce, which both wanted.)

In the Queen's Bedchamber

Tales of adultery, especially among the highborn, have always gripped the interest and imagination of the populace. Homer's account of the havoc wrought by Helen of Troy when she deserted her lawful husband Menelaus and decamped with Paris, still fascinates us, as do the medieval romances of royal adulteries, like those of Guinevere and Lancelot or Tristan and Isolde.

Gossip about the extramarital frolics of kings and queens of earlier times not only brought a bit of color to brighten the lives of their subjects but even today serves as entertaining fare for television audiences and competes for ratings with more mundane sit-coms about adultery among the homey, like "Soap." Hints and innuendos, not to mention outright "confessions" by alleged participants ready to turn a quick penny, of adulterous affairs with presidents, congressmen, and others of high estate excite the imagination of the public and stimulate the sale of newspapers, magazines, and books.

Women's adulteries have held a particular fascination for readers, perhaps because sexual infidelity of women has always been regarded as more heinous and "unnatural" than men's and been more harshly punished. Thanks to the consummate artistry of their creators, two of the best-known adulteresses of nineteenth-century literature — Anna Karenina and Emma Bovary — enthrall us to this day.

And what of the novelists of our own time — Joyce, Lawrence, Miller, Updike, Bellows, Mailer, Malamud, Roth, Lessing, Oates — the list is endless — where would they be without the stuff of infidelity to spark their creativity and inform the content of their work? (John Leonard, the critic, says that adultery is the obsession of novelists.) In fact or fiction, the subject of infidelity quickens the blood and lights up the imagination.

Our Next-Door Neighbor

Closer to home and surely more relevant to our own lives than the amorous exploits of rock stars or the high and mighty is curiosity about the love life of our neighbors. A married man may boast to another in the shower room or over lunch about his "fantastic lay" last night; a married woman may confide to her dearest friend or in the confessional atmosphere of her therapy group the acquisition of a lover. But by and large sexual infidelity, despite the bombardment of verbiage about the salubrity of open marriage, swinging, and mate-swapping, is still considered wrong by the average American and is likely to be kept secret.

Facts and Figures

In the U.S., sexual fidelity in marriage has always been an ideal. In a Roper poll (1974) asking informants to rank those factors they regarded as most important to a good marriage, fidelity ranked near the top of the list. Indeed, when I asked the question of the most profligate man I know, he replied, very seriously, "Love and fidelity." Yet we know that infidelity is widespread. While the extent differs according to class and culture, with the gradual homogenization of our society through the influence of the media, the differences are dwindling.

How prevalent is marital infidelity in our middle-class culture today? While I do not agree with Virginia Satir that our traditional code of monogamy is "a myth . . . the fact is frequent polygamy," or with Cuber and Haroff that monogamy is "a colossal unreality . . . [a] collective pretense," there is no denying that adultery is a not uncommon reality in the lives of many married couples.

Hard facts are difficult to come by. Spotnitz and Freeman[2] estimated that in some parts of urban society up to 90 percent of American husbands engage in extramarital sex. The Life Extension Institute, on the other hand, puts the figure as low as 25 percent for the general male population.

The most reliable overall statistics still come from the Kinsey Institute's research on sexual behavior in the male and female. Kinsey and his associates found that over 50 percent of the men and 25 percent of the women reported extramarital sex experience, most of it "one-night stands" and occurring by and large by the age of 40. They found that among white middle-class males the likelihood of marital infidelity increased with each passing year up to middle age.

How much these figures have changed in the past 25 to 30 years since the Kinsey reports, in view of the so-called sexual revolution, the greater reliability of contraception, the increase in premarital sex, and the women's liberation movement, is anyone's guess. Dr. Paul Gebhardt, director of the Kinsey Institute and one of its original research workers, in 1968 hazarded the guess that the overall figures at that time would more likely be 60 percent for males and 25–40 percent for females.

In a more recent survey (1970) sponsored by the Playboy Foundation, Morton Hunt found relatively little increase in extramarital sex since the Kinsey reports, with one notable exception: a marked increase among married men and women under 25. He saw this as an indication of a breakdown in the traditional double standard. He also thought that the current climate of opinion permitted people to talk about such matters more openly and more honestly than before.[3]

In a more recent nation-wide survey by Pietropino and Simenauer, 30 percent of the husbands and 17 percent of the wives admitted having extra-marital affairs.[4] In another survey by the same authors of sex behavior of men only between the ages of 18 and 65, more than one half the men under 55 and one third over 55 said they had had extramarital relationships. According to this survey, the younger the man the more likely he was to favor extramarital sex.[5] The sociologist Lewis Yablonsky declares that on the basis of his studies at least half of America's married men are adulterous.[6]

Attitude Toward Adultery: The Past

Public attitude toward adultery, whatever the private practice, has varied widely over the past three hundred years and has reflected the moral climate of the age. In Restoration England, with the lax morality of its privileged classes, perhaps as a reaction against the strict Puritanism of the Cromwellian era, adultery among the gentry was a source of amusement and wit in the drama of the day.[7] In seventeenth- and eighteenth-century France, where marriages among the rich and highborn were arranged for economic or political advantage, adulteries by the male were of little moment, acknowledged by friends with a wink and a smirk, and with a sigh or a shrug by the wife, who, more likely than not, was carrying on her own clandestine affair.[8] At the same time there were lamentations and dire predictions by the clergy and moralists deploring the licentiousness of the age. As for the folk of low estate, we know little. On the one hand, we would surmise that religious scruples and fear of hell and damnation would tend to keep vagrant sexual desires more or less in check. On the other hand, the large numbers of illegitimate children among the poor would seem to belie this assumption.

With the ushering in of the Romantic era in the nineteenth century, the idealization of the "pure" woman, the fusion of love and sentimentality in marriage, and the worship of home life as a refuge from the world of commerce made monogamy and the preservation of family life one of the highest goals of bourgeois society. Public figures who openly violated the code of monogamy were treated harshly. The political career of the great Irish nationalist leader, Charles Parnell,[9] was destroyed because of his ten-year liaison with Kitty O'Shea, whose husband refused to divorce her. George Eliot endured social ostracism for twenty years for living with her undivorced lover.[10] As in all societies, however, there was also the hidden underbelly of decadence and depravity among the upper classes, as has recently come to light in a spate of books about the "other Victorians."

Attitudes Toward Adultery: The Present

Today the Seventh Commandment, which once boomed with the stentorian voice of Jehovah, now has a quaint ring to it, like jingle bells at the Christmas season. We live in confusing times. We are in the midst not so much of changed social and cultural conditions or of changed moral values as of uncertain ones. The earth quivers a little under our feet. It is hard to stand firm. Jerry, the hero of John Updike's novel, *Marry Me*, sums up our dilemma. "Maybe," he says, "our trouble is that we live in the twilight of the old morality, and there's just enough to torment us, and not enough to hold us in."

The contradictions between our preachments and our sexual practices — as in other areas of modern life, I might add — are glaring. Even less reconcilable are the disparate pronouncements of our latter-day saints, the psychological experts. Each contender waves the flag of mental health, our mid-century substitute for morality, as the irrefutable criterion for or against infidelity. Here are a few samples:

"Infidelity, like alcoholism or drug addiction, is an expression of a deep basic disorder of character."[11]

"Infidelity is often a neurotic and sometimes psychotic pursuit of exactly the man or woman one imagines one needs . . . it is primarily a return to behavior characteristic of adolescence or earlier."[12]

"Infidelity is . . . psychologically unhealthy. . . . It is a sign of emotional health to be faithful to your husband or wife."[13]

On the other side of the fence stand the scoffers of such outmoded virtues as fidelity. If this were merely an intellectual debate, laurels would have to be handed to the latter, who, by and large, speak louder and are more articulate and amusing than the defenders of the domestic hearth.

Perhaps the best known and most popular of this camp is Albert Ellis, Ph.D. He not only believes that adultery reinforces the stability of many marriages; he finds it conducive to mental health. "Extra-marital adventure is here to stay," Ellis assures us, and to assist the timid or novitiate, he has written a book entitled *A Guide to Extra-Marital Adventure*, in which he advises the reader on such sundry matters as "etiquette and techniques for extra-marital adventure," "overcoming emotional problems about extra-marital adventure," and even, for those who worry about it, "how to handle the problem of children in these adventures."

Sociologists Cuber and Harroff write: "We were struck by the sizable group of people . . . involved in adulterous relationships of many years' standing, who were enriched and fulfilled through the relationship."

In an elegant essay, O. Spurgeon English, Professor of Psychiatry at Temple University and an eminent psychoanalyst, writes: ". . . there are certain people of either sex who, for their mental and emotional welfare, have a very significant need to seek a certain type of person with whom they can give sexual relations more significance than they can obtain in a marriage." Dr. English mentions several kinds of incompatibilities that may exist in a marriage, "some of them with high symbolic meaning, [which] leave one spouse or the other constantly in need of some important elements he can only find elsewhere. . . . Who is to decide which are the cases which constitute a mental health necessity or which are only an expression of hedonistic behavior?"[14]

Dr. Gerhard Neubeck, director of the Minnesota Family Study at the University of Minnesota, adds his authoritative weight in favor of adultery for many spouses. Dr. Neubeck sees adultery as a "sensible solution," "a supplement to the marriage relationship," since "marriage cannot serve to meet all the needs of both spouses at all times."[15]

To bolster their argument, advocates of extramarital

relationships remind us that man is by nature a polygamous animal and they point to the polygamous sexual customs among other societies and other mammals. They quote the impeccably reputable anthropologists, Ford and Beach, who found in a survey of sexual customs in 185 preliterate societies that "only about one-sixth of those societies restrict sexual activities to a single mate. The rest grant formal approval of certain types of extramarital liaisons, or at least tolerate them."[16] And, if further reinforcement is needed, they point to the custom among certain Eskimo and Arabian tribes of offering one's wife to a guest for the night as a token of hospitality.

That man is a polygamous animal few will deny. But in this context it is a spurious argument. Man is also a violent animal, given to killing his own kind. One would hardly use this aspect of his nature as a defense of murder.

Freud, in *Civilization and Its Discontents*,[17] saw the interests of civilization as opposed to the interests of man's sexual drives. Where they conflict with the demands of society, man must deflect or sublimate his sexual aims. It is this eternal war between id and ego — between man's instinctual wishes and social reality — Freud posits, that makes for man's eternal discontent.

What are we to make of these contradictions? They cry out for the need to re-examine the values that have guided civilized man for the past hundreds of years in the light of our present era. Passions (or the Id, to use a Freudian term) have changed little, if at all, since upright man first roamed the earth. How they have been harnessed — and passions must be harnessed if society is to survive — and toward what goals, have varied from age to age. Which virtues are enduring, whatever the age, serving Man's ultimate good as an individual and as a social being? And which are vestigial and no longer serve Man's and society's needs in this, our post-industrial, nuclear age?

To deal with these questions within the frame of fidelity, we must first examine those forces both extrinsic and intrinsic to marriage today that make fidelity difficult for large numbers of decent, well-meaning, responsible men and women.

Sociocultural Forces

Our Judaic-Christian tradition of monogamy, to which our society gives lip service, is being nibbled away by the vast social changes that have been going on. We are drubbed from every side by advocates for looser marriage bonds. As far back as 1929 Bertrand Russell wrote, "There can be no doubt that to close one's mind on marriage against all approaches of love from elsewhere is to diminish receptivity and sympathy and the opportunities for valuable human contacts. It is to do violence to something which, from the most idealistic stand-point, is in itself desirable. And like every kind of restrictive morality it tends to what one may call a policeman's outlook upon the whole of human life — the outlook, that is to say, which is always looking for an opportunity to forbid something."[18]

Magazine articles and books abound extolling the benefits of extramarital relations for "greater personal enrichment." "Marriage Yes! Monogamy No!" blazons forth from the cover of *Forum* magazine as an enticement to purchase the issue. Even "family" magazines like *The Ladies' Home Journal* or *Redbook* carry articles in almost every issue on such matters as how to cope with the adulterous husband, the "other woman," and whether "to tell or not to tell" of one's own inconstancy.

Best-seller books like the O'Neills' *Open Marriage*, while not explicitly promoting adultery, point to the failure of monogamy and the value of outside relationships to enhance "self-growth." The O'Neills write: "In societies around the world in which man has been enjoined to become sexually monogamous in marriage he has failed. He may fail gloriously, impudently, nonchalantly, regretfully, or guiltily, but he *always fails* [italics mine] in numbers large enough to make that failure significant. And that leaves us to an inevitable question: Is it the 'unfaithful' human being who is the failure, or is it the standard itself?"[19]

The erotization of our environment by the mass media insidiously affects our attitudes, if not our behavior, toward sex in general and outside marriage in particular. Even some sectors of the Catholic Church, the last bastion of absolute moral teachings, have bent the Church's traditional doctrine to allow for extramarital sex. A publication entitled *Human Sexuality*,[20] written by five scholars under the auspices of the Catholic Theological Society of America, emphasizes personal fulfillment above procreation as the primary purpose of sex and asserts that extramarital sex can be a good.

Other social and economic changes in the last several decades have tended to loosen marital bonds. The unprecedented affluence of our middle-class population, coupled with the ease and swiftness of transportation, make possible the gratification of desires heretofore inconceivable, except in fantasy, without pots of money. In John Updike's novel, *Marry Me*, the protagonist, after getting the children settled in school in the morning, drives from her Connecticut home to LaGuardia airport in New York and flies to Washington for a few hours' dalliance with her lover, returning home only a little late for supper.

One of my interviewees, a middle-aged executive in New York, tells his family some cock-and-bull story about conferences at his West Coast office, then flies to Paris every so often for a weekend rendezvous with his latest amour. Few people, even among the well-to-do, can afford such luxurious "sinning." But the occasional dinner, gift, hotel room, and other accoutrements of an extramarital affair are within the reach of many middle-class people who need or want the heightened excitement of an affair.

The women's movement has undoubtedly had its unsettling effect upon marriage. It has helped to liberate many married women from the confines of *"Kinder, Küche, und Kirche"* and has taken them into the marketplace, where the likelihood of meeting men, some on the prowl, is obviously greater than in their own back yard. This does not mean that the married woman who works in an office or factory is more likely to engage in hanky-panky than the suburban housewife baking carrot cakes and toting the kiddies off to school. It does mean that the opportunities for turning infidelitous fantasies into reality, were she so inclined, are greater, given the laws of proximity, for the woman away from hearth and home all day in the company of male colleagues than if she were sitting by her fireside doing needlepoint.

The women's movement has also begun to liberate men and women from the bonds of the "double standard" that have regulated their lives over the centuries. Some women, overzealous to assert their equal rights with men — and with their sharpened awareness of themselves as sexual beings, capable of sexual responsiveness at least as great as that of the male — have waged their battle for equality in the sexual arena, adding a notch in their belts, like their male counterparts, for every conquest. In some instances their sexual politics have backfired to the detriment not only of their marriages but of their own well-being.

The very climate of our time encourages infidelity. In an age when advertisements, the media, lecturers, authority figures, urge "Do It," "Yes You Can," "If you've got it, flaunt it" — when a prevailing moral guide for the perplexed is "If it feels good, it is good" — the quest for "skin pleasure," wherever it may lead, be it in a massage parlor, a pick-up's bed, or Plato's Retreat, becomes an end in itself. Loosening of old restraints and envy of the imagined sexual freedom of one's peers rouse feelings of discontent in the bored or restless married person, and add fuel to vagrant sexual yens. The husband and wife who find contentment in each other's company, in family and home, are looked upon as "squares," and are derided by the sexual avant-garde with supercilious disdain or patronizing amusement.

CHAPTER

16

Why Infidelity?

"Because it's there."
— *Sir Edmund Hilary*

Despite its prevalence, marital infidelity, like sin, is almost universally disapproved of. It is regarded even by the infidelitous as somewhat shameful, as was found in a study by Bernard Greene and colleagues.[1] In our "psychology-oriented" culture, in which psychological "reasons" are sought to explain deviant or asocial behavior ("it's his Oedipus complex"; "because she hated her father"), "understanding" infidelity is no exception. To my question of "why," my informants gave replies that ranged from "Because it's there" to complaints about chronic sexual frustration at home. None, I might add, was as painfully honest as Howard, the protagonist in Hilma Wolitzer's novel, *In the Flesh*,[2] who, when asked by his astonished wife, whom he claimed to love, why he was leaving her for another woman, replied, "How should I know?"

In addition to my own interviews, I turned to the comprehensive studies by social-science investigators of the subject. Following is a distillation of their findings on the reasons given by their informants for their infidelities.

Marital Incompatibilities and Sexual Deficits

Seventy-five percent of the men and 35 percent of the women, according to Morton Hunt,[3] gave sexual dissatisfaction at home as the prime reason for seeking sexual gratification outside the marriage bed. About half of my own male informants and one-fourth of my female ones gave this reason. Most of the men wanted, or felt they needed, more frequent and more varied sexual relations than their wives permitted. "She doled out sex like it was medicine," one man said. Another said, "She used sex for barter. No money, no sex."

Many complained that their wives were "frigid" or unresponsive, merely tolerating sexual intercourse as their marital duty. One man told me, "When I try to make love to Elizabeth she behaves like a martyr. She makes me feel like a brute." Some men said they went to prostitutes or other hired persons for oral or anal sex their wives refused. (A patient who complained of his wife's sexual inadequacy because she did not perform fellatio, and for which he went to prostitutes, admitted he had never asked her for it, as he considered it demeaning.)

A 40-year-old housewife, married twenty-one years and mother of four children, had what she considered a satisfactory sex life though she had never experienced orgasm. This did not concern her until she became involved in a consciousness-raising group in her church and learned she was "entitled" to it. Now she felt deprived. Instead of discussing the matter with her husband, she engaged in an affair with his friend, whose flirtatious "propositions" she had heretofore been amused by but never taken seriously. With him too, however, she was inorgastic. Guilt-ridden over her adultery and now thinking there was something wrong with her, she became depressed and eventually found her way into treatment.

Boredom versus Excitement

Boredom seems to be a frequent precipitant of infidelity. In his study, Morton Hunt found that two-thirds of the women and half the men, "normal people who had controlled their extramarital desire for years," blamed boredom — a feeling of emptiness in their marriage, their jobs, their lives — as the major reason for their first infidelity. Among my sample it was not so much boredom as the obverse side of the coin — a desire for excitement, a taste of honey. It was the challenge of the chase — or of being chased — that prompted their first infidelity.

While in some marriages husband and wife become closer as time goes by, their life together more fulfilling, in others monogamy spells monotony. For them the passing years take a slow, insidious toll. They grow farther apart until there is little left between them but strands of habit and a plodding resignation to life's prosaic demands. Communication narrows down to a few stereotyped subjects: bills, money problems, the children, hassles on the job, neighbors, the dripping faucet that needs fixing, new furniture.

According to sociologist Mervyn Cadwallader, "Beautiful romances are transmuted into dull marriages . . . the relationship becomes constricting, corrosive, grinding and destructive. The beautiful love affair becomes a bitter contract."[4]

Meaningful work, which in earlier periods of history men could take pleasure and pride in, has become a vanishing experience for many. A lucky few find excitement and challenge in their work. But for many people — perhaps for most in our compartmentalized, computerized economy — work becomes routine, stultifying, a dead end. Afraid to make a break for fear of an uncertain future, they feel trapped. An inevitable restlessness engulfs them. Opulent sexual fantasies pervade their imagination. (A famous author once told me that his fondest fantasy was "winning the Nobel Prize and having endless orgies." He won the Nobel Prize eventually. I don't know about his orgies.)

Some bored spouses, through an act of will or religious conviction or moral scruples or timidity, are able to subdue their desire for sexual adventure and settle for a rich fantasy life. Others become ripe for an affair. The course one takes depends upon many tangled, complicated, intangible factors, not least of which are societal restraints and the sturdiness of one's conscience on the one side, and the power of the attraction on the other.

Curiosity

Akin to the desire for excitement is curiosity. In Greene's study, half of his 750 respondents gave curiosity as a reason for their infidelity. "I've always been very curious about women," a man is quoted, ". . . I love my wife but my curiosity gets the upper hand."

None of my respondents gave "curiosity" as an outright reason for their extramarital sex, but it was implicit in many remarks. "I kept wondering what she was like in bed." "He looked so sexy, I wondered if I'd have an orgasm with him." (This from an inorgasmic woman. Answer: No.)

The man and woman who had little sex experience before marriage may wonder if they are missing something by confining their sexual life to one person as they see an endless procession of monogamous years ahead. As time and habit blunt their passion, they may grasp an opportunity, if it presents itself, to get what, if anything, they think they may have been deprived of.

Desire for Variety

According to one survey, 40 percent of admitted male adulterers gave as their reason the wish for "new sexual experiences." This had little to do with their marriages, with which many were quite content. A divorced colleague in her middle 30s told me, "When I get 'itchy,' my friends' husbands are only too glad to oblige." Most of these men, she said, had "okay" marriages. Yet they felt no compunction about sleeping now and then with their wife's friend. Did she not feel she was betraying her friendship with the women, I asked? She laughed. "Not at all. I'm doing them a favor. I've made better lovers out of their husbands for them," she said.

Unconscious Retaliation

Unconscious retaliation against a spouse, even a loved spouse, for some deep, undeclared hurt may prompt an adulterous affair. Larry M confessed to his wife Marie that he had been carrying on an affair for almost a year with Janine, her best friend. Marie was very upset but felt she had no right to protest, since two years before she herself had been sexually involved with a fellow employee. After her affair ended, when the man took another job, she found herself telling Larry about it. He behaved "nobly" at the time, was "very understanding," and "forgave" her. The matter was presumably forgotten. But not, apparently, in Larry's unconscious. The fact that he let Marie know about his relationship with Janine (which would have been easy to keep secret) and that his "grand passion" for Janine faded immediately after he had "confessed" to Marie, indicated that at least one motivation for the affair was revenge for the humiliation and sense of betrayal he had silently suffered by Marie's infidelity. Now he was even.

Acting out a Fantasy

Sometimes an affair of a sporadic nature and of short duration that seems to be an eye-for-an-eye retaliation for the discovery of a spouse's infidelity has other unconscious origins. Emily G, a faithful wife for ten years, slept with five different men during a weekend workshop away from home, presumably to "get even" with her husband after she learned of his "quickie" affairs on his frequent out-of-town business trips. In her first therapy session after that fateful weekend she "explained" her strange behavior by saying she was merely acting like her philandering husband when he was away from home. Further investigation revealed that on the unconscious level she had identified herself with the women she called "Charlie's whores." Prostitution fantasies are very common, if not universal, in women, including the most virtuous of wives. Sometimes, under the spur of some special circumstances, a woman will act them out.[5]

A Cry for Attention

It has been said that the purpose of the affair is to regain the spouse. A neglected husband or wife may enter into an affair not merely to assuage his or her loneliness but, by revealing it either accidentally or with conscious intent, to provoke a response from the spouse. Here the "other" woman or man serves primarily as a pawn in one's bid for affection from the spouse.

Elaine, a suburban housewife married seven years, housebound by her three small children, felt increasingly neglected by her ambitious husband, who was spending longer and longer hours at his office and his weekends poring over files at home. Unable to voice her discontent directly to her husband — after all, he was working so hard for the sake of his family — she poured out her complaints to her neighbor Gloria, whose husband Jerry, was quick to console this "office widow" with his amorous attentions. A few well-aimed hints about Jerry's sexual advances elicited her husband's jealousy and, at long last, an open discussion of her feelings of neglect.

Character Problems

The reasons given by some men and women to justify their adultery may be a defense against unconscious needs too painful or frightening to deal with. Besides, it is always easier — and more acceptable — to blame the other partner ("She's an awful nag") or on circumstances ("He lost his job and we had to move in with the in-laws whom I hate") than to face one's own shortcomings.

Perhaps the largest group of men and women whose unconscious needs precipitate their infidelities are those with personality or character defects.

The Infantile or Immature Character: "I can resist everything except temptation," quipped Oscar Wilde in *Lady Windermere's Fan*. The epigram may have been witty banter to Wilde, but to some people it is a way of life. "Instant gratification," we call it in today's parlance. These are people who have never grown up. Like the infants they have remained, they seek to gratify their every desire. As soon expect the tide to keep from ebb and flow as to expect such a person to remain fidelitous to anyone or anything for long.

Not long ago I attended the fortieth wedding anniversary of a famous artist. He is well known not only for his canvases but for his endless pursuit of beautiful young women. His charming wife is a proud, self-assured, mature woman who had obviously made her peace long ago with her husband's sexual predilections. Once, in a moment of intimacy, I asked her how she felt about his escapades. "It bothered me at first," she said. She had felt aggrieved, humiliated. His declaration of his love for her and his assurance that the girls were nothing more than momentary diversions did not assuage her pain. But in time, as she saw the pattern of these affairs repeat themselves, knowing they would end as soon as "the foolish girl" capitulated to his blandishments, she wrote them off as J's "fun and games." What if he fell in love with one and wanted to marry her, I asked? She laughed. "That couldn't happen, the lamb needs me," she said. Then, in a quiet, assured voice, with a scarcely contained smile, she added, "He couldn't get along without me. We both know that."

The Narcissistic Character: Closely akin to the infantile character is the narcissist. In the Greek myth, the fatal flaw of Narcissus is his inability to return anyone's affection. One of his spurned lovers prays for vengeance to the goddess Retribution, who causes Narcissus to fall in love with his own reflection in a pool of water. He finally dies of exhaustion from his vain efforts to kiss his reflected image and is condemned to an eternally frustrated infatuation with his reflection.

Psychoanalysts suggest that, in the narcissist, because of some distortion or deprivation in the infant's relationship to its mother in the first year or two of life, when, in the normal course of emotional growth the child develops what is called "object constancy," the process of a loving, give-and-take relationship with another person has been arrested. Narcissists have little or no capacity for empathy — that is, for appreciating or sharing another person's feelings. Since loving means making another person one's center, they are incapable of loving.

Narcissists are often the most charming and delightful of persons. In social situations they may appear to be interested in their companion but upon scrutiny one realizes that the interest is primarily in order to elicit the other's admiration. The "other" serves as a mirror to confirm their self-image. There is the story of the starlet who regales her dinner companion with non-stop chatter about herself, her career, her likes and dislikes, her hairdresser, etc., then turns to him and says, "Now let's talk about you. How did you like my last picture?"

According to Christopher Lasch,[6] narcissistic men are often highly successful in bureaucratic organizations that require the manipulation of people — a skill at which narcissists are adroit — at the same time avoiding any deep personal attachments to fellow workers.

We tend to think of the stereotypic narcissist as woman — that cool, distant, maddening, inaccessible beauty — La Belle Dame Sans Merci. Freud describes narcissistic women as capable only of loving themselves "with an intensity comparable to that of the man's love for them. Nor does their need lie in the direction of loving, but of being loved; and that man finds favor with them who fulfills this condition."[7]

Narcissistic women hold a great fascination for a certain type of man. These women tend to make poor wives. Incapable of truly loving another, yet endlessly demanding love, they often become, in the words of one psychiatrist, "tyrants of the bedroom."

Women have no monopoly on narcissism. Indeed, as I listen to today's young single women complain about the passive, self-centered men they increasingly find themselves stuck with, I think that Freud's description might well include the male of the species as well. Narcissistic men tend to avoid marriage or to marry late in life if it serves their needs. Narcissistic men can be quite comfortable in marriage as long as the mate caters to their needs, adores them, and keeps nourishing their self-esteem.

If both partners are narcissistic — and from my experience this is not infrequently the case — they can manage to work out a modus operandi that is agreeable to both, at least for a time. Indeed, the marriage can be quite happy in its fashion, since each sees in the other their reflected image and both are willing, if not eager, to avoid the emotional intimacy that makes marriage between mature adults both so fulfilling and so trying at the same time. These are often the "fun couples," whose ostensibly jolly "swinging" and multipartnered sexual sprees we hear of or read about and that titillate our imagination and, perhaps, our envy. Since they are unable to make, let alone sustain, a deep, binding, committed relationship with others, extramarital affairs are of little moment to the narcissist. And with no capacity for empathy, he (or she) cannot understand why their infidelities should anger or grieve a more mature spouse.

Should the narcissistic couple have children, they are generally regarded as decorations or appurtenances, or, on the other hand, nuisances, if they're a bother. These marriages can be wrecked by the arrival of children, whose demands for love are more than these parents bargained for. And God help the child if it turns out to be plain. Therapists' offices are full of disturbed youngsters who failed to fulfill the narcissistic expectations of narcissistic parents.

The Don Juan Character: A familiar adulterer is the Don Juan character, the man who needs constant proof of his masculinity by a "body count" of the women he has managed to bed. Some of these men use the prevailing cultural scene — "everybody does it" — to hide from themselves their boundless need for reassurance of their masculinity.

Psychoanalysts believe that the Don Juan character endlessly pursues women in an effort to deny his unconscious homosexual wishes. Such men, they say, often tolerate and even in some subtle way, encourage their wives to "play around" and then to describe their sexual encounters in order to gratify vicariously their repressed homosexuality.

Whether or not the psychoanalytic interpretation is sound, the Don Juan type seems driven to unceasing conquests of women, especially beautiful, talented, or prominent women, to be displayed as an emblem of their "masculine" power.

Then there is the fellow who can't resist the challenge to seduce every attractive woman that comes within his orbit. This self-same man may deny himself without much struggle the tempting dessert to keep a slim figure, give up tobacco for the sake of his health, arise at 6 A.M. to jog three miles before breakfast, but to forego a pretty female is asking too much of himself.

I do not want to give the impression that lusting for a pretty woman — for every pretty woman — is anything but "normal." I have yet to see a healthy adult male who fails to preen himself when a beautiful female enters a room — straighten his tie, jut out his chest, firm his jaw, and suck in his belly. I refer here to the man who *must* possess every attractive woman he meets. George F. Gilder believes that such men need constant concrete proof against the ever-gnawing uncertainty of their sexual prowess. "Man is less secure than woman," he writes, "because his sexuality is dependent upon action. . . . For men sex is an indispensable test of identity. . . . Unless his maleness is confirmed by his culture he must enact it repeatedly."[8]

Dona Juana: Females are not immune to the Don Juan syndrome. One such woman was Fanny Taub (not her real

name), whom I first met in college. She was one of the most
brilliant students I knew, an outstanding scholar in her field.
She was also very homely. Tall, slightly stooped, her flat, sexless figure was always draped in shapeless, nondescript
clothes. Her frizzy hair, thick-lensed glasses, teeth in braces,
and receding chin didn't help her appearance. I doubt if
Fanny had a single date in college.

Some ten years later I met Fleur Talbot, an elegant
woman, one of the chief editors of a prestigious publishing
house. She turned out to be my college classmate Fanny. She
had not only changed her name but her appearance. Contact
lenses revealed her astonishing blue eyes. The braces of college days had done wonders to transform the shape of her
buck teeth and receding chin. Her fashionable coiffure (or
was it a wig?) gave proof to her hairdresser's skill. But the
greatest triumph lay in her svelte figure, an accolade to the
artistry of Yves St. Laurent or whoever designed her clothes.

We renewed our acquaintance and I subsequently
learned something of her life. She had married a chemistry
professor by whom she bore two little girls, unfortunately as
homely as she had been in her youth. (I trust they will not
have to wait as long as poor Fanny did in order that money,
cosmetics, and the beautician's skill turn them into pretty
girls.)

Although she had made a "good" marriage to a husband who cared deeply for her, Fanny-Fleur had what
amounted to a compulsion to "collect" young men, not ex-
cluding her husband's graduate students. Her flattery, her
ready wit, her interest, real or pretended, in the person, man
or woman, with whom she was talking, were fatally seductive.
For her husband's sake she kept her endless little affairs secret. But she was not averse with women friends to drop a
hint of a budding affair with some "young genius" whom she'd
discovered in the course of her work. Like her male counter-
part, once having conquered, she lost interest in her catch.

I wondered whether this compulsive need to woo and
win young men was to make up for the humiliation she must

have suffered in her adolescent years. I wondered too whether, when she looked in the mirror, she still saw that plain, owlish, uncomely girl she had once been and whether her endless pursuit of masculine adulation was the insatiable effort to exorcise that painful image.

Depression

Often a man or woman will enter into an extramarital affair to ward off depression. Such persons may not know why they are depressed, or even that they are depressed. Howard, the protagonist in Wolitzer's novel who was leaving his wife for another woman despite an apparently happy marriage, knew he was depressed. When asked why he was depressed, he said it was "because it started to rain when he was at the ball game, and the men pulling the tarpaulin over the infield seemed to be covering a common grave." Anatole Broyard, in a perceptive review of the book, wrote: "He saw himself in that common grave with a common wife and two common children. There was only one thing to do: the uncommon. Go out and find a grand passion. Close your eyes and grunt." As Howard is about to leave, Paulette, his wife, in desperation, yells, "We're all going to die, Howard! You're not the only one!" "She realizes," writes Broyard, "that it is not another woman Howard is running after but life itself. Stability means stasis to him, or death, and he thinks he can outrun it. A new woman is a form of sympathetic magic that will make him a new man."[9]

Aging

The man getting on in years may find that more time elapses before desire stirs for his wife. This, and the occasional erectile failure, can be blows to his self-esteem. While a man may have an affair because he no longer loves his wife, more likely it's because he no longer loves himself. "His ego," writes Linda Wolfe, "rather than his heart or his genitalia is in need."

For many of the middle-aged adulterous men I interviewed I felt it was not so much lust as an upsurge of the romantic desire to attain the unattainable and to taste what they feel they may have missed. Their marriages grown stale, their work uninspired, the quest for something new, for fresh pleasures clamor. "I want! I want!" shouts Henderson, Saul Bellow's middle-aged protagonist in *Henderson the Rain King*. If, like Henderson, the man has plenty of money, affairs become a kind of fringe benefit of wealth and power. A suite at the Regency, a weekend skiing at Zermatt while the wife is enjoying the sun and surf in Florida, are within easy reach of the well-heeled adulterer.

The rich have no monopoly on adultery. The less financially blessed, with a bit more imagination, can manage an affair almost as easily, though it may mean only a date at the Whitney Museum, a stroll through the park, and an afternoon's dalliance "on sick leave" at an obliging friend's flat.

For many men, the approach or arrival of middle age is indeed a critical period. Like other life crises, this one too eventually subsides. I have known many a man who, after a series of transient flings in his middle years, settles down into staid old age, warming himself with romantic memories of his earlier, less judicious years.

While the approach of middle or old age is upsetting to many men, it poses a special threat to women in our youth-oriented culture. The marked increase in first infidelity among women over 35 cannot be ignored.

Time's relentless toll on their bodies is dismaying to all women, to some more than others. The mature woman, while regretting the graying hair (which she may decide to "touch up"), the droop of her bosom (which she remedies with a well-fitting bra), the slackened belly muscles (which she tightens with exercise), looks forward to the new experiences this phase of her life may bring. She finds satsifaction in her improved skills, be they in the kitchen, the office, the social situation, or on the tennis court. With more knowledge and art in the use of cosmetics and clothes, with more self-assur-

ance, and generally with more money at her command, many
a middle-aged woman is more attractive than her pretty adolescent daugher.

As for extramarital sex, while the mature fidelitous wife
may find the thought of an "affair" exciting, she has no trouble saying "No" to the blandishments, however sugar-coated,
of a hopeful seducer and to whatever lustful feelings she may
harbor. By and large her self-esteem as an attractive woman is
;sufficiently gratified by a harmless flirtation, the compliments
of a dinner partner, the admiring glance of a male colleague,
the embrace of a guest in the kitchen.

In contrast, the less mature aging woman may find it
not so easy to say "No," especially if her stock in trade has
been her youth and beauty. To her the tiniest wrinkle is a
disaster, the microscopic sag of the chin a tragedy. Every
crumb of recognition of her attractiveness is manna from
heaven. She feeds on the stranger's avid glance, the salacious
innuendoes of a Don Juan at a cocktail party, the "proposi-
tion" of her neighbor at the barbecue. She becomes a push-
over for an affair, especially if she finds her marriage dull, her
husband tiresome.

I confess I was surprised to learn in my own research
for this book how many women had had their first extramarital
affair after ten or fifteen years of marriage. Some "fell into it"
impulsively.

"I don't know how it happened," reported Marian G,
38, a Catholic suburban housewife, mother of three children.
"I'd known Jack for years. He used to work for Bob when he
had his own business. Well, he came over one night around
nine to borrow Bob's power saw for some renovation he was
doing on his house. Bob was at a union meeting and I didn't
expect him home till after ten. Jack said he'd wait for Bob. He
needed his advice on this job. I offered him a drink. As I
handed him the glass, he pulled me down on the couch where
he was sitting and began kissing me and telling me he was
crazy about me and always had been. Next thing I knew we
were making love right there. Lights on, television going,

Marcy and Kit asleep upstairs. I don't know what got into me. I was so excited, like I was sex-starved, though Bob and I get together every Saturday night. I can't remember when it was so good. I was terribly ashamed afterward. I made him leave right away. When Bob came home I told him Jack had come over for the saw. But that's all I said. I was afraid he might suspect something from how I looked — I wondered if it showed on my face. But he never asked me anything more about Jack's visit. I guess he never thought a young man like Jack would be interested in an old bag like me. Now Jack keeps calling me every day. He wants to see me again. Keeps saying how much he loves me. So far I've refused. When I remember how it was like with him I wonder if I'm a fool to hold out."

At this point she began to complain about Bob — how he neglected her for his work, how he spent most of his time with his woodworking in the basement or on his union activities; how he never noticed when she was wearing a new dress or had a new hairdo; how he expected her to have the in-laws over every Sunday for dinner.

I suspected that this litany of complaints was a prelude to seeing Jack again. I was not wrong. She subsequently told me that Jack had come over several times during the day. I do not expect the affair to last much longer, as she is too frightened and guilt ridden. She is terrified her neighbors might know and of what Bob might do if he found out. And she is too filled with guilt to enjoy the lovemaking. Indeed, she has never again experienced the ecstasy of that first impulsive capitulation. But however her conscience may deal with the brief affair, it has been of some salutary benefit to Marian by making her feel like a desirable woman again.

I was even more surprised to learn in the course of my research how many postmenopausal women — staid, serious, plain-looking women married twenty years or more — were involved in extramarital affairs. Some of these have been long-enduring relationships continued from their younger days. Others occurred late in life.

Tall, heavy-set, gray-haired Gertrude L, in her late fifties, a physician, is mother of three and grandmother of six children. A faithful wife for over thirty years, she had a brief affair with a man who sat next to her on a flight to Colorado, where she was to attend a conference. The man, about her own age, an executive in the communications industry, happened to be booked at her hotel. They had dinner together, found each other very congenial, shared many interests (his daughter was a medical student), and ended up spending a happy weekend together.

Before her marriage at 27 to Bill, also a physician, Gertrude had had many lovers, some concurrently. After marriage, however, she "settled down" and became a devoted wife and mother as well as a splendid physician. Although she had numerous close friends among her male colleagues, she felt no sexual desire toward any of them.

Hers is a good marriage. She and Bill care deeply for each other, share the same tastes and interests, and on the whole are very compatible. "This thing with John," she said, "had nothing to do with my marriage. It was just something nice that happened." John telephoned her after her return to the city and she had lunch with him on one occasion but the affair was not resumed. "It made no sense," she said. "I'm not good at playing games. Or hiding things. If it went on I'd have to tell Bill. And I wouldn't want to hurt him or jeopardize our marriage. It wouldn't be worth it." She was one of the few women I interviewed who felt no guilt about the event. In fact, she was quite pleased that a sophisticated man-of-the-world like John had found her sexually attractive. "It gave me a lift," she added.

Vestigial Remains of Childhood

As mentioned earlier, we drag our childhood with us — into our marriages, our parenthood, our divorces, our old age — indeed, into our graves. Anyone who has worked with couples in marital distress is impressed by how often their troubles stem from childhood feelings toward their parents or siblings that have never been laid to rest and that return, like uneasy ghosts, to haunt and torment their love-hate relationships with those closest to them in adulthood — husbands, wives, lovers, children.

Some turn the spouse into a stern parent. There is, for example, the man or woman who has never properly worked through the normal rebelliousness of adolescence. Such a person's infidelities may be an acting-out of that rebelliousness against real or imagined parental restrictions now projected onto the spouse. "You can't tell me what to do. I'm going to do what *I* want, not what *you* want."

Then there is the man or woman who unconsciously turns the spouse into the ever-indulgent, ever-forgiving "mama." With these people adulterous affairs are of little consequence, fun and games that have little to do with their relationship to "mama"-spouse. A patient complained that her husband would "confess" his affairs, always brief and not infrequently with one of her friends, expecting her "understanding" and forgiveness after adding the disclaimer that they meant nothing and in no way impinged on his love for her. An only child of a widowed mother who had indulged his every wish, the patient's husband expected her to fulfill the same role with him. She was furious with him, not only for his betrayals but for telling her about them. "Who the hell wants to know about his dirty little screwings?" she shouted. "Who does he think I am, his mother-confessor who has to give him absolution?"

Not uncommonly there is the man or woman who manages to feel as neglected or unloved by the spouse as he or she had been by the parent. He or she may enter into an adulterous affair that, by confession or accidental discovery, is at bottom a plea to the spouse for the love and attention longed for in childhood. There is the woman whose father, in her childhood, made her mother miserable because, in her mother's words, he was a "skirt chaser." In her own marriage she began to accuse her husband of having other women and before long turned herself into an unhappy, martyred wife.

A patient, married to a young man her own age of another ethnic group, found herself continually getting involved with a series of men all of whom were twenty or more years her senior. In treatment she learned that her unconscious incestuous love for her father, against which she had protected herself by her "exogenous" marriage, broke through in these compulsive affairs, shortly after her father's death.

"Unfinished business" with siblings may also get in the way of a mature adult relationship with the spouse. A patient who loved her husband was dismayed at finding herself in bed with her husband's closest friend. This had happened before with two other of his friends. In the course of treatment she saw the connection between this behavior, which she disapproved and was ashamed of, and her intense childhood rivalry with her twin brother, whom she felt had been favored by her parents. She was still living out this rivalry with a brother surrogate, her husband.

In such cases, where fixations on early love objects or neurotic conflicts motivate a person's behavior, his or her adultery may indeed have little to do with the relationship to the spouse, distressing though it may be to all concerned. Sometimes the passage of time and the vicissitudes of life may help the person get through those critical phases in the developmental process in which he or she has been stuck and to move on to a more mature level of functioning. Sometimes, however, the person may need professional help to untangle the snags.

Female Infidelity[10] versus Male Infidelity: Are they Different?

Although many of the same factors that play a part in male adultery also apply to women — (marital discord, sexual incompatibility, depression, character disturbances, dread of aging, desire for excitement, need for raised self-esteem, boredom, curiosity, or just plain lust) — infidelity has a different meaning to the woman than to the man.

To the adulterous woman infidelity is more emotionally

charged, less compartmentalized, more pervasive in her thoughts and feelings. It is not easily shrugged off as "just one of those things."

And it generates more guilt. One has only to recall once more those classic examples of adulterous women in literature, Emma Bovary and Anna Karenina, to see in stark form its emotional repercussions. While I have yet to hear of an American middle-class woman swallowing poison or throwing herself under a train as a consequence of her adultery, neither have I met many who did not admit some guilt feelings over her extramarital goings-on, even when she described her husband as a bastard and justified her adultery as retaliation for his philandering. In contrast, most of the adulterous men I interviewed, at least those under 40, voice no such feelings of guilt.

Although there is decidely less adultery among women than men, women need claim little moral credit for their greater marital virtue. From time immemorial punishment of the woman for adultery, ranging from social ostracism to banishment, stoning, and other forms of torturous death, has made discretion the better part of valor. Besides, until not so long ago most of a woman's youthful years, when she is presumably more desirable and desirous, were occupied with child-bearing, child rearing, family cares, and household duties. Time and opportunity for sexual relations outside the marriage bed, had there been the inclination, were limited. Moreover, religious and social restrictions were greater, as were the risks of an unwanted pregnancy.

But most decisive in preserving her marital virtue, I believe, was until relatively recently her economic dependence on her husband. Her security, indeed, sometimes her very survival — depended upon her dedication, her loyalty, her obeisance to her husband. Fidelity was her security blanket.

There is controversy these days as to whether women harbor the same "importunate, undifferentiated lust that infects all men." George Gilder claims they do not. He writes that women have always shown "greater sexual control . . . in every society throughout history and anthropology."[11] He backs his argument with data from Ford and Beach, who found that, except for a few primitive tribes, even in polygamous societies with no ban on sexual activity by either sex, females do not equal males in promiscuity.

Most feminists claim they do, a claim supported by the spate of current fiction by women novelists. (Erica Jong's heroine in *Fear of Flying*, whose obsessive fantasy is of a "zipless fuck," is a prime example.) Women's greater chastity, they say, has been an artifact of an oppressive patriarchal society.

The adulterous women I interviewed sought more than relief from sexual tension. Most of them sought some semblance of love or affection, preferably both tendered and received, in the extramarital relationship. They need to gild their infidelities with a patina of romance. Underneath that patina, however, in some instances, lay less palatable forces of which they were dimly or not at all aware. One of these was revenge.

Revenge

"A woman always has her revenge ready," said Molière. To revenge herself on Jason for abandoning her to take another wife, the legendary Medea cut their children's throats and sent his new bride a golden robe that burned her to death when she donned it.

"Sweet is revenge — especially to women," said Byron.

I believe, though I cannot prove it, that revenge is a more frequent motivating force behind a woman's adultery than a man's. Cuckolding a husband is one of the few symbolically lethal weapons a woman, especially a jealous woman, has to "get even" with him for his infidelities. What better way to avenge herself for the humiliation an adulterous husband may have caused her than by letting him know, however accidentally, that she has been found desirable by another man, one presumably more perceptive of her charms than is her insensitive spouse? At the same time it can help restore her self-esteem.

Equal Rights

Akin to revenge as one motive for a married woman's "playing around" is that of resentment of the greater sexual freedom allowed men in our society. "What's sauce for the gander is sauce for the goose," claims the feminist as she takes a series of lovers to prove her sexual equality with men. More often than not, the "other man" has been chosen not so much as an object of affection as one of defiance against an outworn double standard of morality. True, the most ardent feminist is unlikely to engage in extramarital activity if she cares deeply for her husband and feels committed to him. Should, however, her marriage be seriously flawed, she may take a lover, claiming as justification women's "sexual oppression for centuries."

CHAPTER
17
Effect of Infidelity on Marriage

"They were as fed horses in the morning: every one neighed after his neighbour's wife."
— *Jeremiah 5:8*

Does infidelity harm a marriage? When I was very young, and like most young things, cocksure about my opinions, I firmly believed infidelity irreparably wounded a marriage. Though time might heal the wound, scar tissue would remain. Given recurring wounds and enough scar tissue to coarsen and uglify the original soft skin of love and trust and loyalty, the marriage, in its real sense of a deep commitment of two people to each other, was over, though the couple might remain together for the rest of their lives. Thus spoke Jane College.

I came by this stance naturally, having been brought up in a Puritanical household and nourished on a rich diet of romantic nineteenth-century novels. A vivid memory from my childhood haunts me to this day. It was of one of my innumerable aunts weeping hysterically in my mother's comforting arms. I was about six and presumably playing with my dolls in another room, but my consuming curiosity about the world of adults compelled me to eavesdrop shamelessly. I could glean only puzzling bits of information through my aunt's sobs — enough, however, to figure out that Uncle Harry was "seeing another woman." That must be a most dreadful thing, I deduced, to make my aunt so unhappy.

As several years passed and I had occasion to learn the "inside story" of many marriages through my work, I modified my youthful stance. I concluded then that while infidelity need not destroy a marriage it was either a symptom of immaturity or neurosis on the part of the adulterer or a symptom of something seriously amiss in the marital relationship. Whichever, it was nonetheless bound to injure, subtly or obviously, the marriage bond. If unknown to the partner, it posed an invisible barrier of guilt and secrecy between the couple that tarnished it. If known to the partner, it caused pain and humiliation, destroyed trust, and inevitably frayed the marriage tie.

In our country, where marriage, by and large, is based on love, loyalty, and trust, and where monogamy and fidelity are the professed ideals, the first time a husband or wife learns that the spouse has been unfaithful can be a devastating experience.[1]

George L, 32, married four years, came into treatment because of depression and potency difficulties that developed after he learned of his wife's affair for the previous six months with his friend Bud. He expressed his feelings thus: "When Lillian told me, I felt the bottom drop out from under me. I was destroyed. It wasn't just that she betrayed my trust. It was that she let another man come in and ruin our privacy. That mole on the inside of her left thigh. I loved it, that round black spot on her incredible white skin. It was our secret. That son of a bitch, now he was in on it too. I can't get the thought of those two in bed together out of my mind — my bed! I keep wondering, was it better for her with him than with me? Did she pull his hair and cry out when she came? I know I shouldn't feel possessive, but I do. Now when I start to make love to her the thought of him straddling her comes into my head and I'm finished." He cried. "She cut my balls off," he added. George admits that he still loves Lillian but he says he will never be able to trust her again. He asks, "How do you live with someone you don't trust?"

How one reacts in our monogamous society to the knowledge of a spouse's infidelity depends upon many things, including one's character, one's emotional needs, and on practical, all-too-often financial considerations. Some, like

° 246 °

George, react with humiliation, grief, and depression; others, with anger, outrage, ultimatums, or retaliation. "I still care for Harry," his wife said, after telling me he was a "chippy-chaser," "but I lost my respect for him." Lucy wonders whether Fred is "carrying on" with his new secretary, after having learned of his affair with the previous one. Now she never drops in at his office, as she used to, being careful to ring up first. And George, who feels he can no longer trust his wife, will probably always remain a little wary or suspicious when she smiles upon his friends.

Some close their eyes to it. A notorious ladies' man told me that his wife is "completely blind" to his affairs. His wife revealed to me that she only pretended to be blind. "So long as the children and I come first, I can put up with his *mishugass*," she said. "It doesn't take anything away from us." So she takes comfort in the outward accoutrements of a "successful" marriage. She counts her possessions, her social position, and the accomplishments of her children.

Some women resign themselves to the role of victim: "It's a man's world," or reassure themselves: "All men are like that." Some men as well as women are so fearful of loneliness and other terrifying disruptions of their lives that they prefer to suffer humiliation, injured pride, and lowered self-esteem rather than risk any threat to the stability of the marriage.

Whatever the outward reaction, where there had once been love, there is bound to be pain at what is felt as its betrayal:

> " 'Tis not love's going hurt my days
> But that it went in little ways."[2]

Benefit to the Marriage

At first glance it is hard to believe that a situation that evokes pain, guilt, conflict, bewilderment, and grief could eventuate in lasting benefit to all the parties involved. Yet in my work as a family therapist I have seen it happen. Couples who seek professional help when the continuance of their marriage is threatened by the intrusion of a "third party" may, in the long run, profit both as individuals and as partners from the experience. For pain, if not overwhelming, can lead to learning and growth. Under the skilled guidance of a therapist, the couple is helped to take a clear-eyed look at their relationship. With encouragement they dare to talk honestly with each other, sometimes for the first time in their married life, and to express their grievances openly. They come to a better understanding of themselves and each other and how each may have unwittingly contributed to the impasse in which they find themselves. Sometimes they need help to reconcile themselves to the weaknesses or foibles of their mate — and to be aware of their own. Clearing the air of the negative aspects of the relationship frees them to see the strengths in it, if what they really want, underneath the bitterness and guilt, is to remain together and to make that difficult, trying, frustrating institution called marriage work.

Ameliorating Discontent

A marriage grown stale for lack of tending may yet serve many needs of the partners who have no wish but to remain together. But discontent with the monotony of their lives may drive one (or both) to seek diversions that might lift them out of the dreary routine of their daily existence. What's more exciting than "an illicit romance?" Like on television!

The secrecy alone adds an excitement that spills over into one's "real life" and makes it more tolerable. "The secret," writes George Simmel, "produces an immense enlargement of life. . . . The secret offers, so to speak, the possibility of a second world alongside the manifest world; and the latter is decisively influenced by the former."[3]

Charlotte G, 35, mother of two children, 8 and 10, has been married for eleven years to Ralph, 38, an electronics engineer. A laboratory technician, Charlotte has been sexually involved with Jim, 44, her employer, a radiologist, for almost two years. He is also married and the father of two sons.

Charlotte tells the following story: "I realized my marriage was a mistake almost from the beginning. I'm a live wire. I love a good time. Ralph is a homebody. He'd rather watch the ball game on TV than go anywhere." When asked why she married him, she says, "I knew Ralph all my life. Our families were friends from the Old Country. I liked Ralph, but more like a brother. He was always hanging around our house, he was a pal of my brother. I knew he liked me but I paid no attention to him. You see, I was crazy about another guy, a no-gooder. When this guy left me, after we went around together for four years, I was heartbroken. By then most of my girl friends were married and my mother kept nagging me that I should get married. So I married Ralph. He's a good person — kind, a good provider, a wonderful father. I have nothing to complain about. Another woman would consider herself lucky to be married to such a steady, reliable person. But to me he's like . . . like a sack of flour."

She says she knows it's wrong — she was brought up as a Catholic — but as long as the affair doesn't threaten her marriage — and neither she nor Jim have any intention of disrupting their marriages — she doesn't see why she should give it up. She admits some feelings of guilt: "I hate the lying when I get home late from work, and I know I'm cheating on my husband." But she quickly rationalizes her behavior. "I'm not taking anything from Ralph or the children. I think I'm a better wife and mother, more content with what I have at home now that I have this for myself. I used to yell and scream at the kids for the least little thing; now I'm much nicer to them — more patient. And I'm nicer to Ralph. I used to snap his head off, I was so irritated with him. My job, which I love, and Jim, make it easier for me to put up with his quiet boring ways."

Charlotte is a woman of rather shallow emotions with little capacity to love another deeply. The very lack of real intimacy (aside from physical intimacy) with Jim makes it possible for her to keep her extramarital sex life separate from her "real life." In this respect she is like many men who claim that the gratification they get in casual sex encounters ameliorates their discontent at home and makes them better husbands and fathers.

Most of the adulterous women I interviewed were unlike Charlotte in this regard. Their guilt, the secrecy, the risks and fear of discovery, while heightening their excitement, created great emotional tension that disturbed not only their relationship with their husband but with their children as well.

· Benefit to a Person

One of the most illustrious persons in modern history, whose travail over the discovery of her husband's secret romance with her secretary forged her into a remarkable example of strength and courage for the entire nation, was Eleanor Roosevelt. When, after thirteen years of marriage, she accidentally learned of Franklin's affair with Lucy Mercer, "her world seemed to break into pieces . . . Franklin's love was the anchor to which her self-confidence and self-respect were secured, and now that anchor was cut. The thought tortured Eleanor that, having borne him six children, she was now being discarded for a younger, prettier, gayer woman . . . that her husband's love belonged to someone else."[4]

Franklin was always flirtatious. Serious Eleanor, though jealous, treated his flirtations lightly, knowing she did not satisfy "the frivolous side" of him, as long as she was sure of his love for her. Her discovery of his love for another woman threw her into total despair. "She emerged from the ordeal a changed person. She realized that she could not achieve fulfillment through someone else, that she had to build a life and develop interests of her own. She ended her subordination to her mother-in-law, changed from a private to a public person." Twenty-five years later she wrote about that terrible time of her life to Lash: "The bottom dropped out of my own particular world, and I faced myself, my surroundings, my world, honestly for the first time. I really grew up that year."

Eleanor and Franklin continued to live together but their relationship changed. Lash writes: "She no longer allowed herself to be taken for granted either as a woman or as an instrument of his purpose. Her relationship with her husband not only stands as one of the most remarkable in American history but had considerable effect upon its course."

At the time of Roosevelt's inauguration in 1932 — fifteen years after she learned of her husband's adultery — "the wound" writes Lash, "was still open, still painful. She was a woman of sorrow who had surmounted her unhappiness and managed to carry on, stoical toward herself, understanding and tender toward others. She turned her sorrow into a strengthening thing." Lash asserts that the Mercer affair as well as her husband's paralysis, had become for Eleanor "occasions of personal transcendence and growth."

Keeping the Marriage Intact

Sometimes a "meaningful relationship" with a third party, unbeknown to the spouse, may keep a marriage going smoothly through middle age and beyond.

Dr. M, 58, is the chief of the department of immunology at a prestigious hospital. He has been married almost thirty years, has no children. His wife, who has never worked outside the home, keeps busy with social and community activities. Dr. M has had a number of brief affairs in the course of his marriage, none of much emotional consequence. Fifteen years ago, upon paying a condolence call on the widow of a young assistant in his department who died of leukemia, he fell passionately in love with her. After several months of wooing her, they became lovers. He would have divorced his wife to marry her at the time but she was reluctant because of her two pre-adolescent children.

Dr. M and Augusta have remained lovers and friends through all the years, though for the past five or six years, except for a rare weekend when he is attending a conference in another city and she can join him, they have had no sex relations. He telephones her every day, sees her about once a week. Augusta is a curator at a museum and is dedicated to her work. She is also a rather good painter.

"Augusta is everything Dolly isn't," Dr. M said. "Serious, thoughtful, sensitive, understanding. She's the most intelligent and interesting person I know. That includes my male colleagues. I can discuss anything with her — my work, my worries, even my wife. She's a wonderful listener. It isn't as though she's young or beautiful, though I find her very attractive. She's almost as old as Dolly. And not near as pretty. You know Dolly. Cute as a button. I think the men in the department envy me my adorable wife. But she bores the hell out of me. When I get home, dog tired, she chatters away about her bridge hand, recounts the latest episode in Laverne and Shirley, fills me in on the gossip she picked up at the Women's Auxiliary luncheon. On our trips she spends her time shopping. To her Florence is where she picked up five pairs of Ferragamo shoes because they'd cost twice as much here. Venice is where that Murano vase on the buffet came from. The other night at a small dinner party at our house we were talking about the movie "Midnight Express" and the subject of Istanbul came up. So Dolly pipes up, 'Daddy, isn't that where you bought me my gold chain in that funny bazaar? Where they weighed it on a scale to tell you the price?"

He's never told Dolly about Augusta. "She'd be devastated. She'd never understand. The joke is there's been practically no sex between Augusta and me for years, but Dolly would never believe that. Why it's such a sin if you're a married man to have a woman as a close friend is beyond me. It's okay to kid around and make passes at someone else's wife, but friendship — unless she's a colleague — that's taboo. Yet having Augusta in my life is like an anchor for my marriage. Keeps it secure."

There are many kinds of infidelities. Each answers a different need, has a different meaning to the man or woman involved, and affects the marital relationship differently.

The Prostitute or Pickup: Some married men (and a rare woman) occasionally engage in brief, casual sex encounters with a stranger whom they will probably never see again and whose name they may not even know. Many of them do not consider these contacts a betrayal of their marriage vows, since there is no emotional involvement with the temporary sex partner. For some these fleeting encounters with a depersonalized sex object toward whom they feel no responsibility provides an intense physical gratification they no longer find (or may never have found) in the connubial bed. Sometimes the very risks involved in sex with a stranger — venereal disease, robbery, even physical violence — heighten the excitement. Some utilize the experience to live out perverse sexual fantasies;[5] others, who may suffer potency difficulties at home, to prove their masculinity. All my informants who admitted having been with prostitutes or pickups insisted that these experiences, kept secret from the mate, in no way affected the marriage. However, many of them also admitted that this "hit-and-run sex," as one man called it, did leave them with some worry (about V.D.), guilt feelings, and lowered self-esteem.

The Call Girl: The advertisement read: "Wanted: Attractive, intelligent girls between 18 and 30 for elegant private escort service. Experience in modeling, dance and theater preferred." The address was that of a luxurious apartment house in a fashionable section of the city. A reporter for my neighborhood newspaper, posing as a prospective employee, answered it. She found that this so-called escort service was just a call-girl service, of which there are many in New York and other large cities. This one was patronized largely by out-of-town businessmen and other wealthy men. (In 1976 the cost was $100 an hour. It's probably twice that today.) The madam assured the reporter that the operation was strictly "high class" and that she dealt exclusively through referrals. She boasted that her service did a big business among consulates and embassies of nearly every country at the UN. Many corporations use her "escorts" to entertain their out-of-town executives at conventions and other occasions. "We offer the man nighttime company and sex with no hassles," she said.

There are the occasional out-of-town capers of the married man on a business trip, for whom fleeting liaisons with a call girl, often in the company of colleagues or business associates, mean little more than an evening's entertainment. These ventures into "forbidden territory" fulfill the desire for erotic pleasure, often of a perverse nature, in a sensuous atmosphere — which they otherwise dare only to fantasy about. At the same time they avoid the intimacy of a relationship in which the desires or personality of an unpaid partner intrude.

Call girls come closer to the old-fashioned courtesans than do the ordinary run of prostitutes. Generally better-looking and more psychologically knowledgeable (and more expensive) than bar girls or streetwalkers, they offer more than hit-and-run sex. Indeed, if I am to believe some of my informants, they often act as a paraprofessional therapist insofar as they offer a sympathetic ear to their client's troubles, bolster the ego, or restore the confidence of a man who needs assurance that he can still function well sexually. It also gives him an opportunity to abandon traditional sex roles and experiment with practices he'd heard or read about. A psychiatrist I know told me that he has on occasion sent a patient suffering from impotence or a homosexual patient who was distressed by his homosexuality to a certain psychologically (as well as sexually) knowledgeable call girl with good results.

In a study of 1242 men who visited 64 call girls in one establishment[6] Martha Stein reported that most of them were married, in their 40s, "agreeable, reasonably attractive, upper-middle-class men, businessmen or professionals," with "good middle-class manners." They came "to get sexual release, to find ways to make sex more exciting, to make themselves feel worldly, or desirable, or manly, to have attention paid, to act out sexual fantasies that continued to absorb their mental energies, and for combinations of these and other reasons." Most of the men had heavy work schedules, felt harassed and burdened by responsibilities, and used to visit "to counteract tensions induced by performance pressures in other areas of their lives."

Some of the men developed an on-going relationship with a particular girl in the establishment, with whom they would discuss their business and marital problems. Indeed, talking with her about their problems or confessing a secret worry was an intrinsic part of the transaction.

Regarding their marriages, none of the men felt that his call girl visits impinged on his marital relations in any way, except perhaps to stabilize or improve them. Many of the men who came to gratify sexual needs unsatisifed at home were committed to their marriages. They felt that whereas an adulterous relationship with a friend might threaten their marriage, the use of the call girl's services did not. Others who had satisfying sexual relations with their wives came because call girls gave them an opportunity to have a variety of partners, to talk openly about sex, and explore various sexual innovations they did not feel free to try with their wives.

Some men complained that they and their wives had grown apart and that their wives paid no attention to them. But they had no wish to terminate the marriage. Visits to the call girls answered a sexual and psychological need the marriage no longer served. Other men asserted that they loved their wives deeply but that the economic demands of their family to maintain an upper-middle-class standard of living forced them to overwork themselves, and when they came home at the end of the day harried and exhausted, they had neither time nor energy to enjoy sex. Their role of breadwinner had pre-empted their role as husband and lover. In the setting with the call girl — usually in the middle of the day as an escape from their business — they could relax, find relief from performance pressures, and replenish their energies. For men who suffered from sexual dysfunctions with their wives, success with a sexually skilled call girl gave them needed reassurance about themselves.

A Rebuttal

While sexual contacts with prostitutes, be they "high-class" call girls or cheap streetwalkers, may not threaten the institutional aspect of marriage, there can be unwitting side effects. The necessary secrecy about these extramarital sexual excursions widens whatever gaps in communication may already exist between a husband and wife. For the man who has a good relationship with his wife, including a satisfactory sex life, but feels he must have variety, excitement, and whatever other needs these occasional, brief, impersonal paid adventures gratify, they probably do little or no harm to the marital relationship beyond the communication gap. But the man who uses prostitutes to alleviate or compensate for sexual frustrations or dysfunctions with his wife — and most of the men I interviewed, as well as those in the Stein study, gave this as their prime reason for paid sex — may be exacerbating the situation at home. Discussion of sexual discontents, difficult at best, can be avoided if they are alleviated by these sexual outlets. Relieving the symptom makes it easy to ignore the cause. Sexual incompatibilities or dysfunctions that might be helped by professional intervention or even, sometimes, just by airing them, go unresolved and often end up in a cessation of sexual relations between husband and wife altogether.

The Love Affair

The love affair is another story. It is ironic that love, that transcendental emotion, that gift of God to humankind, should pose the greatest threat to marriage. The "one-night stand," the casual sex encounter, which one might expect to pinch the spirit and demean the marriage, is often brushed aside as of little or no consequence. But to be married and fall in love outside the legal boundaries brings guilt, confusion, anxiety, and pain to the "transgressor" and, if known, fear and unhappiness to those near and dear.

Perhaps it is our awe of love's mysterious essence — and our romantic tradition — that makes us so deferential to its demands. A friend, on the eve of her fourth marriage, said to me, "I hope I'll never fall in love again." She took for granted that should she hear love's piper whistling, she must follow his beckoning, though it lead her straight to the sea.

A love affair does not necessarily threaten a marriage unless it is already on the rocks. I have known a number of men and women who were content with their marriage and family life, wanted to keep them intact, yet needed the excitement, the secrecy, the very risks of a love affair to counterbalance and quietly bear the responsibilities and burdens of their daily lives. It is only when one or the other in the adulterous relationship demands marriage or threatens to end the affair that trouble and grief may ensue. It is often at this point that the affair becomes known to the spouse, either because the mate is obviously upset or because the affair is "confessed." It is the rare man or woman who can carry on a secret love affair and eventually end it without disturbing the even tenor of his or her married life.

The psychiatrist O. Spurgeon English believes that a love affair can enrich a person. He writes: "It [the affair] is a relationship to which each person brings the best of himself — his best moods, his best hopes, his best thoughts in admiration and expression of devotion. Each person offers the best he has to bestow upon the other. . . . Each partner carries within him a high spirit of being entertaining as well as being capable of producing in the other the highest sense of self-awareness known to a human being."

A love affair, despite the miseries entailed, revitalizes a man or woman. It revives the pale fire of almost forgotten romantic longings and makes it glow. Whatever the risks, for some it's worth the candle.

Here's Joe, at 45, a business executive, in a relatively happy marriage and with no wish to break it up, who is carrying on an affair with Jean, 22, the secretary of a colleague.

"Sure, I still love Sally. She's a good wife and mother. I've really no complaints. But to Sally I'm just good old steady, reliable Joe. She takes me for granted. And she never misses a chance to tell me I'm getting fat and my hair's getting thin. To Jean, I'm the greatest — handsome, clever, sophisticated. To Sally dinner at the Four Seasons is just another evening out on the maid's day off. To Jean, taking her to an Italian bistro in Soho where the waiter greets us like welcomed guests and I teach her the difference between Bollo Soave and Lugano Rufino is high adventure. To tell you the truth, it's not so much a sex thing. Sally's much better in bed than Jean. But Jean strokes my ego. 'I love a mature man,' she says, when it takes me a long time and once is all I can manage. . . ."

English continues: ". . . no man or woman is as good in marriage as he is in his trysts; the man with a lovely woman who also needs, appreciates, loves, and even honors the tryst . . . finds this to be a periodic escape from the unexciting routine events of daily existence. Each marital partner, on the other hand, knows too well the other's patterns of behavior in everything, including sex. It may be that they feel nothing negative toward each other for which they can hold resentment. But they lack the capacity to see anything highly interesting, glamorous, attractive, or glorious in their relating, nothing for which either would offer that intensity of glad pleasure on meeting which would elicit the emotional satisfaction and even elation of the 'other one.' "[7]

Dr. English's observations are all too true. A woman showed me a sheaf of poetry written to her by her lover. He turned out to be the quite prosaic husband of a friend who, I'm sure, would have been even more astonished than I by her husband's poetic flare. A man I knew, an upstanding citizen and home-loving, uxorial fellow, died suddenly at 55 of cardiac arrest. In going through his effects, his wife, an opera singer who herself had a few not-so-secret affairs, which she claimed she needed to compensate for her boring, predictable, stuffy husband, discovered he had carried on several discreet affairs of his own, including a long relationship with her dramatic coach.

In the course of my research for this book I have come to agree, however reluctantly, with Morton Hunt, who wrote: "The evidence, I believe, clearly shows that in some circumstances an extramarital affair severely damages the marriage, the participants, and even such innocent bystanders as the children; in other circumstances it does none of these things, and is of no consequence; and in still other circumstances it benefits the marriage by ameliorating discontent, or shatters the marriage but benefits the individual by awakening him to his own emotional needs and capabilities. I therefore believe that each extramarital act ought to be judged as morally evil, morally neutral, or morally good, according to the totality of the circumstances and the effects on all concerned."[8]

Fidelity

Fidelity in marriage, like commitment or devotion, is a human ideal all of us strive for and only some of us reach. Fidelity, like love, cannot be legislated. A person must have the wish — and the capacity — for it. In the final analysis, fidelity in marriage — where love exists — depends upon how much a man or woman is blessed with maturity, and what we used to call "character," and a regard for those homely virtues, so commonly mocked today, of loyalty, responsibility, and trustworthiness. That person is fortunate who can say, "I have been loyal to my commitment to my mate, not because I have not lusted or been tempted to lie with another, not because of fear of God or other people's opinion, not because of lack of opportunity, but because I cared deeply enough for my mate to consider his or her welfare before my desire."

If this were the best of all possible worlds, made up of the best of all possible people, willing and able to put devotion before desire, concern for another before gratification of one's own immediate needs, living up to the ideal of fidelity would be no problem. As matters stand, in this imperfect world inhabited by imperfect, vulnerable creatures, driven by needs we are scarcely aware of, besieged by wild fantasies, and exposed to earthly temptations from every side, to many men and women the concept of marital fidelity remains an unrealized ideal.

PART FIVE

Affirmation

"When two people are at one in their inmost hearts,
They shatter even the strength of iron or of bronze.
And when two people understand each other in their inmost hearts
Their words are sweet and strong, like the fragrance of orchids."
— I-ching

CHAPTER

18

A Good Marriage

"And the end of all our exploring
Will be to arrive where we started
And know the place for the first time."
— *T. S. Eliot*

"Happy families are all alike," *Anna Karenina* begins. I scan in my mind the happy marriages I have known among friends, relatives, and patients as well as those in biography and fiction, and right off they contradict Tolstoi's statement. Not only is each of them different from the others but, to paraphrase the rest of his famous remark, each is happy in its own way. The same can be said of the good marriage.

"The Smiths have a good marriage," my husband commented after we had spent a pleasant evening in the warm ambience of their home. I agreed. The Smiths have been married twenty-two years and have two children, currently away at college.

What do we mean by "a good marriage"?

A long marriage is no criterion. It may merely signify a couple's endurance to hang on to a dreary situation for a long time. Nor are the presence of children a criterion, though they can enrich and strengthen the marital relationship. But we have all seen marriages in which the presence of children have frayed or sundered them. And some of the best marriages are childless.

It is not a simple question. As soon as we begin to cope with it, others come to mind. By whose definition? Value judgments derived from one's social, cultural, religious, and even political beliefs would determine one's definition. The criterion for a good marriage as enunciated by a Phyllis Schlafly would differ, I should think, from that, say, of a Germaine Greer, and both would most likely differ from that of Pope John Paul II.

One Man's Meat

Moreover, what may appear to one observer to be a hapless union may be eminently satisfactory to the participants.

On the island where we spend our summers one of the few year-round residents are the Olsens, Hilda, 68, and Sven, 70. Sven, American-born of Scandinavian immigrant stock, is a broad-chested muscular giant of a man. Friendly but inarticulate, he leaves the "socializing" to Hilda, a spare, wiry woman with a quick wit and ready smile. Hilda came from Norway at 14. She worked as a domestic until she met and married Sven at the advanced age of 28. She had resigned herself to remaining an "old maid" or marrying some widower with a brood of children when good fortune sent this 30-year-old fisherman her way. They have four children, all married and living in various parts of the country. Hilda adores Sven. In his own silent way Sven adores Hilda.

Sven makes his living catching live bait, which he sells to the yachtsmen and charter boats plying the bay and ocean. In the winter he traps small game, repairs his fishing tackle and other equipment, and fishes through the ice. Evenings he plays gin rummy with Hilda. He always wins.

The Olsens live in an old houseboat pulled up on shore, which also serves as the bait station. Hilda takes care of the bait business when Sven is off tending the traps. In addition to keeping the house shining clean, Hilda cooks and bakes "three squares a day." "Sven likes to eat good," Hilda says with a laugh as she prepares stews, roasts, pies, cakes, and bread. She also washes and irons, feeds the chickens and rabbits penned in the back yard, plants and weeds the vegetable garden, puts up the harvest for the winter, and repairs the nets that are constantly ripped by the crabs and bluefish Sven catches in them.

Some of us "summer folk" pity Hilda, not so much for her backbreaking labors but because she is so completely subservient to her dominating cock. Sven will not allow her to go ashore without him, not even with friends, for fear something might happen to her. "He's afraid he would be left without his chief cook and bottle washer," we sneer. Even when she occasionally visits neighbors on the island she is in a hurry to return home if "Sven is alone."

When Sven is especially exasperating in his demands, Hilda will say, "He makes me so mad!" But a tiny, amused smile lurks around her lips, like that of a doting mother who unconvincingly scolds her toddler for pulling out the pots and pans from the cupboard, all the while secretly proud of its enterprise.

One morning when she came over to bring me a gift of soft-shell crabs I urged her to stay for lunch. She refused because Sven wouldn't like her to be away too long. "So what if he doesn't," I said in vicarious defiance at this oppressive masculine tyranny over a defenseless female victim. "You have rights too, you know." Hilda gave me a rather superior, pitying smile. City folk, she seemed to be thinking to herself, what do they know of a man like Sven? Strong, powerful, dependable, able to make and fix anything, picks up his two-hundred-pound traps like toys, gave me four children, twelve grandchildren. And he's still a good lover. "Sven wouldn't like it," she repeated as she turned to leave. Unlike her fictional compatriot, Hilda would laugh at the idea of slamming the door behind her.

His and Hers

Still other questions pop into one's head: When we speak of a good marriage, whose are we talking about? The wife's? Or the husband's? "There are two marriages . . . in every marital union, his and hers," writes Jessie Bernard.[1] No two people perceive the same situation exactly alike, particularly if it is emotionally tinged.[2] In so emotionally involved a relationship as marriage, the same gestalt of intimate experiences is often perceived quite differently by the participants. Listening to a husband and wife give their versions of a fight they had, one can scarcely believe it is the same incident they are recounting.[3]

Researchers on such matters report that spouses give different answers to such practical questions as who keeps track of the bills, who does the shopping, who decides where the family goes on vacation. Kinsey found that husbands and wives even gave different reports on the frequency of sexual intercourse.

Honeymooners, one would think, still in the throes of romantic love, whose "hearts beat as one," might more readily agree on the shared events in their newly joined lives than some battle-scarred pair. Not so. In a popular daytime television show, recently married husbands and wives are asked separately such ordinary facts as who proposed marriage, what the spouse likes to do best, or what the spouse would do in a specific situation. The entertainment for the audience comes from hearing the differing responses of the mates to the same question and at their surprise and embarrassment upon learning the other's reply.

No "Average" Marriage

Clearly there is no "average" norm to serve as a yardstick by which to measure the success of a marriage. The heroine of Wolitzer's aforementioned novel asks her erstwhile lover what kind of marriage he has.

"It's really important," she says.

"Average," he said promptly.

Average! What kind of marriage was that? People with average marriages were statistics, were silhouettes in

insurance ads, were bloodless, passionless shadows. I
wanted to know what kind of marriage *they had. I was*
breathless with impatience and with the knowledge that
I had to control myself.

"Mr. K," I said, through my shark's smile. "Nobody has
an average marriage. You can't say that about marriage.
It's a complicated relationship. Fire and ice. Passion,
camaraderie, bonds of sin, love, ecstasy. It's a dangerous,
even a death-defying act."

A glance at the marriages of a few well-known literary figures whose flesh and bones have been exposed to the public view by their biographers or their autobiographies confirms the declaration of Wolitzer's heroine.

Perhaps the most romantic of married lovers in a Romantic age were the Brownings. At the time of their secret marriage, Elizabeth was 40, Robert, 34. Besides their abundant love lyrics to each other, there is documented evidence that after fifteen years of marriage (at Elizabeth's death) they were as tenderly and deeply devoted to each other as they had been at the beginning of their union. One of their biographers, G. K. Chesterson, wrote, ". . . their marriage constituted something like that ideal marriage, an alliance between two strong and independent forces."[4]

In sharp contrast to the Brownings' uneventfully happy marriage was the stormy relationship of Frieda and D. H. Lawrence. To the outsider it looked like a terrible marriage — a misalliance between two neurotic, egotistical, willful (sometimes silly) individuals. To begin with, they came from widely different backgrounds — this in a rigidly hierarchical society. Lawrence, the son of a coal miner, was a schoolteacher; Frieda, the daughter of a German baron who had once been the governor of Alsace-Lorraine, was the wife of a university professor. When they met they fell under the spell of what Ortega y Gasset called "the erotic seizure" and ran off together, Frieda abandoning her three young children (for which she felt eternally guilty). Like most passionate lovers, there were times when they hated each other passionately. Perpetually at war, indulging in violent and exhausting fights (including physical attacks on each other), they nonetheless admired each other inordinately and fundamentally were happy together.

In her autobiography Frieda wrote: ". . . it was a hard life with him, but a wonderful one . . . I felt the wonder of him always. . . . What does it amount to that he hit out at me in a rage, when I exasperated him, or mostly when the life around him drove him to the end of his patience? I didn't care very much. I hit back or waited till the storm in him subsided. We fought our battles outright to the bitter end. Then there was peace, such peace. I preferred it that way. Battles must be. If he had sulked or borne me a grudge, how tedious! What happened, happened out of the deep necessity of our natures."

And later she wrote, "To understand what happened between us, one must have had the experience we had, thrown away as much as we did and gained as much, and have known the fulfillment of body and soul. It is not likely that many did." She reported that once she asked him, "What do I give you, that you didn't get from others?" and he replied, "You made me sure of myself, whole." And at the end, as he lay dying, Lawrence told her, ". . . nothing has mattered but you, nothing at all."[5]

Another well-publicized happy marriage was that of Virginia and Leonard Woolf. Leonard adored his sick, brilliant wife, to whom he devoted his life. She in turn loved this "penniless Jew" (insofar as she could love anyone). She was grateful for his infinite care and graciously accepted her physical and emotional dependence on him. They shared many interests, most notably the establishment and running of the famous Hogarth Press. In her suicide note to Leonard (Virginia suffered many depressive episodes throughout her life) she wrote: ". . . I want to tell you that you have given me complete happiness. No one could have done more than you have done. Please believe that. But I know that I shall never get over this; and I am wasting your life . . ."[6]

Sex and the Good Marriage

What about the quality of the sexual relationship as a measure of a good marriage? Logic tells us to expect a direct connection between good sex and a good marriage. Facts show that it ain't necessarily so. "A happy marriage entails dovetailing of needs and expectations, but not necessarily a high degree of sexual satisfaction," writes the psychiatrist Peter A. Martin.[7]

Research findings of other authorities on human behavior also show that while in general there is a correlation between good sexual relations and a happy marriage, it is not an imperative. And the countless surveys on "marital satisfaction" that have been spawned in the last two decades agree. They indicate that after the erotic fireworks of courtship and early marriage have fizzled out, sex relations tend to become perfunctory over time.

My own interviews confirmed these conclusions. Among my informants I found that while mediocre or unsatisfying sex caused distress to one or both partners, it did not mortally wound the marriage unless other, more conflictual problems were also present.

A Good Fit

"A good marriage is when the rocks in his head fit the holes in hers." Marital patterns are infinite in their variety.[8] Among the most common are: the traditional pattern, in which the husband is the dominant partner, the wife, the submissive one; the not unusual reverse combination of the strong, aggressive female married to a passive, sometimes weak, male (in the extreme form, the Maggie and Jiggs stereotype, a standby of comic strips and vaudeville jokes); the mom-and-pop variety in which the parental role has superseded the spousal role; and the companionate pattern. In the last, increasingly characteristic of today's middle-class "young marrieds," each partner fulfills his or her traditional role; i.e., the husband is the main breadwinner and protector of the family; the wife, who may or may not be employed outside the home, is the primary homemaker and nurturer of the children; but both take responsibility for running the household and child rearing.

There are other fairly successful marital relationships that, for want of a better term, I shall call "neurotic."[9] These are marriages of otherwise "normal" individuals whose mates serve some unconscious infantile, perverse, or other morbid need. One such is the marriage that quite obviously recapitulates the early parent-child relationship. All of us live out many roles with our spouse. The wife serves at different times as mistress, mother, sister, or child to the husband; the husband, as lover, father, brother, or child to the wife. In these particular relationships, however, the couple seems to be reliving prominently a pattern that had been very emotionally gratifying in childhood in which they are rigidly stuck. Most frequently it is that of parent and child.

One such marriage is that of the Rs, who have been married eighteen years. They have no children. Ralph was 30 years old at marriage; Theresa, 36. She had been his mother's nurse and during the last four months of his mother's life had lived in the R home. Theresa not only provided good nursing care for his mother, who was suffering from cancer, but looked after Ralph's creature comforts as well. Ralph, an only child, had always lived with his mother. It was hardly a surprise when Theresa and Ralph were married soon after the mother's death.

Theresa indulges Ralph, as his mother had before her, in his every wish. Although she is constantly nagging at him with a litany of "do this," "don't do that," like an overprotective mother her naughty son, Ralph pays her no mind. He is her pampered little boy, a role he had always basked in with his mom. Theresa even turns a blind eye to his frequent infidelities, which he makes little effort to hide. Both are quite content with their marital arrangement.

The V marriage of twenty-two years is almost a carica-
ture of a neurotic relationship that works. Oscar V is an eminent physician, 18 years older than his wife, Lydia. Lydia
suffered a miscarriage in the first year of marriage, has had no
pregnancies since. Lydia is a tiny thing, weighing under a
hundred pounds, blonde, delicate, with a high piping voice, a
faint lisp, and a coy, flirtatious manner. Dr. V cossets his
"darling girl" like a pet lamb. He considers himself the most
fortunate of men to be the proud possessor of so exquisite a
creature. He showers her with gifts. Lydia had trained to be a
singer before her marriage, a potential career she still mourns.
At gatherings in the V home, with a little coaxing from Dr. V,
Lydia entertains the guests by singing Schubert lieder in a
small, pretty voice. After twenty-two years Dr. V still listens
to her sing in rapt adoration. (He assumes his guests too are
enraptured.) The Vs seem to fit each other's needs like the
proverbial hand in glove.

Some spouses, like identical twins, complement each
other; one "acts out" for the other. "It is often seen that bad
husbands have very good wives," Francis Bacon wrote. An
example of such a marriage in reverse in that of the Fs. "Poor
Louie," their friends say. "Such a sweet gentle guy. To be
cursed with such a mean shrew of a wife. Did you see how
badly she treats his sisters?" Poor Louie? Lucky Louie! To
have a wife who can "act out" his mean hostile wishes toward
his relatives, leaving him free to be altruistic and kind to them
and gaining at the same time the sympathy of his friends for
his unfortunate marriage.

And we are all familiar with marriages (one's own, perhaps?) in which one partner is cautious, perfectionist, "uptight," what the psychologist calls obsessive, and the other
spontaneous, careless, a "free spirit"; yet they work well. Although she may complain about his rigidity, he about her
heedlessness, each secretly admires and is gratified by the
other's traits. They are a good fit.

Then there is the Pygmalian-Galatea phenomenon: the
worldly educated gentleman who married a waif and grooms

her into a sophisticated lady. The reverse — elegant lady and uncouth lad — while less common, is not infrequently seen in the literary and entertainment worlds. Akin to this type is the man or woman who marries a person of dubious character in order to "save" or "reform" him or her, thereby gratifying an unconscious "rescue fantasy."[10] (I have known several police officers who married prostitutes.)

There is also the classic example of the man or woman who comes from a background of chronic marital strife, vowing to avoid like the plague anyone remotely resembling the presumably despised parent of the opposite sex, only to end up with a replica of him or her. In my work with wives of alcoholics this was a common story. Most of them had had alcoholic fathers. (Their unconscious identification with their masochistic mothers was often a powerful force that propelled them into the arms of a man not unlike their fathers.)

Examples of neurotic interaction in marital relations are legion. These marriages can work for a lifetime as long as their interdependent neuroses remain locked together, immobilizing them against change. Trouble arises when unanticipated growth of one, stimulated by some new situation or some emotional change (sometimes a result of therapy), disturbs the precarious balance and throws askew the finely tuned reciprocal relationship.

A Pragmatic Reply

As I study the many varieties of durable marriages, so disparate yet each successful in its fashion, there seems to be no encompassing answer to my original question: "What is a good marriage?" One can only reply that a marriage which works more or less well for both partners, separately and together, most of the time, can be called a good marriage. That reply, while logical, leaves me discomfited. I prefer rather to call these marriages "good enough."[11]

My own definition of a good marriage would transcend the "good enough." (Though, given the human condition, a "good enough" marriage should be good enough.) To me a good marriage would partake of certain qualities in the relationship between husband and wife beyond "a good fit." They would include the following:

Good Companions

"Good marriages, in literature as in life, partake more of friendship than romance . . ."[12]

A good marriage is one in which husband and wife enjoy each other's company. They feel easy in each other's presence. They generally, though by no means always, like to do things together and are seldom bored with each other. This does not imply "togetherness," that shibboleth that a few decades ago was touted as the Scotch tape that kept a family intact. (Remember the slogans — The family that plays together — or prays together — stays together?)

Nor need they share the same interests, though it is an added bonus when they do. The Gs have one of the best marriages I know, yet they enjoy quite different outside pleasures. Mr. G, a biologist, is an avid fisherman who flies to Canada every year for a week's salmon fishing. Mrs. G gets seasick at the mere sight of a fishing boat. A teacher of handicapped children, in her spare time she is an amateur horticulturist who exhibits prize-winning dahlias at national flower shows. Mr. G doesn't know one flower from another. "To Jim all flowers are roses," Mrs. G laughs. The Gs share other interests, however — books, the countryside, and, best of all, joy in their three young grandchildren. They also take a genuine interest in each other's work. But they respect the spouse's private pleasures and grant each other "space" to indulge them.

Good Talk

"A meet and happy conversation is the chiefest and noblest end of marriage," wrote John Milton.

A good marriage is one in which husband and wife enjoy talking — and listening — to each other. One of the intrinsic pleasures of friendship is the sharing of thoughts, perceptions, and experiences with another. This pleasure takes on an added dimension when augmented with the sexual and domestic intimacies of marriage: sharing the joy of an ecstatic union or the dismay of a failed one; the concern over a rash in his groin or her menstrual cramps; the annoyance of an overflowing toilet or cockroaches under the kitchen sink; worry over the baby's diarrhea; happiness at the miracle of his first steps or at his graduation from high school.

In a good marriage the partners are not afraid to talk about their feelings toward each other, especially their warm feelings. (A patient told me that her husband of twenty-two years, a good, kind man who, she feels certain, cares deeply for her, has never been able to say the words "I love you.") They can also be silent together in comfort. Neither feels "locked out" when the other is engrossed in his or her own interests or thoughts.

A breakdown in communication is a common source of trouble between husband and wife. Neither really hears what the other is saying because each is concerned with his or her own feelings. So they talk past each other. Or they unconsciously distort what is said to conform to their own misperceptions. A patient with a deep sense of inferiority interpreted almost everything her husband said as a criticism of her. For example, if he refused a second helping of food at the dinner table or added salt to a dish, she interpreted this as a sign that he didn't like her cooking and was in this indirect way critical of her. (One of the valuable tasks a therapist performs is to help family members learn to communicate openly with one another.)

Good Fighting

In the intimacy of marriage conflict is inevitable, no matter how much husband and wife care for each other. Fighting can be salutary. It clears the air, relieves the tension that is built up when two human beings with different needs try to live harmoniously together. (And there is the pleasure of "making up" afterward.) It is very tempting when one is angry to strike out as the spouse's vulnerable spots. In many a marriage one spouse seems ever on the alert to pounce upon and lay bare the failings of the other, to chip away at the mate's self-esteem, seeming to derive a perverse pleasure or sense of power at making small change of the other.[13]

In a good marriage one tries not to hit below the belt. This does not mean avoiding giving pain at all costs. In life it is sometimes necessary to inflict as well as to endure pain. I refer to the infliction of pain that serves no purpose save for the indulgence of one's own angry passion. Someone said that the difference between a mediocre marriage and a good one is four or five things — left unsaid.

In a good marriage disagreements are dealt with, not evaded or denied. Trusting the other, a spouse is not afraid to express differences of opinion. Many women, particularly if they are economically or emotionally dependent upon their husbands, are all too ready to conciliate in any disagreement for fear of arousing the husband's disapproval or ire. Some men too, particularly passive, submissive men, are not immune from ready capitulation — anything to avoid an argument.

A patient tells me that when he comes home from the office or a meeting later than expected, his tight-lipped, red-eyed wife meets him with a wall of icy silence. He finds himself mumbling apologies, though there is nothing to be apologetic about. He often turns down invitations from colleagues to join them after work for a drink rather than be confronted with a silently reproachful wife. How much less damaging it would be to the relationship were she to shout at him when he came home late: "Where the hell have you been?"

Accommodation

A good marriage requires the ability to accommodate oneself to the spouse's likes, dislikes, and peculiarities without, however, relinquishing one's own. This is easier said than done, for it requires almost constant compromise of one's own desires if some degree of harmony in the marriage is to be attained.

This accommodation is exemplified by the Ws who, to all outward appearances, have an odd kind of stable, contented marriage of thirty years. Mrs. W is always dashing about; Mr. W stays home. They are seldom seen together at gatherings. They have long ago made their peace with each other's disparate personalities, habits, and interests. Mr. W, a brilliant but rather schizoid person, is an inventor. He enjoys above all else puttering in his workshop. He also enjoys listening to music, especially grand opera, of which he has a huge collection of records. In their younger years the Ws attended the opera regularly, although Mrs. W had little interest in the music. ("I can't tell *Pagliacci* from *The Last Rose of Summer*," she once jokingly confided.) What she did enjoy was the social aspects of opera-going — getting dressed up, chatting with friends at intermission, and having supper at a fine restaurant afterward. But it has been many years since they've been to the opera house.

Mrs. W is a lawyer. She is a gay, outgoing busybody of a woman, active in many social causes. She is intensely involved in local politics and is considering running for public office. Mr. W supports her in her social and political activities but he draws the line at participating in the "socializing" these often entail. He feels uncomfortable in crowds, is shy with strangers, and has no talent for small talk. "I never know what to say to those people," he explains when he refuses to accompany his wife to a large affair. When he concedes, under protest, he retires to a corner for the evening, waiting for his wife to go home.

Mrs. W loves to travel; Mr. W hates it. During World War II he had spent several years in active military service both in the European and Pacific staging areas. "I've had enough traveling," he says. "Besides, I can travel all I want in my head." So she goes off without him. She has joined groups on trips to Europe, South America, the Middle East, and

Japan. Next year she plans to go to China. Mr. W doesn't mind her going; he enjoys her tales of adventure on her return.

I asked Mrs. W what the glue was that kept them together. "I find him so interesting," she answered. "He never bores me." Sometime later I asked Mr. W the same question. He smiled, saying, "She's a great old girl." Then, after a pause, he added, "I find her so interesting. She never bores me."

Realistic Expectations

We bring our inner needs to all our relationships. Some of them are met by those closest to us: parents, siblings, mates, lovers, friends, children. Other needs are satisfied in our work or play. And some go ungratified except in fantasy and dreams. Most of the time we are not aware of our inner needs. Indeed, we may unconsciously defend ourselves against them in a manner that belies them to ourselves and others if they go counter to our ego ideals. The macho he-man may, deep inside, long to be cuddled by a "big mamma." The active feminist may be struggling against her deep desire to have children and be looked after by a masterful husband.

When we marry we expect, consciously or unconsciously, that our mate will gratify our innermost needs. It is a grand expectation. It is also a pipe dream. No one, not even the most devoted mother of a new-born infant, can be expected to fulfill all of another's needs. In a good marriage one comes to terms with the reality of our expectations. One does not blame the spouse if our expectations were unrealistic. (The woman who marries a gambler expecting to "reform" him is in for disappointment.)

The following example illustrates one woman's unfulfilled, unrealistic expectations that doomed the marriage:

Jane R, 33, a successful commercial artist, married the top executive of the advertising agency for which she worked. Tom, 48, a handsome, sophisticated divorced man, was considered "quite a catch" by Jane's friends. With both their generous incomes they were able to live very well. They entertained lavishly, traveled frequently, and altogether appeared to be enjoying an enviable married life.

After nine months of marriage Jane developed headaches and a nervous twitch of the right eyelid. When a thorough medical examination revealed no physical pathology, Jane was referred for psychotherapy. In therapy it soon became apparent that although she was making great strides in her career, what Jane really wanted was to stay at home "in a little white cottage with a picket fence and roses climbing on it and four beautiful little kiddies playing in the back yard," she confessed, mocking herself for her "old-fashioned" desires. "Had she discussed having children with Tom?" I asked. "Only once," she said, "before we were married. And then it was in a kind of bantering way." Tom has two adolescent children by his previous marriage, whom he considered "a pain in the ass. When they see me all they ever want is money," he grumbled. He told Jane he didn't think he had the makings of a good father.

In the course of treatment Jane took courage and voiced her wish to have a child. Tom was shocked. "Not on your life," he had said. "At my age?" Children were the last thing he wanted. Joint counseling seemed indicated. But Tom refused even to consider it. Not many months later the couple separated and eventually were divorced.

Sometimes a person expects gratification for dependency needs that the other cannot supply. Marilyn, 22, a pretty, self-centered woman, married Robert, 28, an up-and-coming attorney, who had been captain of his college football team and was a champion skier and mountain climber. To Marilyn's disappointment, this rugged athlete, whom she had looked to as a "big daddy," turned out to be, in her words, "a six-foot-four baby with a red beard."

Patience

A good marriage requires patience — patience to ride out the inevitable rough storms that rock every marriage. Even the most solid marriage goes through crises that threaten its stability. In my grandmother's day, if a woman had a serious fight with her husband she could pack up the kids and go to her mother's house across town. After a few days' cooling off and apologies from a contrite spouse, she and the kids would return home. These days, Mother lives in a two-room apartment halfway across the country.

Today, with society's greater tolerance of divorce, there is less social pressure to keep a marriage intact. Separation and divorce become a viable option. Sometimes a couple is too quick to take this option when with patience they might have worked things out.

"I have the angries!" shouts Sue Jean, married twelve years and mother of two children. She ticks off a long bill of complaints to her bewildered, uncomprehending husband. The women's liberation movement, which has done so much for men as well as for women in making them aware of the inequities women have endured over the centuries, has shaken up many a marriage. In some instances this has been all to the good. It has spurred the growth and development of the pair and in the long run improved their relationship. In other instances, however, it has wrought havoc. I have known women who, in a fury of hitherto repressed rage at their subjection, needlessly broke up their marriage, to the emotional (and financial) detriment of their husbands, their children, and themselves.

Mature Love

Finally, the indispensable ingredient of a good marriage is mature love — concern for the other, and respect for the integrity, individuality, and privacy of the other. Smiley

Blanton defines mature love as "a relationship in which each helps to preserve and enlarge the life of the other . . . a love . . . free of childish compulsions to exploit, to dominate or to destroy. It is based on an acceptance of one another's specific biological nature, with the recognition that man and woman are complementary, not hostile, to each other. . . . Mature love thrives on a realistic basis of equal exchange which sets up a benign circle of mutual pleasure, reassurance and inspiration."[14]

Whatever life's hardships, marriage is that benign circle within which lies sanctuary.

Then and Now

THEN AND............

To My Dear and Loving Husband

"If ever two were one, then surely we.
If ever man were lov'd by wife, then thee;
If ever wife was happy in a man,
Compare with me ye women if you can.
I prize thy love more than whole Mines of gold,
Or all the riches that the East doth hold.
My love is such that Rivers cannot quench,
Nor ought but love from thee, give recompence.
Thy love is such I can no way repay,
The heavens reward thee manifold I pray.
Then while we live, in love let's so persever,
That when we live no more, we may live ever."
— Anne Bradstreet
(1612?–1672)

All the While

"Upstairs to my downstairs
echo to my silence
you walk through my veins shopping
and spin food from my sleep

"I hear your small noises
you hide in closets without handles
and surprise me from the cellar
your foot-soles bright black

"You slip in and out of beauty
and imply that nothing is wrong
Who sent you?
What is your assignment?

"Though years sneak by like children
it stays as unaccountable
as the underpants set to soak
in the bowl
where I would scour my teeth."
— John Updike
(1932–   )

NOTES

IN THE *Introduction*

1. For a statistical and descriptive analysis of the differences in sexual practices among social classes in the United States, see Alfred C. Kinsey, Wardell B. Pomeroy, and Clyde E. Martin, *Sexual Behavior in the Human Male*, Philadelphia: W. B. Saunders, 1948.
2. Parental behavior and child-rearing practices of the "blue-collar" class differ in many respects from those of the "white-collar" class. In general, working-class parents are stricter, more authoritative and more demanding than are middle-class parents that their children conform to external proscriptions. Middle-class parents are more likely to want their children to be self-directing, well-rounded, and given "worthwhile" experiences. To discipline the child, the working-class parent is more likely to use physical punishment, the middle-class parent reasoning and appeal to guilt. The latter is more likely to seek the "newest" child-rearing methods, to try to "understand" the child's behavior rather than to judge and deal with it in moral terms.

   Attitudes toward higher education, particularly for females, differ. In the rural Illinois mining town where I grew up, with its large proletarian immigrant population, a girl, upon finishing high school, was expected to get married or go to work in the Big Ben Clockworks until she got herself a husband. Few "blue-collar" families even thought of her going to college. Among my urban middle-class professional friends, the refusal of a daughter to go to college is regarded as a calamity.

   For a full discussion of class differences in family structure, child-rearing practices, and social attitudes, *see* E. James Anthony and Therese Benedek eds., *Parenthood: Its Psychology and Psychopathology*, Boston: Little, Brown, 1970; Mirra Komarofsky, *Blue Collar Marriage*, New York: Vintage, 1967; Lee Rainwater, *Family Design, Marital Sexuality, Family Size and Contraception*, Chicago: Alden, 1965; John Dollard,

Caste and Class in a Southern Town, Garden City, New York: Doubleday Anchor Books, 1957.

3. On the occasion of her 75th birthday Margaret Mead, asked about her three marriages, said that they had all been interesting marriages. "It wasn't so much that they didn't work out — they got used up." *New York Times*, December 16, 1976.

CHAPTER 1: *The Marriage Bond*

1. Here is anti-marriage propaganda carried to extremes: "I feel that the personal relationship of marriage must undergo a revolution . . . the roles of male and female must be completely redefined, no, eliminated. I do not see this as possible in the present relationships of marriage . . . The only alternative, as I see it, is communal living . . . It may be that our only solution will be the dissolution of marriage, with the foundation of all-female communes to eliminate the burdens placed on women." Barbara Balogun, "Marriage as an oppressive institution/collectives as solution," *Voices from Women's Liberation*. ed. L. B. Tanner, New York: New American Library, 1971.

2. Bureau of the Census, *Current Population Reports*, Series P. 20, No. 297. "Number, Timing and Duration of Marriages and Divorces in U.S.," June 1975.

3. Gore Vidal, *New York Review of Books*, June 4, 1977.

4. Ferdinand Lundberg, *The Coming World Transformation*. Toronto: Doubleday Canada Ltd., 1963.

5. National Center for Health Statistics. *New York Times*, Nov. 16, 1980.

6. Evelyn M. Kitagawa and Philip M. Hauser, *Differential Mortality in the U.S.*, Cambridge, Mass.: Harvard University Press, 1973.

7. Jane Brody, "Marriage is Good for Health and Longevity," *New York Times*, May 8, 1979.

8. Jessie Bernard, *The Future of Marriage*, New York: Bantam Books, 1972.

9. The following surveys and research studies concur in their findings that, overall, married people are happier than single people: *National Opinion Research Council General Social Survey*, 1972 and 1973; Angus Converse and Willard L.

Rodgers, *The Quality of American Life*, New York: Russell Sage Foundation, 1976; Norbal D. Glenn, "The Contribution of Marriage to the Psychological Well-Being of Males and Females," *Journal of Marriage and the Family*, Vol. 37, 1975.

10. According to the National Institute of Mental Health, in 1975, 89.9 married persons per 100,000 Americans 14 years and older were admitted to psychiatric hospitals. The rate for those who had never married or were widowed was 685.2 per 100,000 — *7½ times higher* than for married persons. For the separated and divorced it was 865.6 per 100,000, — *almost ten times higher* than for married persons. (Italics mine.) *See* Jane Brody, op. cit.

11. Denis de Rougemont, *Love in the Western World*, translated by Montgomery Belgion, New York: Pantheon Books, 1956.

12. Erikson, in his well-known eight stages of psycho-social development in the life of an individual, each with its own particular crisis, calls the stage after adolescence (in which the crisis to be passed is that of finding one's identity) the stage of "intimacy versus isolation." He writes, ". . . The young adult, emerging from the search for an insistence on identity, is eager and willing to fuse his identity with that of another. He is ready for intimacy, that is, the capacity to commit himself to concrete affiliations and partnerships and to develop the ethical strength to abide by such commitments, even though they may call for significant sacrifices and compromises." For a successful marriage, says Erikson, it is necessary to pass through this stage. From Erik H. Erikson, *Childhood and Society*, 2nd ed., New York: W. W. Norton, 1963.

13. John Cheever, *Falconer*, New York: Alfred A. Knopf, 1977.

14. Carson McCullers, *The Ballad of the Sad Café*, Boston: Houghton Mifflin, 1936.

15. Rainer Maria Rilke, *Letters to a Poet*, New York: W. W. Norton, 1934.

16. Edward M. Waring, in "Marital Intimacy, Psychosomatic Symptoms, and Cognitive Therapy," states that marriages of patients with chronic psychosomatic illness are characterized by specific incompatibilities, primarily by a profound lack of interpersonal intimacy. The couple does not share feelings or engage in self-disclosure. They are unable to discuss personal matters or private thoughts or beliefs. The author believes that

the psychosomatic symptoms may be used by the ill partner as an indirect attempt to overcome a frustrating lack of communication. (Dr. Waring utilizes cognitive family therapy to enable the spouses in such marriages to open up to each other, thereby increasing intimacy. By so doing he states that the psychosomatic symptoms of the patient have been improved.) *Psychosomatics*, Vol. 21, No. 7, July 1980.

17. "The Sorrows of Travel," *Harpers Magazine*, February 1978.
18. Medical findings show that the onset of illness frequently follows the death or divorce of a spouse. *See* Jane Brody, op. cit.
19. Sigmund Freud wrote: ". . . the act of defloration has not merely the socially useful result of binding the woman to the man; it also liberates an archaic reaction of enmity toward the man, which may assume pathological forms, and often enough expresses itself by inhibitions in the erotic life of the pair, and to which one may ascribe the fact that second marriages so often turn out better than first. The strange taboo of virginity — the fear which among primitive peoples induces the husband to avoid the performance of defloration — finds its full justification in this hostile turn of feeling.

". . . psychoanalysts come across women in whom the two contrary attitudes — thraldom and enmity — both come to expression and remain in close association. There are women who appear to be utterly alienated from their husbands and who can yet make only vain attempts to separate from them. As often as they try to turn their love to some other man, the image of the first who is nevertheless not loved, comes as a barrier between . . . these women still cling to their first husbands, in thraldom, truly, but no longer from affection. They cannot free themselves from him because their revenge upon him is not yet complete; and indeed, in extreme cases they have never even let the vengeful impulse reach their conscious minds." *See* "The Taboo of Virginity," *Collected Papers*, Vol. IV. London: Hogarth Press, 1925.

CHAPTER 2: *Why Marriage?*

1. "First [matrimony] was ordained for the increase of mankind according to the will of God, and that children might be brought up in the fear and nurture of the Lord, and to the praise of his holy name.

"Secondly, it was ordained in order that the natural instincts and affections implanted by God, should be hallowed and directed aright . . ." — Solemnization of Matrimony, Holy Trinity Church, London.

2. The young account for most of this increase. Today there are eight times more unmarried couples under 25 living together than 10 years ago. (Some of the reported increase may be due to a greater frankness in replying to census questions.)

3. A study of 1063 freshmen women at City University of New York, asked to project themselves fifteen years in the future, revealed that most of them wanted marriage, children, and a career. *See* Gilda F. Epstein and Arline L. Branzaft, "Female Freshmen View Their Roles as Women," *Journal Marriage and Family*, Vol. 34, November 1972.

4. Disraeli is said to have stated "Every woman should marry — and no man." Diogenes, when asked what is the proper time for a man to marry, said "A young man not yet, an old man, never."

5. Gilder, George, *Sexual Suicide*, New York: Quadrangle, Times Book Co., 1975.

6. Menander, back in 300 B.C., called marriage "a necessary evil"; nineteen centuries later, Cervantes called it "a noose." Literature is full of epigrams and witticisms making fun of marriage. For example, Socrates, being asked whether it was better to marry or not, replied, "Whichever you do, you will repent it." And the 17th-century playwright William Congreve, in *The Double Dealer*, wrote, "Tho' marriage makes man and wife one flesh, it leaves 'em still two fools." Closer to our own times, Lord Chesterfield, Samuel Johnson, William Thackeray, Oscar Wilde, G. B. Shaw, not to mention the wits and wiseacres of our own age, like H. L. Mencken, Alexander Woollcott, and Ogden Nash, enjoyed mocking that hoary institution.

7. Interview, *New York Times*, March 3, 1981.

8. Kathryn Perutz, *Liberated Marriage*, New York: Pyramid, 1975.

9. Edward O. Wilson, *On Human Nature*, Cambridge, Mass.: Harvard University Press, 1978.

The anthropologist C. Owen Lovejoy holds with Wilson that the sexuality of human beings, which is not confined to the brief period of female fertility in the menstrual cycle, evolved not for reproductive purposes, but to strengthen and maintain the pair bond.

Notes

Recent fossil discoveries in Ethiopia give great credence to Wilson's and Lovejoy's hypotheses. In 1973, Dr. Donald Johanson, a paleoanthropologist, discovered the skeleton of a prehuman female who walked erect nearly four million years ago. (*See* Donald C. Johanson and Maitland A. Edey, *Lucy, The Beginning of Humankind*, New York: Simon & Schuster, 1981.) Now, bipedalism has long been considered a human characteristic. Since the earliest known true human, *Homo erectus*, appeared two million years ago, the appearance of bipedalism in a prehuman creature two million years *earlier* has forced paleoanthropologists to reconsider their assumptions about the early stages of human evolution. It has been theorized on the basis of scientific evidence that *Homo* began to walk erect as his brain enlarged and he began to make tools. In order to use his forelimbs for toolmaking, his hind legs alone began to serve for locomotion. Since the earliest stone tools were made two million years *after* Lucy lived, how can scientists account for Lucy's erect walk?

Johansen and Edey conjecture that bipedalism is linked to the origin of pair bonding and the nuclear family. They reason thus: The earliest proto-humans (sometimes called *hominids*), like chimpanzees, reproduced slowly. Moreover, each baby needed five or six years of nurturing. In a food-rich tropical forest, the female could provide food for her offspring without the assistance of the male. However, as climates turned more sharply seasonal and food-rich environments began shrinking millions of years ago, food sources became farther away. An evolutionary opportunity was opened for a new, ape-like creature that could evolve a means of reproducing faster or surviving longer. Monogamous pair bonding developed, in which the male helped gather food for his family. With food sources far away, the best foraging method was for the pair to split up, gather food, and bring it back to share with the offspring at home. Bipedalism arose, Johanson and Edey theorize, because it allowed the hominids to carry food long distances to feed their families.

10. "The attachment relationship is in many ways the foundation of all our later affectionate or loving relationships, and is considered essential to form the more sophisticated, less instinctually bound relationships of mature life. This first bond is

overwhelmingly important in determining the capacity and the quality of all other later significant relationships." Willard Gaylin, *Caring*, New York: Alfred A. Knopf, 1976.

11. Selma Fraiberg, *Every Child's Birthright*, New York: Basic Books, 1977.

12. For a brilliant description of the first three years of a child's life, see Louise J. Kaplan, *Oneness and Separateness*, New York: Simon & Schuster, 1978.

13. For a detailed analysis of the normal separation-individuation process in the psychological development of the infant through the third year of life, I would refer the reader to the most definitive research work on the subject: Margaret S. Mahler, Fred Pine, and Anni Bergman, *The Psychological Birth of the Human Infant*, New York: Basic Books, 1975.

14. Gaylin, *Caring*

CHAPTER 3: *Marriage Yesterday and Today*

1. *See* the novels of Edith Wharton and Henry James.

2. *See* Christopher Lasch, *Haven in a Heartless World*, New York: Basic Books, 1977; and Kenneth Keniston and the Carnegie Council on Children, *All Our Children: the American Family under Pressure*, New York: Harcourt Brace Jovanovich, 1977.

3. The women's movement has helped to expand employment opportunities for females. Women are challenging the traditional notions of what was fitting work for them. By 1977 women were holding 18% of the nation's blue-collar jobs, including many in the construction trades. (The figures are undoubtedly much higher today.) Women serve these days on the police force, in the Army and Navy, as railroad engineers, telephone linesmen, plumbers, carpenters, in mines, and in other occupations traditionally "men's work."

4. *New York Times*, May 17, 1978.

5. In a *New York Times*-CBS news poll taken of 1603 adult Americans from all parts of the nation and representing different races, religions, ages, and occupations, 48% said they believed that marriages in which both partners share the tasks of breadwinner and homemaker make a much more "satisfying way of life"; 43% preferred the traditional marriage in which the husband is exclusively the provider and the wife exclusively a

homemaker. As might be expected there was a wide disparity in views between young and old. Of the youngest age group, 18–29-year-olds, only 27% preferred the traditional marriage; among those over 45 years old, 59% chose it. *See New York Times,* November 27, 1977.

6. Belva Plain, author of the best-selling novels, *Evergreen* and *Random Winds,* in an interview said, "In my day, from the age of 12 on, you just thought about getting married and having a family."

In a 1980 Roper poll on American Women's Opinions, 94 percent of American women favor marriage, although 52 percent redefine the "traditional" marriage of male as breadwinner and female as housewife to that of both sharing earnings and home-making responsibilities. *New York Times,* March 14, 1980.

See Betty Friedan, *The Feminine Mystique,* New York: W. W. Norton, 1963; Carl N. Degler, *At Odds: Women and the Family in America from the Revolution to the Present,* New York: Oxford University Press, 1980; John Stuart Mill, *The Subjection of Women: Three Essays,* London: Oxford University Press, 1912.

7. Erik H. Erikson, *Identity: Youth and Crisis,* New York: W. W. Norton, 1968. In *Childhood and Society* Erikson writes ". . . This fear of being left empty and, more simply, that of being left, seems to be the most basic feminine fear, extending over the whole of woman's existence. . . . No wonder, then, that the anxiety aroused by these fears can express itself either in complete subjection to male thought, in desperate competition with it, or in efforts to catch the male and make him a possession."

8. In a study of 231 dating couples, all of whom were strong supporters of egalitarian relationships, to determine "the ideals or values that people hold about power . . . and the style by which one person is able to influence another," Dr. Susan L. Kaplan and colleagues at Stanford University found that while the women in the sample "did not have to resort to placating and appeasing to achieve their ends, they were still not comfortable proposing their ideas and opinions directly." Even the most influential and powerful women in the sample used frequent questioning, an indirect though effective style to get

their point of view across. Kaplan noted that ". . . direct assertion by proposing ideas while stating opinions is still not a
power strategy of choice for women when interacting with
men." "Researcher Probes Sex Roles and Power," *Psychiatric
News*, February 18, 1977.

9. Mary Jo Bane, *Here to Stay: American Families in the Twentieth
Century*, New York: Basic Books, 1976.

10. Caroline Bird, *The Two Pay-Check Marriage*, New York: Rawson
Wade, 1979. Since 1966 the highest divorce rate has been in
the marriages of working women in their 20s.

   Many other factors contribute to divorce besides the increased tensions and pressures on the woman who holds a job
and runs a household, or the marital conflicts that may flare
up over who does what housekeeping chores. For the young
economically independent wife the temptation to "split" if the
marriage does not fulfill her expectations may be greater than
the desire to struggle through the inevitable difficulties in the
early years of marriage.

11. In 1975, out of over 16 million working couples in the U.S., in
more than two million both husband and wife were in professions, management, or administration. *New York Magazine*,
October 25, 1976.

12. *American Medical News*, October 26, 1979. *See also* Theodore
Nadelson and Leon Eisenberg, "The Successful Professional
Woman: On Being Married to One," *American Journal of Psy-
chiatry* No. 134, Oct. 1977; "The New American Marriage,"
New York Magazine, Oct. 25, 1976.

13. *See* Gilder, *Sexual Suicide.*

14. Many contemporary novels have dealt with this theme. *See* Marilyn French, *The Women's Room*, New York: Summit Books,
1977; Sara Davidson, *Loose Change*, New York: Doubleday,
1977.

15. Life expectancy of men born after 1946 is 67.7 years and of
women 77.1 years as compared with 56.4 for men and 60.7 for
women born a century earlier. Bane, op. cit.

16. The Jewish religion has always recognized women's sexuality and
the responsibility of the husband to gratify her sexually. "Her
food, her clothing and her conjugal rights shall he not with-
hold" (Exodus 21:10). Maimonides summed up Jewish laws on
conjugal relations thus: "Sexual union should be consum-

mated only out of desire and as a result of joy of the husband and wife."

17. Simone de Beauvoir, *The Second Sex*, translated and edited by H. M. Parshley, New York: Alfred A. Knopf, 1953.

18. *See* Leslie H. Farber, "I'm Sorry, Dear," *Lying, despair, jealousy, envy, sex, suicide, drugs, and the good life*, New York: Harper and Row, 1976.

19. For attitudes of young people toward premarital sex, *see* Morton Hunt, "Sexual Behavior in the 70s: Premarital Sex," *Playboy*, November 1973; Kenneth L. Cannon and Richard Lang, "Premarital Sexual Behavior in the Sixties," *Journal of Marriage and the Family*, Vol. 33, 1971; Ira L. Reiss, "Premarital Sexuality: Past, Present and Future," in Ira L. Reiss, ed., *Readings on the Family System*, New York: Holt, Rinehart and Winston, 1972.

20. *See* Ben B. Lindsey and Wainright Evans, *Companionate Marriage*, New York: Arno Press, 1980 (reprint of 1927 edition); Margaret Mead and Rhoda Metraux, *A Way of Seeing*, New York: William Morrow, 1974.

21. The greatest number of divorces occur between the fifth and eighth year of marriage.

22. Increasingly men are seeking — and being granted — sole or joint custody of their children. California has an admirable joint custody statute as well as "no fault" divorce.

23. In many present-day Moslem countries, female adultery can be punishable by death. (*See* 1980 television film, *Death of a Princess*.)

24. In 1977 the National Opinion Research Center asked a representative sample of adults across the nation their opinion about extramarital sex. 73% said it was "always wrong" and 14% said it was "almost always wrong." Only 3% did not consider it wrong. Similarly, in a recent Harris poll, three out of four men between 18 and 49 (a period when adultery is most rife) said they regarded sexual fidelity to be "very important" for a successful marriage. *The Playboy Report of American Men: A Study of Values, Attitudes and Goals of U.S. Males 18–49 Years*. Survey conducted by Louis Harris and Associates, Inc., 1979.

25. Linda Wolfe, *Playing Around: Women and Extramarital Sex*, New York: William Morrow, 1975. According to Wolfe, a con-

servative estimate is that 25% of married women, mostly under 30, engage in extramarital sex.

26. Christopher Lasch, *The Culture of Narcissism: American Life in an Age of Diminishing Expectations*, New York: W. W. Norton, 1978.

CHAPTER 4: *Introduction*

1. For a full exposition of the life cycle, *see:* Theodore Lidz, *The Person, His Development Throughout the Life Cycle*, New York: Basic Books, 1969. Erik Erikson (ed.) *Adulthood*, New York: W. W. Norton, 1978. Daniel J. Levinson, *The Seasons of a Man's Life*, New York: Alfred A. Knopf, 1978. Marjorie F. Lowenthal, Majda Thurber, and David Cheriboga, *Four Stages of Life*, San Francisco: Jossey-Bass, 1975. Bernice L. Neugarten (ed.), *Middle Age and Aging*, Chicago: University of Chicago Press, 1968. Gail Sheehy, *Passages*, New York: E. P. Dutton, 1976. George Vaillant, *Adaptation to Life*, Boston: Little, Brown, 1977. Shakespeare, "Seven Ages," *As You Like It*, Act II, Sc. 7.

2. In a *New York Times* news item (August 24, 1980) the Census Bureau reported that for the first time since World War II more women than men were enrolled in college, mainly because "many women over 35 years were seeking higher education."

CHAPTER 5. *Spring*

1. Longitudinal studies of couples over time concur that marital satisfaction is highest for newlyweds, begins to decline with the birth of the first baby, then turns upward when the children leave home. See R. O. Blood, Jr. and D. M. Wolfe, *Husbands and Wives: The Dynamics of Married Living*, New York: Free Press, 1960. Wesley R. Burr, "Satisfaction with Various Aspects of Marriage over the Life Cycle: a random middle-class sample," *Journal of Marriage and the Family*, February 1970.

2. Boyd C. Rollins and Kenneth L. Cannon, "Marital Satisfaction over the Family Life Cycle — a Re-evaluation," *Journal of Marriage and the Family*, May 1974.

The cynical sociologist Willard Walker called the honeymoon "that period while illusions last."

3. Battles over the question of whether there is a maternal instinct have raged for generations but never more fiercely than in the '60s and '70s, when the current women's liberation movement (which had many predecessors) was in first flower. The psychoanalyst Helene Deutsch states that "motherliness" is an instinctive quality of the feminine character and that pregnancy offers a woman the opportunity to realize her full feminine potentialities. She believes that an instinctive tendency to bear children resides even in women who have never borne any; indeed, even in women who assume masculine prerogatives in order to escape from their vulnerability as females. *Psychology of Women: Motherhood*, Vol. II, Grune and Stratton, 1945.

Therese Benedek, in her classic investigations on the correlation between emotional states and hormonal processes during the menstrual cycle, tends to confirm Deutsch's conjectures. She found from analyzing the dreams and fantasies of women in analysis that in the lutein phase of the menstrual cycle (the period following ovulation, when the chances of conception are greatest) there were definite psychological manifestations of preparation for pregnancy. Therese Benedek and Boris B. Rubenstein, *The Sexual Cycle in Women: The Relation between Ovarian Function and Psychological Processes*, Washington, D.C.: National Research Council, 1972.

Radical feminists hoot at the idea of a maternal instinct. They say that women have been brainwashed through the ages into believing the myth about maternity being instinctive. Having babies, declares Roxanne Dunbar, is a cultural trap to keep women in the slave role in the family. Ellen Peck, founder of NON (Non-Parents), declares that the myth of motherhood as central to a woman's social and sexual definition is "one of history's fallacies."

Shulamith Firestone wants women to be freed from "the tyranny of their reproductive biology" and from child bearing altogether. Ti Grace Atkinson, who identifies men as the enemy, favors artificial, i.e. extrauterine reproduction. Both Firestone and Atkinson advocate the abolition of the family.

In Ellen Peck, A *Funny Thing Happened on the Way to Equality*, Englewood Cliffs, New Jersey: Prentice Hall, 1975.

In my interviews with women who had abortions, a few expressed only relief that the medical procedure spared them the cataclysmic changes in their lives a child (or another child) would create, changes that they were unable or unwilling to cope with. Many women, however, even while expressing relief, also voiced regret (some even repugnance) at having to terminate the pregnancy. A patient who had aborted her first (premarital) pregnancy, continued throughout her married life and the birth of two subsequent children, to consider the aborted fetus her "first born" and secretly marked its birthday, had it come to term, for many years.

4. *See* Greta L. Bibring, "Some Considerations of the Psychological Processes in Pregnancy," *The Psychoanalytic Study of the Child*, Vol. 14, 1959.

5. Freud considered pregnancy a "period of bliss," since he believed it gratified a basic biological and emotional need in the woman.

6. *See* Jesse O. Cavenar, Jr. and Nancy T. Butts, "Fatherhood and Emotional Illness," *American Journal of Psychiatry*, April 1977. Gregory Zilboorg, "Depressive Reactions Related to Parenthood," *American Journal of Psychiatry*, 87: 1931. T. Freeman, "Pregnancy as a Precipitant of Mental Illness in Men," *British Journal of Medical Psychology*, 24: 1951. W. H. Wainwright, "Fatherhood as a Precipitant of Mental Illness," *American Journal of Psychiatry*, 123: 1966.

CHAPTER 6: *Summer*

Note: I have not dealt in this book with the special problems of parenting a chronically ill or disabled child, or a child of divorce, a stepchild, or an adopted child. For readers interested in these subjects I would refer them to: Edith M. Stern and Elsa Castendyck, *Care of the Handicapped Child*, New York: A. A. Wyn, 1950; Group for the Advancement of Psychiatry, *The Joys and Sorrows of Parenthood*, New York: Charles Scribner's Sons, 1973; Verda Husler, A *Handicapped Child in the Family*, New York and London: Grune & Stratton, 1972; William C. Kvaraceus and E. Nelson Hayes, eds., *If Your Child*

Is Handicapped, Boston: Porter Sargent, 1969; Brenda Maddox, *The Half Parent: Living with Other People's Children*, New York: M. Evans, 1975; Claire Berman, *Making It as a Stepparent: New Roles/New Rules*, New York: Doubleday, 1975; Anne W. Simon, *Stepchild in the Family*, New York: Pocketbooks, 1964; Edith Atkin and Estelle Rubin, *Part-Time Father*, New York: Vanguard Press, 1976; J. Louise Despert, *Children of Divorce*, Garden City, N.Y.: Doubleday, 1953; Richard Gardner, *The Parents Book about Divorce*, Garden City, N.Y.: Doubleday, 1977; Bernard Steinzor, *When Parents Divorce*, New York: Pantheon Books, 1969; M. D. Schechter, "Observations on Adopted Children," *Archives of General Psychiatry*, 1960; Betty Jean Lifton, *Lost and Found: The Adoption Experience*, New York: Dial Press, 1979; Jane Rowe, *Parents, Children and Adoption*, London: Humanities Press, 1966.

1. Ten percent of marriages are childless. In half of these the childlessness is involuntary. In the other half (which the couples prefer to call "child-free" rather than "child-less") the decision not to have children is deliberate. Advocates of the child-free marriage claim it is more "liberating," allowing the couple more leisure to develop their own "potential." They declare that society exerts subtle pressures on both sexes from childhood on to believe that a woman's destiny is to bear children — a "hype," the insidiuous purpose of which is to keep women in subjection and "for tribal or national . . . aggrandisement." Indeed, several years ago an organization called NON (Nonparents) was founded to counteract what it termed "pronatalism" — "any attitude or policy that is pro-birth, that encourages reproduction, that exalts the role of parenthood." All quotes from Ellen Peck and Judith Senderowitz, eds., *Pronatalism: The Myth of Mom and Apple Pie*, New York: Crowell, 1974.

Most people, however, would agree with Benedek that parenthood, whether one has children or not, is a natural phase in the life cycle of an adult. *See* Therese Benedek, "Parenthood as a Developmental Phase," *Journal of the American Psychoanalytic Association*, VII: 1959.

"Parenthood is a manifestation of 'natural man' and, as such, is governed by the laws of biologic processes that are universal." Introduction, E. James Anthony and Therese Benedek, eds., *Parenthood: Its Psychology and Psychopathology*, Boston: Little, Brown, 1970.

Freud claims that the main satisfaction of being a parent — which means renouncing one's own self-centered needs in favor of gratifying those of one's offspring — is narcissistic; that is, it gratifies the wish to re-create in the child one's own image.

As for my own position, along with other "experts," I waffle. I do not believe there is a universal "instinct" for motherhood or fatherhood. Neither do I believe the creation of human life and the rearing of children in a family is merely a learned social activity ingrained through centuries of custom and imposed by society for its own purposes. I do believe that beyond any narcissistic wish to reproduce oneself in offspring or any sense of social obligation to perpetuate the race, there is an inner need in most (though by no means all) mature men and women to parent the young, a need to "mother" (or "father") a helpless, dependent child, that transcends our self-centeredness. I believe this need is what we are responding to when we stand entranced before the window of a pet shop and watch with delight the cavorting of kittens and puppies; when we try to comfort a crying child who has lost sight of its mother in the supermarket; when we adopt a Vietnamese orphan although we already have four kids of our own.

2. Erikson defines generativity as "primarily the interest in establishing and guiding the next generation, or whatever in a given case may be the absorbing object of a parental kind of responsibility." Erik H. Erikson, *Childhood and Society*, New York: W. W. Norton, 1950.

3. Sigmund Freud, Contributions to the Psychology of Love. "The Most Prevalent Form of Degradation in Erotic Life," *Collected Papers*, Vol. IV (1912), London: Hogarth Press, 1925.

4. *See* Anne Roiphe, *Up the Sandbox!* New York: Simon & Schuster, 1970.

CHAPTER 7: *Autumn*

1. Barbara Fried, *Middle Age Crisis*, New York: Harper and Row, 1967.

2. Boswell is said to have asked Dr. Samuel Johnson, "Is not the fear

of death natural to man?" "So much so, sir," replied Dr. Johnson, "that the whole of life is keeping away thoughts of it."

3. Edmund Bergler: *Revolt of the Middle-Aged Man*, New York: Grosset & Dunlap, 1967.

4. John Updike: "I Will Not Let Thee Go, Except Thou Bless Me," in *Museums and Women and Other Stories*, New York: Alfred A. Knopf, 1972.

5. *See* Sue Kaufman, *Diary of a Mad Housewife*, Garden City, N.Y.: Doubleday, 1967.

6. Allen Wheelis, *The Seeker*, New York: New American Library, 1962.

7. H. L. Klemme, "Mid-Life Crisis," *Menninger Perspective*, June-July, 1970.

8. One of the best novels of our time depicting the dilemma of the middle-aged woman is Doris Lessing, *The Summer Before the Dark*, New York: Alfred A. Knopf, 1973.

9. John Updike conveys this feeling poignantly in one of his short stories, "Solitaire" (in *Museums*) as the hero ponders with awe the phenomenon of being "the father of others. . . ." "He wondered if they [his growing children] loved him as he had loved his father, wondered what depth of night sky would be displayed by his removal. They formed a club from which he was excluded. Their corporate commotion denied him access."

10. Angus Campbell, "The American Way of Mating," *Psychology Today*, May, 1975.

11. James A. Fitzgerald, "Middle-life Crisis of the Physician," *New York Journal of Medicine*, December 1, 1973.

12. Elliot Jacques, "Death and the Mid-Life Crisis," *International Journal of Psychoanalysis*, Vol. 46, 1965, writes: "The individual has stopped growing up and has begun to grow old. A new set of external circumstances has to be met. The first phase of adult life has been lived. Family and occupation have been established . . .; parents have grown old, and children are at the threshold of adulthood. Youth and childhood are past and gone, and demand to be mourned. . . . The paradox is that of entering the prime of life, the stage of fulfillment, but at the same time [they] are dated. Death lies beyond . . . the reality and inevitability of one's own eventual personal death that is the central and crucial feature of the mid-life phase. . . .

Death . . . instead of being a general conception, or an event experienced in terms of the loss of someone else, becomes a personal matter. . . ."

13. *See* Ruth Goode, *A Book for Grandmothers*, New York: Macmillan, 1976.

CHAPTER 8: *Winter*

1. The term "old age," like "middle age," can only be defined in our culture within a very broad range. As everyone knows, there is a marked difference in the biological aging process among individuals of the same chronological age as well as a great diversity in life styles and in psychological responses and adaptational patterns to that process. To try to encompass these disparities within an arbitrary time structure would be restrictive. However, for the sake of conveniently dealing with this subject within the framework of this book, I am assigning the onset of what I call "early old age" somewhere around 65, when retirement looms or becomes an actuality; and the onset of "late old age" somewhere in the 70s. Moreover, no matter how young one *feels*, this is how one is regarded by the younger generations.

2. *See* Malcolm Cowley, *The View from 80*, New York: Viking, 1980.

CHAPTER 9: *The Family as a Social Institution*

1. Pitirim A. Sorokin, *Social and Cultural Dynamics*, Vol. IV, 1937.
2. *Raising Children in a Changing Society*, The General Mills American Family Report 1976–77 conducted by Yankelovich, Skelly & White.
3. In Scott G. McCall, ed., *The Sociological Perspective*, Boston: Little, Brown, 1968.
4. Discontent with the nuclear family as a pattern for marriage and particularly for rearing children is nothing new in American life. In the 19th century many "utopian" communities and communes, based on various ideologies that presumably would make for a better way of life, were established. Few, if any, survived. The thousands of "hippie" communes of the '60s and '70s were largely a counterculture movement, a revolt against the prevailing bourgeois middle-class society (from

which most of their members came). Practically all failed, sooner than later. (One survivor is Walden II, in Virginia, though it has changed radically in form and practice since its beginnings.)

The best-known utopian family experiment is the Israeli kibbutz. (Four percent of Israel's population live in kibbutzim and other forms of collective and cooperative settings.) In the kibbutz the children live from infancy on in groups with their age peers and are looked after by specially assigned persons. However, there is a close, affectional relationship with their parents, whom they see daily or as frequently as they wish. The kibbutzim, which began as pioneering cooperative agricultural settlements (many today are industrialized), were based on certain ideological convictions of their founders: the equality of women with men, particularly in work, and the emancipation of women from traditional "female" social roles; abolition of the patriarchal authority of the father; democratic education for the children; and the perpetuation of socialist values and ideals. Since the 1880s, when the first kibbutzim were established, there have been many social and economic changes, including the greater involvement of parents with children. But the basic kibbutz philosophy has remained firm. *See:* Bruno Bettelheim, *The Children of the Dream*; London: Macmillan, 1969. Melford E. Spiro, *Kibbutz Venture in Utopia*; Cambridge, Mass.: Harvard University Press, 1956. Also, same author and press, *Children of the Kibbutz*, 1958. Rosabeth Kanter, *Commitment and Community: Communes and Utopias in Sociological Perspective*, Cambridge, Mass.: Harvard University Press, 1972.

5. I have used Lawrence Stone's *The Family, Sex, and Marriage in England, 1500–1800*, New York: Harper and Row, 1978, as my principal source for this section. This truncated version of family life from the 16th to the 19th century, which was drawn largely from middle- and upper-class English life, applied equally to family life in America after the landing of the Pilgrims in 1620, who brought with them the social, legal, religious, and ethical practices of the mother country. Hawthorne's *Scarlet Letter* gives a vivid picture of the rigid codes that governed the lives of our Puritan forebears. As in England, these Puritan standards were relaxed in 18th-century

America as social conditions, at least for the middle class, became less harsh.

For a history of the origins of the family, *see:* E. Wester-mark, A *Short History of Marriage*, New York: Macmillan, 1926; F. Engels, *The Origin of the Family, Private Property, and the State*, Chicago: Charles H. Kerry, 1910; S. Freud, *Totem and Taboo*, New York: W. W. Norton, 1952.

6. Historical romances like *Ivanhoe* and *Robin Hood* give a good picture of kinship families.
7. Keniston, *All Our Children*
8. Lasch, *Haven*
9 Elliot R. Morse and Ritchie H. Reed, eds., *Economic Aspects of Population Change*, Vol. 2, Commission on Population Growth and the American Future, U.S. Dept. of Agriculture, Govt. Printing Office, Washington, D.C. 1972. This estimate was made before galloping inflation of the last decade.
10. Bane, *Here to Stay*
11. "Saving the Family," *Newsweek*, May 15, 1978.
12. Talcott Parsons and Robert F. Bales, *Family Socialization and Interactional Process*, Glencoe, Ill.: The Free Press, 1955.
13. "The Ties Don't Bind," *New York Times*, Aug. 26, 1976.
14. Keniston, *All Our Children*
15. Underlying the mood of optimism, the report indicated, were many symptoms of strain. The most pervasive was the conflict between the traditional expectation that parents should sub-ordinate their own needs to those of the children and the new preoccupation with self-fulfillment. The respondents split al-most equally into two camps on this issue: the "traditionalists" and the "new breed."

The former were more willing to sacrifice for their chil-dren, believed in stricter discipline, demanded respect for au-thority figures, were ambitious for their children, and felt strongly that boys should be raised by different standards from girls.

The "new breed' believed parents "have the right to lead their own lives, but in exchange children don't owe them any-thing later." They were more permissive with their children but gave their own self-fulfillment priority over their obliga-tions to children. Interesting enough, however, while the "new breed" discarded many of the values by which they were brought up, when it came to teaching the children they hung on to them, such as respect for authority, the importance of hard work, saving, and patriotism.

The same proportion of both groups (over 70%) disapproved of sexual relations outside marriage. Both groups also disapproved of mothers with young children working except out of necessity. Almost 79% of all the parents believed that children of working mothers were worse off than were those of mothers who stayed home. (Working mothers were equally divided on this issue.)

CHAPTER 10: *The Blood Knot: The Family and the Individual*

1. Leslie Farber, *Lying*, etc.
2. The social anthropologist Ashley Montague condemns the family for its "systematic production of physical and mental illness in the members." The writer Susan Sontag goes even further in her condemnation of the modern family, which she calls "a psychological and moral disaster, a prison of sexual repression, a playing field of inconsistent moral laxity, a museum of possessiveness, a guilt-producing factory, a school of selfishness." In Jane Howard, *Families*, New York: Simon & Schuster, 1978.

   Some of the most virulent attacks on the family have come from radical feminists who regard the family as the enemy of women, a "baby trap" devised by a patriarchal society to keep them oppressed and subservient to the master sex. "Families perpetuate themselves and their bad values by educating children to see them as the only model for adult life. . . . The nuclear family must be destroyed, and people must find better ways of living together." Linda Gordon, "Functioning of the Family," *Voices from Women's Liberation*.
3. *New York Times*, April 14, 1978.
4. Keniston writes of the parental "malaise" that consists of having no guidelines or supports for raising children and the feeling of not being in control as parents, and the widespread sense of personal guilt for what seems to be going awry. He takes for granted that "we live in a society where parents must increas-

ingly rely on others for help and support in raising their children." *All Our Children*
5. *New York Times*, March 6, 1977.
6. Lawrence H. Fuchs, *Family Matters*, New York: Warner, 1974.

CHAPTER *11: Love and Marriage*

1. Jonathan Freedman, *Happy People*, New York: Harcourt, Brace, Jovanovich, 1978.
2. In a nationwide poll by the Roper Organization (1974) 87% of the women and 77% of the men, when asked what they considered the primary reason for getting married, answered, not surprisingly, "Love."
3. For a full discussion of the subject *see:* Morton Hunt, *Natural History of Love*, New York: Alfred A. Knopf, 1959.
4. Henry Miller, *Nexus*, New York: Grove, 1965.
5.   Phebe: Good shepherd, tell this youth what 'tis to love.

       Silvius: It is to be all made of sighs and tears; . . .

                It is to be all made of faith and service; . . .

                It is to be all made of fantasy,

                All made of passion and all made of wishes,

                All adoration, duty, and obedience;

                All humbleness, patience and impatience,

                All purity, all trial, all observance. . . .

       — Shakespeare *As You Like It*, Act V, Scene II.
6. There have been many studies on the biochemistry of psychic states, including that of "being in love." A recent study that has gained much public attention is that of Donald F. Klein and Michael Liebowitz of the New York State Psychiatric Institute. Examining the "chemistry" of love, they found that in a state of love there is an outpouring of a chemical substance in the brain called phenylethylamine, which is similar to amphetamine. "Love brings on a giddy response comparable to an amphetamine high," Dr. Liebowitz said, "And the crash that follows breakup is much like amphetamine withdrawal." Klein and Liebowitz studied a group of "love junkies," women with a life pattern of forming disastrous love relationships. The scientists found that the withdrawal of love "may drain the body's store of a potent mood-altering chemical [phenyl-

ethylamine], one that chocolate has in rich supply." The good doctors found that many of these women went on chocolate binges when depressed. "The binging may be an attempt at self-medication," Dr. Liebowitz added. *The New York Times,* Jan. 22, 1980.

Dr. John Money, professor of medical psychology and pediatrics at Johns Hopkins University School of Medicine for many years has been studying the brain pathways associated with love and sex and has recently published an encyclopedic book on the subject, *Love and Love Sickness: The Science of Sex, Gender Difference, and Pair Bonding,* Baltimore and London: The Johns Hopkins University Press, 1980.

7. My own preferred explanation leans toward that which Aristophanes expounded at the banquet attended by Socrates and fellow philosophers, where they discoursed on love. Aristophanes declares that "of all the gods [Love] is the best friend of men, the helper and the healer of the ills which are the great impediment to the happiness of the race." He then goes on to describe the nature of man and how love came into being. According to him, primeval man was a spherical creature with eight limbs, two faces, and two generative organs facing in opposite directions. "Terrible was their might and strength, and the thoughts of their hearts were great, and they made an attack upon the gods . . . Doubts reigned in the celestial councils. Should they annihilate the race then there would be an end of the sacrifices and worship which men offered to them; but on the other hand, the gods could not suffer their insolence to be unrestrained. At last . . . Zeus discovered a way. He said, 'Methinks I have a plan which will humble their pride and improve their manners; men shall continue to exist, but I will cut them in two and then they will be diminished in strength and increased in numbers; . . . They shall walk upright on two legs'. . . . He cut men in two . . . as you might divide an egg with a hair; . . .

"After the division the two parts of man, each desiring his other half, came together, and throwing their arms about one another, entwined in mutual embraces, longing to grow into one; they were on the point of dying from hunger and self-neglect, because they did not like to do anything apart. . . . Zeus in pity of them invented a new plan: he turned the parts of generation round to the front, for this had not always been

their position, and they sowed the seed no longer as hitherto like grasshoppers in the ground, but in one another; and after the transposition the male generated in the female in order that by mutual embraces of man and woman they might breed, and the race might continue . . . so ancient is the desire of one another which is implanted in us, reuniting our original nature, making one of two, and healing the state of man. Each of us when separated, having one side only like a flat fish, is but the indenture of a man, and he is always looking for his other half. . . . And when one of them meets with his other half, the pair are lost in an amazement of love and friendship and intimacy, and one will not be out of the other's sight . . . even for a moment: these are the people who pass their whole lives together; yet they could not explain what they desire of one another. For the intense yearning which each of them has toward the other does not appear to be the desire of lover's intercourse, but of something else which the soul of either evidently desires and cannot tell . . . Suppose Hephaestus . . . (would) come to the pair lying side by side and say to them, 'What do you people want of one another?' they would be unable to explain. And suppose further . . . he said: 'Do you desire to be wholly one; always day and night to be in one another's company? . . . if this is what you desire, I am ready to melt you into one and let you grow together'. . . . there is not a man of them would deny or would not acknowledge that . . . this becoming one instead of two, was the very expression of his ancient need. And the reason is that human nature was originally one and were whole, and *the desire and pursuit of the whole is called love*" (italics mine). "The Symposium," *The Works of Plato*, 3rd edition, Jowett translation, selected and edited by Irwin Edman. New York: Random House, 1956.
8. Psychoanalysts differ in their theories on the source of love. Among the various psychoanalytic exegeses, I shall mention here only a few. Freud, in propounding his dual theory of instincts (Eros and Thanatos), thought that Eros (love) sprang from the sexual instinct but in an "aim inhibited" or sublimated form. (*See* Freud's "Instincts and Their Vicissitudes," *Collected Papers*, (1915) Vol. IV., London: Hogarth Press, 1925.)

Theodore Reik, Freud's renegade pupil, differed from his

erstwhile master on this matter. He thought that love was a psychical power in its own right, quite apart from the sexual instinct. In passionate love sexual and tender feelings were united and directed toward the same person, but they came from two separate domains. To bolster his thesis, Reik pointed out that there can be sex without love and love without sex. (*See* Reik's *Of Love and Lust*, New York: Farrar Straus & Giroux, 1941.)

Eric Fromm thought that love was an imperative for doing away with unbearable feelings of isolation. Our need to love, he maintained, lay in the experience of separateness and the resulting need to overcome the anxiety of separateness by union with another. (*See* Fromm's *The Art of Loving*, New York: Harper and Row, 1962.)

9. Theodore Reik, *From Thirty Years with Freud*, New York: Rinehart, 1940.

10. William Proxmire, when he was chairman of the Senate Budget Committee, withdrew federal funds from the National Science Foundation for a study by two social psychologists on falling in love. Proxmire objected to the study saying, "I believe that 200 million Americans want to leave some things in life a mystery, and right at the top of things we don't want to know is why a man falls in love with a woman and vice versa."

11. Richard A. Bollinger, "Whatever Happened to Marriage?" *Menninger Perspective*, Fall, 1976.

12. Smiley Blanton, *Love or Perish*, New York: Simon & Schuster, 1956.

13. Bertrand Russell, *Marriage and Morals*, Garden City, N.Y.: Garden City Publishing Co. 1929.

14. Freud differentiated between two kinds of love among adults, one that he called anaclitic, the other narcissistic. In the first the lover seeks in his or her beloved the giving, nourishing mother or the protecting, providing father. In the second, the lover seeks in the beloved an idealized self. If the love is returned the lovers feel as though they have become part of each other — they merge. (In the course of a good marriage, both kinds of love exist and blend.)

15. Quoted in Gerald R. Leslie, *The Family in Social Context*, New York: Oxford University Press, 1973.

16. Sigmund Freud, "Analysis of a Phobia in a Five-Year Old Boy" (1909), *Collected Works*, Vol. X. London: Hogarth Press, 1955.

17. Sigmund Freud, "Thoughts for the Times on War and Death," *Collected Papers* (1915), Vol II. London: Hogarth Press, 1925.

CHAPTER 12: *Sex in Our Time*

1. Kinsey et al., *Sexual Behavior in the Human Male; Sexual Behavior in the Human Female.*
2. Masters and Johnson, *Human Sexual Response.*
3. Shere Hite, *The Hite Report*, New York: Macmillan, 1976. The intention of the book, Ms. Hite wrote, was ". . . to share how we have experienced our sexuality, how we feel about it, and to see our personal lives more clearly, thus redefining our sexuality and strengthening our identities as women."
4. Sandra Kahn, *The Kahn Report*, New York: St. Martin's Press, 1981.
5. Morton Hunt, *Sexual Behavior in the 1970's.* New York: Dell, 1974.
6. Joseph Epstein, *Divorced in America*, New York: Penguin, 1975.
7. Autobiographies of actors, actresses, singers, and writers, among them Lauren Bacall, Shelley Winters, Susan Strasberg, Lillian Hellman, Joan Crawford, Joan Schary Robinson, and Dory Previn, baring their sex lives, have rolled off the presses in hundreds of thousands of copies. An item in the *New York Times* (July 26, 1980) reports an interview with Shelley Winters, celebrating the publication of her bestseller: "I'm throwing a party for everybody mentioned in the book, including all my former husbands and lovers . . . for about four hundred people. It's for everybody who helped me lead my uproarious life." (The news item lists some of the famous men she mentions in the book as having been her lovers.) "Of course," Miss Winters adds, "I didn't have all that many men in my life. Considering today's women's lib attitudes, I was a piker."
8. Bonnie Prudden, *Ladies' Home Journal*, August 1977.
9. Paul Robinson, *The Modernization of Sex*, New York: Harper & Row, 1976.
10. Francine du Plessix Gray, author of that estimable novel, *Lovers and Tyrants*, in an interview with an editor of *Book Digest*, when asked whether the explicit sex scenes in her book helped its reception, answered: "I think the fact that it had some explicit sexuality — which is the chic thing to do — turned some people on to buy it. For totally understandable commer-

cial reasons the publishers played that up, calling the book 'erotic' and so on."

11. Harold I. Lief, Professor of Psychiatry at University of Pennsylvania School of Medicine and Director of the Center for the Study of Sex Education in Medicine, describes the spectrum as follows: Approximately 10% are totally inorgasmic; 20% can reach orgasm with masturbation; 40% are potentially orgasmic with coital stimulation by the partner; 10% are high responsive, with multiple orgasm during coitus. *Medical Aspects of Human Sexuality*, April 1977.
12. Norman Mailer, *The Prisoner of Sex*, Boston: Little, Brown, 1971.
13. *See* Paul D. Mozley, "Woman's Capacity for Orgasm after Menopause," *Medical Aspects of Human Sexuality*, August 1975.
14. Frank Caprio, *The Sexually Adequate Female*, New York: Citadel, 1953.

CHAPTER 13: *Sex in Marriage*

1. Havelock Ellis, *Studies in the Psychology of Sex*, Vol. I., Introduction, New York: Random House, 1940.
2. Karl and Anne Taylor Fleming, *The First Time*, New York: Simon & Schuster, 1975.
3. John F. Cuber, "The Natural History of Sex in Marriage," *Medical Aspects of Human Sexuality*, July 1975.
4. In a study of 345 married persons below 40 and married for an average of 11 years, one-third reported long periods with no sex, some for eight weeks or more, most commonly because of marital discord. Jane E. Brody, *New York Times*, April 20, 1977.
5. Gay Talese, *Thy Neighbor's Wife*, New York: Doubleday, 1980.
6. Sigmund Freud, "Contributions to the Psychology of Love. The Most Prevalent Form of Degradation in Erotic Life." (1912) *Collected Papers*, Vol IV., London: Hogarth Press, 1925.
7. Mailer, *Prisoner*

CHAPTER 14: *Trouble in Paradise: Sexual Problems*

1. In the female the most common sexual dysfunctions are: anaesthesia (no feeling), inorgasmia (no orgasm), vaginismus (involuntary clamping shut of the vaginal muscles making

penetration impossible), and dyspareunia (pain in coitus). Sometimes there is actual revulsion against the sexual act and sometimes, though it is rare, nymphomania.

In the male, common sexual dysfunctions are impotence and premature ejaculation. Retarded ejaculation is another, though rarer, dysfunction. Sometimes, though rarely, there is satyriasis. In nymphomania and satyriasis there is an insatiable desire for sex.

2. In Aristophanes' *Lysistrata*, the Athenian women bring an end to war by refusing to make love with their soldier-husbands.
3. Merle S. Kroop, "Are 'Frigid' Women Capable of Love?" *Medical Aspects of Human Sexuality*, December 1977.
4. In an article by Leonard R. Derogatis, Jon K. Meyer, and Bridget W. Gallant, "Distinctions between Male and Female Invested Partners in Sexual Disorders," reporting on a study of 48 couples in which only one partner was sexually dysfunctional, the authors found that the asymptomatic husbands were more distressed, more anxious and depressed, more self-depreciative, more "paranoid" in their style of thinking — as though somehow they were to blame for their wives' dysfunction — than were the asymptomatic wives, who were more tolerant, more relaxed, and felt less responsible for the husbands' dysfunctions.

   The authors hypothesized that "because our culture assigns disproportionate responsibility to the male in sexual matters, the additional accountability associated with this culturally determined role definition may act to generate higher levels of conflict and symptom manifestations in the male partner." The study proved their hypothesis to be sound. They concluded that "This [difference] is attributed, in our interpretation, to the gender specificity of the role model of 'lover' in our society. For the male, this role definition carried with it primary responsibility for the sexual gratification of both his partner and himself and it appears that a surprising number of men and women have 'colluded' to make this role model a reality." *American Journal of Psychiatry*, 134:4, April 1977.
5. Ruth Moulton, "Some Effects of the New Feminism," *American Journal of Psychiatry*, January 1977.
6. The long-standing belief that 90% of impotence cases are emo-

tional in origin is being seriously questioned as a result of research being done at Beth Israel Hospital in Boston, which found that certain hormonal abnormalities can produce impotence. It is now believed that perhaps one-third of sexually impotent men have hormonal derangements which can be successfully treated with hormone therapy. From article, "Impotence Linked to Hormone Abnormality," Jane E. Brody, *New York Times*, February 19, 1980.

7. Masters and Johnson, *Human Sexual Inadequacy*, Boston: Little, Brown, 1970.

CHAPTER 15: *Forsaking All Others: The Question of Fidelity*

1. Erikson defines fidelity as "the ability to sustain loyalties freely pledged in spite of the inevitable contradictions of value systems." Erik H. Erikson, *Insight and Responsibility*, Lectures on the Ethical Implications of Psychoanalytic Insight, New York: W. W. Norton & Co., 1964.
2. Hyman Spotnitz and Lucy Freeman, *The Wandering Husband*, Englewood Cliffs, New Jersey: Prentice-Hall, 1964.
3. Morton Hunt, *Sexual Behavior in the 1970's*, New York: Dell, 1974.
4. Anthony Pietropino and Jacqueline Simenauer, *Husbands and Wives*, New York: Time Books, 1979.
5. Anthony Pietropino and Jacqueline Simenauer, *Beyond the Male Myth*, New York: Time Books, 1974.
6. Lewis Yablonsky, *The Extra-Sex Factor: Why Over Half of America's Married Men Play Around*, New York: Time Books, 1979.
7. *See* the Restoration comedies of Richard Brinsley Sheridan, William Congreve, and William Wycherley.
8. *See* Olivier Bernier, *Pleasure and Privilege: Life in France, Naples and America, 1770–90*, New York: Doubleday, 1981. According to Bernier, almost everybody in high society slept with everybody else and then reviewed their performances for the entertainment of their friends.
9. F. S. L. Lynes, *Charles Stewart Parnell*, New York: Oxford University Press, 1977.
10. Ruby V. Redinger, *George Eliot: The Emergent Self*, New York: Alfred A. Knopf, 1975.

11. Frank Caprio, *Marital Infidelity*, New York: Citadel, 1953.
12. Leon Saul, *Fidelity and Infidelity*, Philadelphia: J. B. Lippincott, 1967.
13. Spotnitz and Freeman, *Wandering Husband*
14. O. Spurgeon English, "Values in Psychotherapy: The Affair." *Voices:* Winter, 1968.
15. Gerhard Neubeck, ed., *Extra-Marital Sexual Relations*, Englewood Cliffs, N.J.: Prentice-Hall, 1969.
16. Clellan S. Ford and Frank A. Beach, *Patterns of Sexual Behavior*, New York: Harper, 1951.
17. Sigmund Freud, *Civilization and Its Discontents*, London: Hogarth Press, 1930.
18. Bertrand Russell, *Marriage and Morals*, New York: Liveright, 1957.
19. George and Nina O'Neill, *Open Marriage: a New Life Style for Couples*, New York: M. Evans, 1972.
20. Paulist Press, 1977. A committee of Catholic bishops has sharply criticized the book, warning that it is not a safe guideline for moral conduct (*New York York Times*, Nov. 17, 1977), and the most recent papal encyclical condemns adultery, along with abortion, contraception, and fornication as mortal sins.

CHAPTER 16: *Why Infidelity?*

1. In a study of 750 cases of marital dysfunction by Dr. Bernard Greene, Clinical Professor of Psychiatry, Abraham Lincoln School of Medicine, University of Illinois, 30% initially reported adultery, but in the course of therapy another 30% admitted having had secret affairs. Bernard L. Greene, Ronald R. Lee, and Noel Lustig, "Conscious and Unconscious Factors in Marital Infidelity," *Medical Aspects of Human Sexuality*, September 1974.
2. Hilma Wolitzer, *In the Flesh*, New York: William Morrow, 1977.
3. Morton Hunt, *The Affair*, New York: World, 1969.
4. Mervyn Cadwallader, "Marriage is a Miserable Institution," *The Atlantic*, November 1966.
5. Buñuel's classic film, *Belle du Jour*, is an excellent example of prostitution fantasies in a virtuous wife. Other fantasies of a forbidden nature, like incest, for example, can be acted out in extramarital sexual activities. See Jean Genet, *The Balcony*.
6. Lasch, *Narcissism*

7. Sigmund Freud, "On Narcissism: an Introduction." *Complete Works*, Vol. XIV, London: Hogarth Press, 1957.
8. Gilder, *Sexual Suicide*
9. *New York Times*, September 11, 1977.
10. For a full discussion of female infidelity see Linda Wolfe, *Playing Around*.
11. Gilder, *Sexual Suicide*

CHAPTER *17: Effect of Infidelity on Marriage*

1. Compare Tess Slesinger, "On Being Told that Her Second Husband Has Taken His First Lover," *Time: The Present*, New York: Simon & Schuster, 1935.
2. Edna St. Vincent Millay, *Collected Poems*, New York: Harper & Row, copyright 1923, 1951.
3. Kurt W. Wolff, *The Sociology of Georg Simmel*, Glencoe, Ill.: Free Press, 1950.
4. Joseph Lash, *Eleanor and Franklin*, New York: W. W. Norton, 1971.
5. Compare clients of brothel in Jean Genet's play, *The Balcony*.
6. Martha Stein, *Lovers, Friends, Slaves*, New York: Berkley, 1974.
7. English, *Values*
8. Hunt, *The Affair*

CHAPTER *18: A Good Marriage*

1. Jessie Bernard, *The Future of Marriage*
2. In the Japanese film classic *Rashomon*, five different accounts are given by five witnesses to an alleged rape.
3. I would refer the reader to Evan Connell's novels, *Mrs. Bridge* (1958) and *Mr. Bridge* (1969), in which the same situations are differently perceived by each spouse.
4. G. K. Chesterton, *Robert Browning*, London: Macmillan, 1951.
5. Frieda Lawrence, *Not I, But the Wind*, New York: Viking, 1934.
6. Quentin Bell, *Virginia Woolf. A Biography*, New York: Harcourt Brace Jovanovich, 1972. *See* also *The Letters of Virginia Woolf*, Volume VI, 1936–41, Nigel Nicolson and Joanne Trautmann, New York: Harcourt Brace Jovanovich, 1978.
7. Peter A. Martin, in *Medical Aspects of Human Sexuality*, May 1977.

8. One of the best known research studies dissecting countless varieties of marital patterns is that of the sociologists Cuber and Harroff. (John F. Cuber and Peggy Harroff, *Sex and the Significant Americans*, Baltimore: Penguin, 1965.) They interviewed 436 "normal" successful middle-class men and women between 35 and 55, on the basis of which they described five types of stable marriages: (a) *Conflict-Habituated Marriage*. In this type the couples fight with each other very often but do not regard this as any reason for dissolving the union. Fighting is their way of being close to each other. (b) *Devitalized Marriage*. In this type the couple started out romantically with love and intimacy, but drifted apart over the years. Although sex has become a bit of a bore, they get along well together and want to stay married. (c) *Passive-Congenial Marriage*. In this type the pair were never deeply emotionally involved with each other. They regard their marriage as a convenient and comfortable way to live while spending their creative energies elsewhere, usually in their careers, social commitments, or community. It is a utilitarian arrangement in which they lead separate lives and harbor no romantic notions about intimacy. Sexual relations with others may or may not be acceptable to the partner. (d) *Vital Marriage*. In this type the couples spend a lot of time together and enjoy each other's company, but they maintain their separate identities and interests. (e) *Total Marriage*. In this type the pair is extremely close, more so than in Vital Marriage. They have what the authors call an "intrinsic relationship," to which all other relationships, including those with their children, are secondary. Some of these people hide their true feelings about their spouses for fear of being laughed at or considered odd because of their extreme closeness; indeed, they are looked upon by many as rather peculiar.

9. *See* Victor Eisentein, *Neurotic Interaction in Marriage*, New York: Basic Books, 1956, for a full description of the psychodynamics of such marital relationships.

10. Sigmund Freud, in "Contributions to the Psychology of Love: A Special Type of Choice of Object Made by Men", (1910), *Collected Papers*, Vol. IV, London: Hogarth Press, 1925, writes: "The trait in this type of love . . . is the desire they express to 'rescue' the beloved. The man is convinced that the loved woman has need of him, that without him she would lose all

hold on respectability and rapidly sink to a deplorable level. He saves her from this fate, therefore, by not letting her go. The impulse to rescue the woman is occasionally justified by her untrustworthy temperament sexually. . . ."

11. I am indebted to the British psychoanalyst D. W. Winnicott for the concept "good enough," a phrase he coined to describe a certain kind of mother.

12. Carolyn G. Heilbrun, "Hers," *New York Times*, March 5, 1981.

   When Colette took up with Goudeket, who became her third husband, she described the relationship as "two tranquil comrades who looked like friends. Oh, the luxury of also being friends! It's hardly believable." *Letters from Colette*, Selected and translated by Robert Phelps, New York: Farrar, Straus and Giroux, 1980.

13. Cf. Edward Albee, *Who's Afraid of Virginia Woolf?*

14. Blanton, *Love or Perish*

INDEX